The Brensham Trilogy

PORTRAIT OF ELMBURY

John Moore was born in Gloucestershire in 1907 and educated at Malvern College. As he himself said, his half-hearted efforts in school and in business were always overshadowed by his keen love of nature study and his irrepressible passion for writing. He spent several years hitch-hiking round the world, writing freelance articles and short stories about his travels, including 'Tiger, Tiger' and 'The Octopus'. Many of his novels are set around Tewkesbury, where he lived for a major part of his life, and with books such as *Portrait of Elmbury*, *Brensham Village* and *The Blue Field* he made his name as an unrivalled chronicler of the English countryside. He died in 1967.

D1424737

The Brensham Trilogy

PORTRAIT OF ELMBURY

JOHN MOORE

UNABRIDGED

PAN BOOKS LTD : LONDON

First published 1946 by Wm Collins Sons & Company Ltd.
This edition published 1971 by Pan Books Ltd,
33 Tothill Street, London, S.W.1.

ISBN 0 330 02868 5

Printed in Great Britain by
Richard Clay (The Chaucer Press), Ltd, Bungay, Suffolk

To
ERIC LINKLATER
with love

CONTENTS

CONFESSION

'Elmbury' is a real place in the sense that I have taken as it were the ground-plan of a real town and built somewhat freely upon it. Likewise this account of the fortunes of its people in the years between the wars is built upon a framework of truth; but I haven't hesitated to alter names, to play tricks with time and geography, and where necessary to import one or two original and purely imaginary wrong-doers in cases where a selection from among our ready-made 'Elmbury' ones might have resulted in an action for libel.

JOHN MOORE

January 1945

PART ONE

THROUGH THE WINDOW

(1913–18)

Background to Childhood – Punch and Judy Show – Beauty in Ugliness – 'Fields – Flocks – Flowers' – A Vision of Piers Plowman – Missed Opportunities – Odd-job Man's Delight – English Eccentrics – The Bourgeois at Play – The Bourgeois at Work – Gallery of Relations – The Colonel – Faces at the Window – Hopscotch, Hoops, Hobbly-'onkers – Pistol, Bardolph and Nym – The Town Scoundrels – Oyez! Oyez! – Passing Acquaintances – The Mystery of Fred – Christmas Fair – Elmbury Goes to War

Background to Childhood

THE LOVELIEST HOUSE in Elmbury, which was called Tudor House, looked out across a wide main street upon the filthiest slum I have ever set eyes on in England. Few people saw anything incongruous in this, for in those days Elmbury was a higgledy-piggledy place, of incomparable beauty and incomparable squalor, and its inhabitants had retained something of the spirit of the Elizabethans, who could enjoy *Hamlet* in the interval between an afternoon at the bear-pit and a visit to the brothel, when both bear-pit and brothel lay within a stone's throw of the theatre.

In Tudor House I spent most of my early childhood. That is literally true, for apart from brief formal 'walks' with Old Nanny we didn't go out much, and since I was erroneously supposed to be 'not very strong' I was always in the condi-

tion of having a cold, of having had a cold, or of being liable
to catch a cold if I got wet. So Tudor House was my world;
and with its winding staircases, its dark oak-panelled corridors, its numerous exciting junk-rooms and attics, and its
curious and delightful back-garden, it provided a domain
wide enough for any small boy.

The garden, especially, was a child's paradise. It was not
too big, so that we knew every stick and stone of it; and
since it was by no means a source of pride either to our
parents or to the occasional odd-jobbing gardener, we could
do whatever we liked in it without reproof. Moreover, it
had an unique and thrilling smell, a sort of jungle smell
made up, I suppose, of damp rotting leaves, wet sandstone
walls, a stagnant well, and dead cats in the nearby river: you
would scarcely term it a fragrance, but we loved it, somehow we associated it with adventure and mysterious things.

No doubt the extraordinarily high walls were the cause of
the garden being so damp. One of these was provided by a
Drill Hall wherein the local Volunteers ineffectually
paraded once a week; another, of tremendous size, un-
scalable even by cats, was a bastion against our next-door
neighbours: it need have been no bigger if the Picts and the
Scots had been encamped on the other side of it. The third
wall, most unnecessarily, shut out the slow river, with its
barges, its rowing-boats, and its immobile patient fishermen. A great oaken door, however, which creaked terrify-
ingly like that which gives entrance to the home of the
omnipotent gods, opened on reluctant hinges to these
delights.

The high walls, which seemed to cloister the garden
rather than to imprison it, were in themselves extremely
beautiful. One of them was made of old red sandstone, and
the other two of that pinkish-orange Georgian brick which
becomes almost incandescent and glows with an inward
light when the sun shines on it. The Drill Hall was covered
with virginia creeper, its leaves redder than robins' breasts
in autumn. The wall-against-the-neighbours was hung with
ivy, a dusty hiding-place for sparrows' nests, for small

yellow moths, and for those big downy brown ones called
Old Ladies. The river wall, of weathered sandstone, was a
background to the most delightful herbaceous border
imaginable, a small-scale jungle in which peonies, stocks,
marigolds and red-hot pokers fought for life, and out of
which triumphantly rose great hollyhocks and even more
gigantic sunflowers, a few of which each season topped the
wall and, having looked towards the Promised Land, bowed
their heads towards it and contentedly died.

For the rest, the garden possessed one climbable tree, a
laburnum, seasonally weeping golden rain; a bush of white
lilac; a sort of shrubbery about five yards square, just big
enough for one thrush's nest each spring; white jasmine on
an outhouse wall; a small wicket-scarred lawn; a 'sand-pit'
in which we children were supposed to play (but we had
better games); and a disused well, with an old ramshackle
wooden cover to it, which we believed to be the entrance to
a monks' secret passage.

Above the garden towered the big house. Its 'backs'
were as beautiful as its façade. You went up some wide,
semi-circular stone steps on to a flagged courtyard around
which stood the half-timbered building, whitewashed
between its sepia oak beams. The back door was a tremendous piece of oak, studded with nails, with a knocker heavy
enough to wake the dead; there were strange scars on the
oak as if someone with an axe had tried to force his way in.
Inside there was a sudden cool darkness of stone-floored
corridors, sculleries, pantries and whatnot, and then the
spice-scented kitchen with Old Cookie, if she were sober,
busy over her pots and pans. Then you came to the hall, its
panelled walls hung with brass ladles, a curious form of
decoration (but pictures would have looked cold and lonely
against the dark oak); then, off the hall, the drawing-room,
very long and light, with big windows and a pale oak
parquet floor – the walls abounding in more brass ladles,
in copper warming-pans, shelves of pewter tankards,
cabinets of valuable china, a housemaid's nightmare; and
then the dining-room, as cosily dark as the drawing-room

was airily bright, with the royal coat-of-arms (we never knew why) carved above the mantelpiece.

There was also a fair-sized room with white enamelled walls, called 'the day nursery', which had a comfortable window-seat beneath its leaded windows, looking out on to the main street. This was the place where my sister and I were most often to be found, with our noses pressed close to diamond-shaped panes, gazing out with lively interest and eager anticipation at the black and gaping maw of Double Alley, which was the name of the slum opposite us. Some of the panes had queer distorting whorls in them, so that from certain angles Double Alley was double indeed; and others were cloudy with a mysterious pinkish cloudiness, imparting to objects seen through them an unearthly flush. Tinted thus, the entrance to the alley, with the usual quarrelsome and gesticulating figures standing about it, was not unlike the yawning jaws of a medieval hell.

Punch and Judy Show

Indeed, even among Elmbury's slums, Double Alley was something to be wondered at. Respectable women drew their skirts closer about them as they passed its nauseous opening; even the doctor and the priest were unwilling adventurers on the rare occasions when they were summoned to visit it; and policemen, who were more frequent visitors, took care to go in pairs when their duties took them there.

One of the most extraordinary things about Double Alley was that little children who lived within it would run about naked, in the full light of day. This served to sharpen the impression which the place gave to strangers, that it was populated by fiends.

We children had no such illusion. We knew very well that the inhabitants of Double Alley were flesh-and-blood. (The blood, indeed, was only too evident on Saturday nights.) Their too-human frailties were daily manifested to us. We knew the names, the relationships, and a large part of the life histories of almost all that piteous riff-raff. The ragged women, the drunken men, the screaming wanton wenches, the rickety children, were more real to us than many of our relations; far more real than the visitors in evening clothes who came to dine with our parents and afterwards played the piano, and sang, in the drawing-room. We never had much use for such singing; but when Nobbler Price came home from the pub roaring and bellowing we thoroughly appreciated the entertainment. It was very much better than *When Lady Betty Walks Abroad* or *Melisande*.

A fair example of Double Alley's inhabitants would be Mr and Mrs Hook. The domestic disagreements of this hot-tempered couple always took place *coram populo*, at the street entrance to the Alley, instead of in the decent seclusion of their own hovel; not through any exhibitionism, I suppose, but simply because, for fighting on the scale practised by them, their hovel was not big enough. We had learned, from nurse-maid's or servant's gossip, enough of Mr and Mrs Hook's affairs to be able to reconstruct the course of their quarrels, which much resembled that of a Punch and Judy show. Mr Hook would return, lurching and staggering, from his festivities, and Mrs Hook, hearing his approach or being warned of it, would rush out to greet him with blows and blasphemy; and in a confused flurry of attack and counter-attack they would disappear together into the Alley's dark maw. There followed an interval during which it might be supposed Mr Hook slept, while his wife providently abstracted what remained of his week's pay from his pockets. Then Mr Hook would wake up, remember an important appointment at the George, and discover that he was penniless. His enormous bellow of rage was the signal for Mrs Hook to run helter-skelter down the Alley to take up station in their traditional battleground at its entrance. There among the chattering anticipatory neighbours she would await, with arms akimbo, the terrible coming of her outraged lord. Again it was just like Punch and Judy. *Whang!* – Mrs Hook clouted him on the side of the head.

Bonk! – Mr Hook countered with a left to the jaw. And so it went on, until some spoilsport fetched a policeman. (Punch and Judy again, you see; these disputants invariably observed the formality and the tradition.) But to the two peaky-faced children who watched with their noses glued to the window it was better than any Punch and Judy show: it was the first taste of real life.

There were others, more colourful if less violent than the Hooks, who took part in this daily pageant which might almost have been staged for our special benefit. (At least we had seats in the front row of the stalls.) There was, for instance, Black Sal. She was mad, she was frequently drunk, and she never washed. When the frenzy was upon her, or when she was full of gin, she would range about the town chanting meaningless obscenities; at other times she practised a kind of coarse and friendly banter, a running commentary upon life and affairs, addressed to all and sundry, but particularly to the Mayor, as she waddled down the middle of the street. These comments were generally expressed in rough and ready rhymes, or in the assonances which modern poets use, which gave them added point. 'Wot's the Town Council but a lot of scoundrels?' she would ask; and there were few found willing to answer her. 'The Mayor has banquets, we ain't got no blankets,' she would declare. All the time she threw quips and jeers over her shoulder as the respectable top-floor windows were opened and the respectable householders peered out. 'Ho! ho! ho!' she would cry. 'Ships yuds is chip this morning!' Sheep's heads were symbols of stupidity: thus she reproved the inquisitive who so rudely stared at her. She would sing, too, improvising as she went along:

> 'Black Sal,
> Jolly old gal,
> What do the Doctor say?
> *He wants to put her away.*
> Poor Black Sal,
> Poor old gal!'

It was related of her, in later years, that she died two deaths. The first occurred in her own home, and when the breath had ceased in her, her husband brought out a bottle of gin and shared it with some of the neighbours, either to celebrate his release from her or to sustain him in his loss. It is recorded that as he poured out the drink he glanced at the corpse upon the bed and remarked, sententiously: 'Black Sal, thee's sarved me many a trick in thy time but never thee's sarved me a trick like this.' But Black Sal, halfway to Gehenna, smelled the gin, hastened back, and finished the bottle. After this first death she survived for many years, until at last, becoming destitute, she was taken to the workhouse where among other indignities she suffered that of being forcibly washed. This killed her: and the chilly hard-hearted Institution provided no bottle of gin to lure her back to life.

Her appearance, in the days when she dwelt in the filthiest cottage of all Double Alley, was horrific in the extreme. She wore a black bonnet, a black shawl, and a black ragged skirt; her bonnet, which was tall, elaborate and decorated with black feathers, gave her the overdressed appearance of a witch on holiday, one of the Weird Sisters gone gallivanting. Her face was almost as black as her clothes. When I began to learn Greek I thought of the Eumenides as Black Sals; but in spite of her frightful appearance, we children never feared her nor imagined that there was anything malevolent about her. She was just another character in the pageant; and when we met her in the street we said 'Good morning, Black Sal,' and she answered politely, 'Mornin', Miss Daphne.'

One more Hogarthian figure, and then I have done with them. Nobbler Price did not actually inhabit Double Alley, but kept a tiny greengrocer's shop nearby; he also possessed a weedy patch of back-garden, abutting on the Alley, and a miserable-looking nannygoat which was tethered to a peg and which demonstrated by its circumscribed nibbling the great truths discovered by Euclid and Pythagoras.

When Nobbler was drunk, he became maniacal. I saw him once careering down the street in his pony-cart, whipping his wretched little pony into a canter, while two stout policemen hung on to the bridle; and when they seemed likely to slow him up he picked up his mongrel dog that rode in the cart beside him and shied it with remarkable accuracy at the nearest policeman's head. It was Nobbler's chief obsession, when he was drunk, that he wanted to shoot his wife, of whom in sober moments he was extremely fond; but while with drunken clumsiness he searched for his shotgun, she would take shelter at a neighbour's house, where she remained until his fit passed. On one of these occasions, in frustrated rage, being determined to shoot *something*, Nobbler went out into his back-garden and shot the nannygoat.

Yet when he was dead, many years later, Mrs Price told me, with tears in her eyes, 'I miss him. . . Yes, I miss Nobbler. You see, sir, *he was so good to I.*'

And indeed the poor demented creature had his good qualities. Between bouts, he behaved to man and beast with the greatest gentleness; he was capable of strong loyalties and deep affections. He worshipped my father (who was often called to quieten him when he was drunk), and after my father's death, when the lovely house had been sold to be turned into an hotel, Nobbler and his wife became for a time its caretakers. It stood empty for months, and once a week – every Sunday morning – Nobbler would walk two miles to bring my mother a draggled nosegay, of peonies, columbines, stocks and marigolds, from the herbaceous border against the sandstone wall.

Beauty in Ugliness

The appalling incongruity between our tall, beautiful house and the squat cavernous Alley opposite; between our parents' smooth-flowing and contented lives and the drunken brawls across the street; between our spoiled and rather pampered upbringing and the ribby nakedness of the slum children: all this sounds very shocking now. But it was part of a larger incongruity with which we grew up, scarcely noticing it: the extraordinary higgledy-piggledi-ness, the rich seething hotch-potch of a thousand ingredi-ents, which was Elmbury itself. Elmbury was a small town, and such are generally supposed to be dull, and to be associated with aspidistras, and to infect the souls of their inhabitants with something mean and crabbed and petty, with ignorant 'provincialism', and with something specially reprehensible and circumscribed called a 'small-town mentality'. But Elmbury wasn't like that at all. It had infinite variety. It was splendid and it was sordid; but it certainly wasn't dull.

Over it and dominating it rose the huge square tower of the Abbey: the finest Norman tower, some say, in the world. The Abbey itself, bigger than many cathedrals, loomed vastly out of its churchyard chestnuts and yews. But there was none of that 'odour of sanctity', which usually belongs to cathedral closes, about the immediate neighbourhood of Elmbury's great church: no cloistered quietude, nothing sanctimonious or grave. Outside the churchyard gates the main road ran north to Birmingham and south to Bristol, and up and down it the heedless traffic flowed. Just across the road, exactly opposite the church, was a good, solid, half-timbered pub; it had a garden hedged with thick impenetrable yews, a secret place hidden from prying eyes, where old men played bowls till the light faded and younger folk played more mischievous games in the twilight. But adjoining this delightful garden (at the bottom of which a willowy stream flowed) was a large horrible red-brick building like a public lavatory; this was the grammar school. And beyond it was an untidy-looking rubbish dump, a noisome wilderness into which the town's sewage was discharged, loved only by rats and terriers and crows and little boys.

At the other side of the Abbey things were equally chaotic. There were more pubs – small squalid ones with spit-and-sawdust bars. There were Elizabethan almhouses, enchanting but scarcely habitable, which American tourists always wanted to buy, lock, stock, and barrel, so that they could carry them home, as explorers' trophies, to the States. There were tumbledown cottages, dirty and overcrowded, with whole families·sleeping in one small bedroom; roses in their pretty little front-gardens, bugs in their beds. There was a dreadful 'Italian Tea Garden' with umbrellas like striped mushrooms shading the tables on the lawn. There were shops which sold trivial souvenirs to visitors. There were allotments, smelling of dead cabbages and live pigs. And there was a pleasant cricket-field, margined by willows and cressy streams, its green turf hallowed by the feet of W. G. Grace who once played there, its pavilion roof still bearing honourable scars from the big hits of Gilbert Jessop.

The town itself, which straggled along the main road for half a mile or so, consisted of a haphazard assortment of ancient half-timbered houses and shops – some of these leaned across the street towards each other, like old wives gossiping – with later Georgian buildings among them, and the inevitable alleys, dozens of alleys, leading off the main road into the ruinous rabbit-warren of Elmbury's slums. There were hundreds of acres of these slums. They were scandalous; they were far worse, probably, than many of the slums in London's East End; but the extraordinary, the almost unbelievable thing about them was that as well as being terrifying they were curiously beautiful. The narrow crooked alleys, fantastical enough by day, at twilight seemed to belong to a Grimms' fairy tale. By the time the moon had risen their metamorphosis was complete; they had dissolved into a monstrous and yet enchanting dreamland, they had become part of a City of Beautiful Nonsense. The tottering hunchback cottages leaned shoulder-to-shoulder like drunken men; if one of them fell down they'd all collapse in a heap. Their ragged eaves nearly met across the alley, fretting the tattered strip of sky into which crooked chimney-stacks intruded dangerously. Nothing was orderly, nothing rational. The chimneys defied the laws of gravity and even the stout oak beams which were the bones of the cottages were not straight, but bent like elbows – as if a forked tree had once stood there and the cottages had been built around it. One expected that when the doors of the dwellings opened there would emerge not people, but hobgoblins and dwarfs; and often enough there did.

The alleys nearest the river – and these were the dirtiest and most insanitary of all – often reminded visitors of parts of Venice; and here it was a common sight during the summer season to see a devoted artist squatting at his easel surrounded by cheeky urchins, ferociously painting a row of filthy and exquisite hovels, and chewing antiseptic lozenges like mad.

'Fields – Flocks – Flowers'

But the way to see Elmbury as a whole, to see it in all its squalor and all its glory, was to climb to the top of a nearby hill, a little hump like an overgrown haycock, curiously called the Toot. From here you could watch the light changing on the Abbey tower, so that sometimes it seemed as insubstantial as a dream, a grey ghost-tower brooding over the town, and at others, especially at set of sun, it smouldered and shone like a glowing affirmation of faith. There are few towers like it in all the world, and one of them is at Caen in Normandy. On a day in June 1944, I lay upon the forward slope of just such a little eminence as the Toot, and watched Caen burning around its Norman tower; and I thought that but for the geographical accident of our English Channel I might have watched Elmbury burn so.

From the Toot you could see, too, how clumsily and how untidily the town sprawled about the church: and how the rivers were a recurrent theme running through its history and the lives of its people. Two broad streams joined at Elmbury among a confusion of small brooks. These snaking waterways almost isolated the town even in summer; and when the floods rose in the winter they sometimes cut it off altogether, so that milk was delivered by rowing-boat and people punted through the back streets. At such times the meadows round Elmbury disappeared beneath a huge inland sea; and no doubt it was this annual flooding that made them so fertile and rich. There never was a greener countryside than those few square miles in which Elmbury was set, and what gave it a particularly fat and sumptuous appearance was the size of those river-meadows, which were large and liberal, pasturing fifty beasts apiece and yielding at haytime not one meagre rick but a whole rickyard. The biggest of all was Elmbury's own field, called the Ham, which lay in the triangle between the confluent rivers and the town. It was something of a legal curiosity, and mixed up in his title-deeds were some of the principles of feudalism, capitalism, distributism, and communism. The hay crop belonged to a number of private owners, including the Squire and the Abbey; their boundaries were marked mysteriously by means of little posts. They did not, however, mow their own hay; the Vicar didn't come down from his vestry with a pitching fork; so the hay crop was sold each year, in little parcels none of which by themselves would have been worth the trouble of mowing. It was bid for by groups of men, little combines, who saw to it that they bought contiguous pieces of sufficient area to make a sizeable rick. But while the hay crop was private property, the meadow itself, the soil that grew the hay, belonged to 'the burgesses of Elmbury'; these burgesses, the householder, the ironmonger, the draper, the chemist, the doctor, possessed no cows or sheep to graze upon it, so they too each season sold the aftermath by auction and distributed the proceeds, according to an ancient law, among the owners of the houses having a frontage on the main street. Nobody got more than a few shillings for his share; but at least every man, woman and child in Elmbury had the right to walk and play in the field, which gave them a good possessive feeling about it. It was always 'our Ham'. In the winter we shot snipe there, and sometimes hares, without let or hindrance. In the spring, when the patches of ladysmocks were silver-white like pools of lingering flood-water, we hunted for plovers' nests and listened to the whistle of the redshanks and the weird sad cry of the curlews which came to the Ham in breeding-time. In May, when buttercups gilded it, and the grass was as high as your waist, the courting couples used its cover for their amorous games, flattening out neat circles where they had lain, as if they had rotated on their axis, which perhaps they had, so unquiet alas is love.

But in June the lovers' hiding-places were laid bare, and those same lovers, probably, were toiling and sweating on the wagons, bringing in the hay. Three big rickyards grew up like little towns. Then, while the quick-growing aftermath painted the field green again, and the ochreous sheep or the white-faced Hereford cattle were turned out to graze on it — then the Ham became more than ever Elmbury's playground. Cricket-pitches, on which the ball broke unpredictably, made brown scars on the turf. From the banks of the river jutted out numberless fishing-rods; little boys with willow-wands conjured up minnows, bigger boys dapped with houseflies for bleak, middle-aged trades-men perched sedately on wicker creels legering for bream, while the more energetic ones, swift of eye and wrist, fished for roach, and the more adventurous wandered here and there, carrying a jar of minnows, live-baiting for perch. The 'gentry', possessing more expensive tools, threw big hackled flies over flopping chub. And the very old, and the very stupid, content with the mere dregs of angling, heaved enor-mous lobworms impaled upon enormous hooks into the deepest and stillest backwaters and then went to sleep until Fate, in the guise of a shiny yellow eel, accepted at last their unheroic challenge.

Meanwhile along the towpath, on summer evenings and Sunday afternoons paraded those who were not immediately concerned with fish: shopkeepers and their wives taking the same leisurely stroll they had been accustomed to take, may-be, for twenty years; mothers wheeling their babies out for an airing; boys and girls 'walking out' prior to courtship; and so on. But even these would pause now and then to watch the motionless or the gently-bobbing float. 'Caught owt, Willum?' 'Nobbut daddy-ruffs and tiddlers.' 'Wants a fresh o' rain, like as not.' 'Maybe. But maybe there's tempest hanging about somewheres.'

Fishermen always have the same excuses.

A Vision of Piers Plowman

I have devoted rather a lot of space to the Ham because it was part of the life as well as the landscape of Elmbury. I have called it the town's playground; by which I mean a very different thing from a playing-field. A playing-field associates itself with serious and organized games and sedate tennis-courts and terrible bouncing gym-mistresses teaching people how to keep fit. We had none of that nonsense. But Elmbury used its Ham for real 'play' – all sorts of play, from catching tiddlers to poaching salmon, from birds'-nesting to tumbling wenches in the hay.

And so, if you had climbed to the top of the Toot on a summer evening, you would have had the vision of Piers Plowman; which he had when he stood upon a higher hill not very far from Elmbury. You would have seen 'a fair field full of folk' stretched out below. It was a very fair field indeed, with the townsfolk going to and fro upon it in the calm of evening; with the silver rivers ribboned all round it, the tumbling weir with small withy-grown islands in mid-stream, the old mill above its placid millpool, and behind it the great Abbey rising up, massive and solid as England's history, and yet as airy-light as a dream.

But I must insist that Elmbury, although beautiful, was not a beauty-spot; for that implies, I think, a rather steril-ized sort of beauty, unspoiled, preserved, and sacrosanct; whereas in Elmbury beauty and ugliness grew up side by side and merged into a single entity, indivisible and unique, in which you could no more easily separate and distinguish those two qualities than you could winnow out the good and evil in the heart of man.

Missed Opportunities

Like wrecks out of a receding tide, the ruins of Elmbury's industries rose up among its slums: a disused flour-mill, rat-run warehouses, a derelict shirt-and-collar factory, and what was left of an establishment which once made mustard.

Three or four industries precariously survived: a big modern flour-mill, a maltster's, a collection of sheds and wharves and slipways where ancient craftsmen who loved their trade built boats of all kinds from canoes to river-steamers. But these concerns were not nearly sufficient to provide a living for a population of five thousand people. The town had known better days; for trade, which once came by river, now followed the railway, and the industrial prosperity of one nearby city, and the social prosperity of another, made a sharp contrast with Elmbury's back-wardness. This was supposed to be the fault of a previous generation of Elmburians, who cold-shouldered the railway until the main-line had gone elsewhere and who, finding spring-waters of remarkable nastiness almost at their front doors, failed to exploit them until half the fashionable world was curing its gout ten miles away. So Elmbury slumbered beside a branch line of the railway, and the ridiculous building which it pretentiously called 'The Spa' saw no Beau Brummells, fell into disuse, and finally became a farmhouse, keeping its name 'The Spa Farm', long after the majority of the people had forgotten why it was called so.

Odd-job Man's Delight

But for their obstinacy, then, but for the short-sightedness of those ancient Elmbury Die-Hards, the place might have been either blackened by belching chimneys or blighted by the withering presence of decrepit colonels drawing out their last meaningless days. Miraculously preserved from both disasters, the little town muddled along contentedly enough in its own haphazard way; and although I suppose a very high percentage of the population must have been technically 'unemployed' there was much less poverty and very much less distress that you would find in similar circumstances in an industrial town. The city-dweller, when he is out of work, is generally helpless; there are few 'odd-jobs' to be had, even if he were adaptable enough to be capable of doing them. But in the country and in the country town it is different; and Elmbury was an odd-job man's paradise. The farmers in the neighbourhood needed casual labour for a dozen seasonal jobs, haymaking, harvest, fruit-picking, turnip-pulling and whatnot; a man could earn a few shillings and a quart of cider almost any day he'd a mind to. There was drovering, and there was timber-felling, and there was rick-cutting; thatching, ditch-cleaning, and hedging. Many of the Elmbury men could turn their hands to skilled and semi-skilled jobs such as these. But there were more individualist odd-jobs too. In those days, if a man knew something about bird-lime and decoys and clap-nets he could catch a dozen linnets or goldfinches on Brockeridge Common in a morning, and be ten shillings the richer when he had caged and sold them. Even the poorest people bred dogs or canaries or pigeons or rabbits in the backyards of their cottages; many worked allotments and kept chickens or pigs as well. Others got their living out of the river, building boats, netting salmon, cutting osiers, dredging sand, setting putcheons for eels. Almost every man and boy, as we have seen, was a devoted fisherman, but almost every one was a still more devoted poacher. There were other ways of catching salmon beside the legitimate nets or the rods of the rich; and there were plenty of people willing to pay half a sovereign for a clean-run fish, no questions asked or answered.

So that was how many of the Elmbury men lived. In the spring they'd do a bit of salmon-fishing, fair or foul; hay-making in June; drovering on Saturday (a walk to the

neighbouring market and a drink in the pubs afterwards);
plum-picking now and then – but this rather as a favour –
for a farmer who was known to be free with his cider;
illegal forays after mushrooms on misty September mornings; a few days' beating when Squire shot his pheasants;
blackberrying; eel-catching at the first autumn flood; and
the winter spent variously in building a new punt for sale
or hire, caulking an old one, mending the salmon nets,
pottering up the river after duck (or perhaps an otter
whose skin would be worth a pound), ferreting for rabbits,
poaching occasional pheasants, collecting betting-slips for
a bookie, or any one of a score of pleasant, profitable, and
adventurous ways.

Now the men who lived in this casual way – and there
were several hundred of them out of our population of five
thousand – possessed two advantages which were rare
enough then and which are almost priceless today: they
were independent of employers; and they were not condi-
tioned to believe in the popular fallacy, that work in itself
is a virtue. They worked when they wanted to work; and
their work was fun. They were, in fact, a sort of privileged
class; and their privilege was one which nowadays only a
few great artists have. It was fortunate for Elmbury that its
population included these few hundred truly free men; they
acted as a leaven upon the whole community.

Their independence of employers gave them a vivid
individuality. In those days, when sweated labour in the big
industrial districts was sapping the vitality of whole populations and turning millions into rather inefficient robots, the
men in the country towns were able to preserve their
intelligence, their humour, and their pride. They still
believed in a vague undefined something which they called
their 'rights'; and for all their poverty, for all the dirt and
squalor in which many of them lived, they actually believed
that they exercised some rights. They may have called
themselves, variously, Conservatives, Radicals and Social-
ists; but I think really they were the last true Liberals. They
believed in Freedom without defining it; but they thought

it was something to do with saying You-be-damned to all tyrants, great and small.

English Eccentrics

It is not surprising that out of such a fertile soil should blossom strange and fantastical characters. These rich and rare ones, who for all their oddity are somehow essentially and exclusively English, seem always to sport and flourish most freely in the atmosphere of the small and ancient towns which lie close to England's heart. ''Tis summat in the air as breeds 'em,' said old Fred Pullin, when I asked him why we had so many queer characters in Elmbury. He was a bit of a curiosity himself, now I come to think of it, that doddering old coachman who had driven my grandfather to his wedding and who followed my father to his grave. He had a remarkably ugly wife who bore the unusual name of Abigail, and when Abigail died old Fred promptly courted and married another one, although at that time he must have been well past sixty.

'It was something in the air that bred them,' and so, in common with many another old-fashioned market town, we had our minor Falstaffs (one in particular who regularly drank twelve pints of beer at a sitting and once ate a whole leg of lamb at a single meal) – our Pistols, Bardolphs and Nyms, our Mistress Quicklys, our Mr Justice Shallow. For of course Shakespeare didn't invent these; they were his for the picking, familiar weeds in Stratford streets; and Elmbury in 1913, apart from a few trifling differences in such matters as drainage, was much the same sort of place as Stratford in 1600. Our little Falstaff was possessed of huge appetites and a vast belly, and was boastful and lecherous and cunning and cowardly yet withal had a twinkle in his watery blue eyes; he only needed a Shakespeare to breathe the immortal spirit into him, and he would have been Old Jack to the life.

We had also our rich eccentrics, lesser John Myttons

whose crazy equestrian feats are remembered still ('Those are the double gates that his lordship jumped one day when his fox crossed the railway') – squires who built strange edifices which are known still as their Follies – cranks who indulged extraordinary hobbies, such as letting loose wild animals in their grounds and surprising their neighbours with antelopes and flamingos. And among humbler folk we had a gallery of merry rascals, scallywags, drunkards and ne'er-do-weels straight from Dickens and Surtees; while as it were at the extreme end of the mental spectrum there were our genuine lunatics such as Black Sal dressed all in sable topped with her great flopping black bonnet, and Poor Tom who thought he had Heaven's commandment to empty the river and who might have been seen almost any day happily baling it out with a leaky bucket.

It is true, of course, that one remembers the freakish and forgets the commonplace; and Elmbury was neither Bedlam nor a scene out of *Henry the Fourth*, but a quiet respectable country town in the streets of which during a morning walk you would have encountered plenty of stolid *petit bourgeois* and prosperous tradesmen who fitted in with the popular conception of small-town dwellers; aspidistra-loving, unenterprising and dull. Yet even some of these had their heroic hours, when they played boisterous pranks upon each other at municipal elections, painting each other's houses with politically odious colours, Tory Blue or Liberal Scarlet, and indulging in schoolboyish practical jokes of the kind that are out of fashion nowadays.

And even some of these, ordinary enough to look at, suffered strange metamorphoses and were beckoned by sudden adventure. There was a rather oafish-looking youth, a country boy called Alf, who came in from a neighbouring village for a game of cricket on Saturday afternoons – who entertained us with his sweeping cow-shots and annoyed us by his unwillingness to chase long hits in the outfield – now who'd have thought that one day our Alf would be playing for England, and making just the same cow-shots and displaying, even at Lord's, the same charming non-

chalance towards boundary-hurrying balls at long on?
There was a ragged boy out of the alleys who when war
came put on the khaki simply because it was better than
rags, and went to France simply because it was more
comfortable than the alley, but who became a sergeant and
at Passchendaele was seized with a divine fury and when all
his officers had been killed led half a company forward
through the mud; and when they had been thinned out to
half a platoon still he led them, until at last he fell; and he
would have won the VC, men said, if there had been anybody left to recommend him.

And there was a modest shy lad, the son of a schoolmaster,
who collected fossils and bits of rock, and who went quietly
off one day without saying where he was going; and when
he came back, years later, we learned that he had been with
Shackleton to the South Pole.

The Bourgeois at Play

Goodness knows, my own relations were bourgeois and
ordinary enough: country doctors, lawyers and auctioneers;
but even they sported a few eccentrics and contrived to
express themselves, when they had a mind to, without any
pettifogging regard to convention and smug routine. My
great-grandfather on my mother's side, going his doctor's
rounds in a gig, encountered one morning a very aggrieved
prize-fighter, pacing furiously up and down beside a
famous landmark called the Four Shires Stone. When he
asked the large and murmurous crowd what was the matter,
my great grandfather learned that they were all very angry
and disappointed because the prize-fighter's opponent had
taken fright and failed to turn up. 'I have a long morning,'
said my great-grandfather promptly, 'what with measles
and confinements and one thing and another, but if somebody will hold my horse I shall be delighted to give the
gentleman a fight if he is willing.' They fought with bare
fists, and my great-grandfather did so much damage to the

prize-fighter's face that he had to stitch it up for him. He is said to have demanded his fee for this service. He then wiped his hands and went on to the confinements and the measles.

His son, my mother's father, inherited the practice, and *his* form of self-expression was to break his bones out hunting. He avoided breaking his neck, however, and miraculously died in bed. By all accounts, he was a man much loved; even the gipsies, whose wandering tribes he doctored, knew him as their friend, and often when he was riding on his twenty-mile round he would stop for breakfast or dinner at one of their encampments. Gipsies have long memories; and only two years ago I was told that the tinkers still talk of him, and his mercurial chestnut mare which danced and pirouetted continually, while my grandfather sat it like a jockey, one light hand on the reins, the other holding his little black bag.

The Bourgeois at Work

My relations on my father's side were much more stolid; they would never, I think, have sat down to a dish of roast hedgehog at a Romany camp fire. They had lived in and about Elmbury for so long, and moreover there were so many of them, that they seemed to have proprietary rights in the place. They were mayors, justices of the peace, churchwardens. Most of them were comfortably off, none of them was rich. Most of them were able, few of them were clever. In fact, they mistrusted cleverness. That was the sort of people they were. Cleverness, they thought, generally got you into trouble; and it was true enough that the only one of them who was really clever finished up by drinking himself to death. His name was Clem; and he was brilliant. He became a barrister, which was outside the family tradition, and upon the threshold of a great career he paused, hesitated, and turned back. He liked the local pub better. But when we children asked what had happened to him, and why Clem who was so gay and handsome did not come to visit us any more, there was always an uncomfortable pause. The family didn't like talking about Clem. 'He was very clever, of course, but cleverness isn't everything.' We had to be content with that.

The others, lacking this terrible handicap of cleverness, prospered moderately and lived long respectable lives. They were all large and substantial, rather like family portraits come to life: Uncle Reg the doctor; Uncle Jim the lawyer; Uncle Tom and my father, the auctioneers. They sat together upon the Town Council; they took it in turns to be Mayor, and Chairman of the local Conservative Association; they administered charities and trusts with meticulous care; they shared a monopoly of the post of churchwarden of the Abbey. The editor of the local paper had little trouble when they died; the same obituary notice, with a few trifling alterations, would serve for all of them. 'He played a prominent part in Public Life.' And that indeed was their tradition; so long as the Public was not too large. Elmbury with its five thousand inhabitants was just big enough; if you ventured into the world beyond, you got mixed up in wider politics, which were administered by clever fellows; and clever fellows were generally shady fellows, and by no means to be trusted.

Gallery of Relations

Beyond all these uncles and their wives, like the widening ripples round a splash in a pond extended a vast complication of distant and yet more distant relations: a network, an inescapable spider's web of kith and kin. Most of them had enormous families; and this resulted in countless cousins.

You might say that this regiment, this veritable Army Corps, was based upon Elmbury. Many of its members lived there; the others, who travelled farther afield, returned there from time to time to go into winter quarters; and unless the accident of death overtook them suddenly, they all came back there to die. I cannot write about

Elmbury unless I mention them too; for they grew about the place as the ivy wraps itself round a tree.

Since even the wandering ones would ultimately return, there was a family tradition that relations must be 'kept up with'. Keeping up with relations was a stern duty; you failed in that duty if you let them fall into desuetude, if they 'got out of touch'. In order to prevent this, you had to write them letters at Christmas and send them diaries on their birthdays; and whenever it occurred to my mother that Aunt Nancy or Cousin Gerald was being neglected, was falling into disuse, she immediately invited the forgotten one to Tudor House in order that the dusty and rusty relationship might be polished up and oiled and put into running order again.

If they could not come to you, it was your duty to go to them. Great-aunt Mary-Jane was bedridden, and wore a nightcap, and looked just like the wolf which frightened Red Riding Hood. We were frequently taken to visit her, in the dark Victorian house at the top of Elmbury High Street, and she gave us curious presents, such as stamps pierced through with a darning-needle and strung tightly on a piece of thread, so that they formed a kind of snake, wriggly and tenuous. Alas, the snake was composed of Penny Blacks and Twopenny Blues; and the five hundred stamps which articulated it would be worth, today, about two hundred pounds if Great-aunt Mary-Jane hadn't in every case poked her red-hot darning-needle through the young queen's head.

Other relations, more mobile, came to visit us; a succession of aunts and uncles, of first and second and third cousins, of cousins goodness knows how many times removed. It took about a year for the wheel to turn full circle; and then, like the second house at the pictures, it began all over again, but one had forgotten the characters which appeared at the beginning; so that the procession of relatives seemed endless indeed.

They did not, however, unduly oppress us. The house was big, and they troubled us children very little, intruding into our privacy only now and then, when my mother no doubt said to them: 'But of course you'd like to see the children . . .' and they, liking nothing less, warmly agreed. So Old Nanny, warned in advance, spat on a handkerchief to rub imaginary smuts off our faces; and we were made ready in the nursery, hair brushed, toys tidied away, ready for the awful visitation – of rich Aunt Blanche or poor Cousin Minnie or fashionable Aunt Doll or soldierly Cousin Farley who was in the Guards, or decrepit old Cousin Tom Holland who'd fought in the Indian Mutiny . . . We shook hands, and they made the usual idiotic remarks, and soon they were gone, to be forgotten until another year brought them like migrants back again.

They did not tarry long in our recollections; and shortly we were back in our favourite window-seat, gazing out through the blurry glass between the leads upon the rose-pink-tinted fantastic little world, and the daily pageant that passed along the town's wide High Street.

The Colonel

Once a year, on Boxing Day, scarlet was the colour of pageantry when the foxhounds met outside the Swan Hotel and afterwards the whole cavalcade tittuped past on its way to the first draw, dappled flop-eared hounds, shining horses, shining leather, shining top-hats. In the summer there was sometimes a meet of the otterhounds, but this was less of an entertainment because there were no horses and no pink coats; instead the participants wore a blue uniform with scarlet stockings which even to us seemed rather odd. I remember chiefly some ferocious-looking women, thus garbed, carrying long poles with which, I imagined, they must surely beat the poor otter over the head. I remember also a man like an elderly gnome who wore a faded green Norfolk jacket and knee-breeches, with a deerstalker hat of astonishing shape to match. These clothes, and something indescribable in the air with which he wore them, marked him without doubt as a man of the forest and the field. He caught my imagination at once, as some sort of older edition of Robin Hood. His face was red and his nose was a brighter red; he had a badger-grizzled walrus moustache and little twinkling blue eyes. We were told he was 'the Colonel'; we never asked what colonel, and it was years before I discovered his name. Then, as you will read, I got to know him well; and I learned from him more than I ever learned from any schoolmaster. But I never forgot my first sight of him, when I watched the meet through the window (as usual, I had a cold). He arrived on a motor-bicycle, which he was unable to control. Skidding to avoid the hounds, he fell off. He picked himself up, grunted angrily, promptly produced a silver flask out of his pocket, and examined it carefully to make sure that it was unbroken. Then he shook it, holding it up to his ear, to make certain that its contents were undiminished. Then, to make doubly sure, he put it to his lips and swigged the lot. As he wiped his moustache he happened to look towards our window; and seeing my face there he suddenly grinned. His ribston-pippin cheeks all wrinkles, he looked like a kelpie. I was enchanted and I grinned back, but it was too late; the hounds were moving off and the Colonel with them, hobbling along on bowed legs and with bent back, as crooked as a hobgoblin.

Faces at the Window

He was not the only acquaintance we made through the day-nursery window – which was on the ground floor, so we could communicate with people who passed by. One wet winter night, when the gas-lamps made blurred yellow pools on the pavement and our breaths condensed on the window-pane, there came out of the shadows suddenly a white-faced little boy, who pressed his nose against the glass and put out his tongue at us. In a moment he was gone; but we had a notion that he was still hanging about close by, so we tapped on the window. Nothing stirred. We tapped again. Then suddenly he poked his head round the corner, pressed his face against the pane, and shouted cheekily – we could just hear him – ' *Who be thee a-tabberin' at?*' Communication was established, and we began to talk, sometimes by shouting and sometimes by signs. Next day he came back, and the next, and after that every night for many months. His name was Alfie, and he told us everything we wanted to know about the lives of the Hooks and Nobbler Price and Black Sal; it seemed to us that he had his being in a wide and immensely exciting world, and greatly we envied him. Greatly he envied us, no doubt, as he stood out in the cold and looked through the window at our toys and our bright hearth. There is still something terrible to me in the thought of the two small white faces pressed against the dividing glass, and the two pairs of eyes each looking out upon an alien and utterly desirable world.

In the spring he suddenly ceased to visit us. It may be he was taken to hospital – he looked pale and frail enough; it may be simply that he preferred bird's-nesting to our company. But for weeks our sense of loss was deep and sharp indeed; we felt like beleaguered citizens must feel, whose last link is cut with the world beyond their invested walls.

Hopscotch, Hoops, Hobbly-'onkers

If Alfie envied our toys, it was true also that we were jealous of the rougher and less sophisticated games in which he and the rest of the Double Alley youngsters took part: marbles, tops, tipcat, hopscotch, hoops and hobbly-'onkers. The latter, also called Conkers, belonged, of course, to the autumn, when the bright glossy horse-chestnuts littered the ground beneath the grave churchyard trees. The other games were also seasonal, though it is not easy to understand why. Tops and hopscotch belonged to the winter, hoops to the early spring, marbles to high summer, and tipcat, as far as I can remember, to summer holidays. There was a strict convention governing these matters: a boy would as soon bowl a hoop in January as a man would ride in Rotten Row in a frock coat and top-hat; yet in March, when the hoop season came in, not a single ragged guttersnipe would be seen without one. They were home-made, of course, as were the ingenious whip-tops which when lashed smartly would fly twenty yards through the air and continue to spin when they came to earth, and which were sometimes slotted so that they hummed like little aeroplanes. As for hopscotch, all that was needed was a piece of chalk; while tipcat demanded merely a peg sharpened at both ends and a stout stick with which to slog it. Only marbles could not be manufactured in Double Alley; you had to buy them, twenty-four for a penny, at any of the little nondescript shops which sold everything from babies' comforters to butterfly-nets. The big glass ones, streaked with tricolour whorls of red, white and blue, cost much more – sometimes as much as a halfpenny each. These were the sovereigns in the guttersnipe currency; and when one rolled down the muddy gutter and fell with a plop through the grating into the drain it was a tragedy indeed.

Marbles had a strange, an ancient, and a poetic termin-ology which Alfie knew and paraded, but which to us was a mystery only half understood; we never truly mastered it. Other games, even more obscure, had wonderful rhymes associated with them, snatches of song, outlandish catches, and curious fragments of mumbo-jumbo which ran like this:

> 'Egdom, pegdom, penny-a-legdom,
>   Popped the lorum gee.
>   Eggs, butter, cheese, bread,
>   Stick, stock, stone dead,
>   Out goes she.'

That sounded like poetry to us, half-heard through the window; it sounds like a sort of poetry to me still.

Pistol, Bardolph and Nym

It must have been about this time that we made the acquaintance of three good-for-nothings whose present disrepute – for they were notorious cadgers, scroungers, poachers and petty thieves – was somewhat mitigated by their past history of great deeds done in distant battles. What battles and where we never knew: Pistol frequently talked airily of Zulus and Afghans, Bardolph was accustomed to use fearful oaths which he said came from the Sudanese, and it was pretty well established that Nym at the age of seventeen had played some minor part in the relief of Ladysmith. However, the Army had discovered before long that the three of them were more trouble than they were worth; so they had returned to Elmbury and to the dark disastrous alleys in which they had been spawned. We would watch them loafing and leering at the Double Alley entrance, chasing the wenches, begging from passers-by, and more than once we would see them borne away to the police-station for some offence of drunkenness or brawling.

Seen through the window, they were to us figures of high romance; we communicated with them by signs, and sometimes to the dismay of Old Nanny held conversation with them in the street. It was Bardolph who taught me how to make my first catapult, and Pistol, I think, from whom I picked up a lot of weird expressive phrases which shocked my parents.

At the age of thirty-five or so, they were already confirmed and incorrigible rogues. Magistrates and police despaired of them. And yet there was nothing mean nor sordid about their misdemeanours. Sheer mischief and a sort of impishness illuminated all their crimes. They had an air and even a kind of grace in wrong-doing; and although officially Elmbury had to regard them as a pest, the majority of people were inclined to look upon them as licensed jesters whom we should be sorry to lose. At Christmas-time they always formed themselves into a ragtime band, with tins and penny-whistles, and held the passers-by to ransom, and went begging from pub to pub until they were too drunk to continue any farther. On these occasions they always made their first call at Tudor House, since it was opposite their starting point in Double Alley, and they would kick up a great and merry row outside the front door, beating on their tins and catawauling their seasonal song:

> 'Arise arise and make your mincepies!
> A frosty night and a col' morning!'

Then my father would go out to them and give them half a crown accompanied by a short lecture on their bad behaviour during the past year; and they would sweep off their caps and cry, 'God bless you, Mr Mayor, and a Merry Christmas and a Happy New Year to your good self and the Missus and the little ones; and so help us you'll never see us in the dock again!' But of course at the first Court after the holiday they'd be up before the Bench once more and my father with a twinkle in his eye would admonish them: 'Your promises are like piecrust, made to be broken . . . Seven days.'

The Town Scoundrels

One annual pageant which gave us much pleasure was the slow and ponderous procession of the Town Council as they marched in a body to church on Mayor's Sunday, which I think was the first Sunday after the election of the Mayor. It was traditional that they should attend on that day at whichever place of worship the Mayor belonged to; and you could pick out by their long faces the Nonconformists who were marching towards the Church of England and vice versa; they had the air of men who know that their reluctant steps lead them towards the dangerous slopes of Hell, yet stern duty compels them on.

Whichever church it went to, the procession, which started at the Town Hall, had to pass our window. It was preceded by the Town Band, which came only second to the Fire Brigade as a comic turn to delight the inhabitants of Elmbury. Behind the band shuffled the Mayor, Aldermen, and Councillors in their appropriate robes; the Town Clerk in his wig: the Town Crier, the Beadle and other officials; and behind them, and out of step (for nobody could march behind the Council and keep step) came the Boy Scouts, Girl Guides, Wolfcubs, Brownies, Church Lads' Brigade, and that despised handful of Territorials who were destined so soon for immortal glory.

On these occasions Double Alley, and the other alleys nearby, would disgorge their ragged hordes, and Black Sal and Nobbler Price, the Hooks and all the rest would line the pavement and laugh till they nearly split their sides. Their laughter was not really unkindly and I think the Councillor who wrote to the local paper complaining about 'the cheap jibes and shallow mirth which travestied a solemn occasion' was talking through his cocked hat. Far from being shallow, the mirth sprang from one of the most ancient and most profound of all the sources of mirth: dressing up. Deep down at the origins of kingship, deeper still at the dark roots of religion and magic, lies the notion of Fancy Dress: and the idea that Fancy Dress may be the symbol of an office, marking a man out from his fellows by virtue of his putting it on.

Now there is nothing very funny, if you believe in magic, in the Witch-Doctor's mask; or if you believe in religion, in the Cardinal's hat; or if you believe in monarchy, in the King's crown; but all would probably seem very funny if you were in the habit of drinking with the witch-doctor or the cardinal or the king in the local pub. In fact, what makes Fancy Dress funny is its incongruity; and it was certain incongruous aspects of the Town Council's parade that made Double Alley roar with laughter. My uncle, who happened to be a good Mayor, matched his robes very well, and gave them dignity, and got dignity from them; nobody laughed at him when he wore them. But if Councillor X sold you bad fish and ran after the wenches when he was long past the age for such frivolity – if Councillor Y was your slum landlord and so mean that he wouldn't repair your roof – you couldn't be blamed for having a good laugh when you saw him shuffling down the street in his robes with a sanctimonious expression on his face and a cocked hat on his head two sizes too big for him. Double Alley's laughter, in fact, was one of the ancient sanctions of democracy; and it was a good thing and a proper thing that Double Alley's representatives should dress up once a year and submit to be tested in what is, after all, only a very ancient method of testing witch-doctors and kings.

There were a few who failed to pass the test; and these were the occasion for the popular mirth. ''Ere comes the Town Scoundrels!' Black Sal would cry; and then she would begin her obscene and libellous running commentary. She would announce *urbi et orbi* that Councillor X was desirous of sleeping with the typist in the Borough Surveyor's Office; that Councillor Y was only on the Council because he was anxious to prevent his slum cottages being condemned as uninhabitable. 'Wot's 'e got 'imself elected for?' was her most devastating question; for say what you will about Double Alley, there wasn't much wrong with its sense of values.

There was only one criterion by which it judged the men who asked for its votes each November: were they disinterested or were they out for themselves? This question cut clean across all Party politics, and Radicals would rather vote for a thorough-going dyed-in-the-wool Tory if they thought he was an honest man than for their own Party's representative whom they suspected of being a careerist. A 'gentleman' could always get on the Town Council; not by reason of a preponderant Conservative vote but because the people thought that one possessing independent means was unlikely to seek election for what he could get out of it.

Unfortunately, 'gentlemen' rarely stood; the Council was discredited by its few careerists and slum landlords; and

when, many years later, a lady actually dared to put up for
election, the oldest, the wisest, and perhaps the crookedest
of her opponents ingenuously warned her: 'I'll tell 'ee 'ow
it be, Missus: the Town Council bain't no fit place for a
lady.'

So it came about that a section of the Borough's representatives was held in general contempt, or at any rate
regarded with cynical amusement; and one of the annual
church-going processions – it must have been the last before
the Great War – provoked a remarkable gesture from the
three warriors whom I have named Pistol, Bardolph and
Nym. They had just come out of the pub; and the procession must have been returning from church, for the Town
Band did not accompany it. Pistol, Bardolph and Nym,
being slightly confused by drink, looked through bleary
eyes at the solemn march-past of slow and shuffling feet
and decided that a funeral was going by. They respectfully
took off their caps. A moment later, however, they caught
sight of the top hat and the blue uniform of the Town Crier,
who was one of their cronies and with whom they were
accustomed to get drunk. Horrified lest it should appear
that they had taken off their caps out of deference to the
Town Scoundrels, whom they despised, they hurriedly
replaced their headgear and took council among themselves
how they could best correct the unfortunate impression they
had made upon their fellows. At last they removed themselves to the farther end of the street, where they again
encountered the procession as it approached the steps of the
Town Hall; and were in time to walk slowly past it, arm-in-
arm, caps cocked at a jaunty angle, and singing in some
attempt at unison a bawdy song, lest anyone should be so
foolish as to believe that they held the robed Aldermen and
Councillors in any respect or reverence.

Oyez! Oyez!

The Town Crier, boon-companion of the three warriors, was at that time a very frail-looking old man with a white beard and a thin quavery voice. Presumably he had been capable of shouting once upon a time; but old age had shrivelled him, throat, lungs and all. He was dried-up and perpetually parched; so that between cries he must needs hobble into the nearest pub to wet his desiccated larynx. He cried, in those days, about four times a week, announcing, say, a furniture sale, a bazaar in aid of the British and Foreign Bible Society, a whist drive and dance, or the fact that Mrs Turner had lost her Persian cat. He was paid according to the number of words, and on the average he got about two shillings a time. But for two shillings he had to cry the event a score of times in different parts of the town; and after each cry he had to buy some beer to cool his burning throat; there was little profit in't. His voice faded to a whisper, but the Council was reluctant to depose him; and at last it was by reason of his failing eyesight, rather than his vanishing voice, that he was compelled to retire. He could no longer see what was written on the slip of paper from which he read his cries; nor was he capable of memorizing it. His long career ended in a toothless mumble.

His successor was a great roaring bull of a man with lungs of brass who had been dustman until the Council promoted him. His voice was like a clap of thunder; when he cried at one end of the High Street we could hear him at the other, a rolling crashing sound as of a distant battle. But you could never hear what he said, though he made so much noise about it, for he accompanied his own voice by frantic ringing upon his loud-clappered bell. I have seen people with their hands pressed to their ears, standing a-tiptoe behind him as he cried and peering over his shoulder to read what was written on the sheet of paper.

Passing Acquaintances

Through the window, we got to know, not only these dignitaries, but the more prosaic members of Elmbury's little community; the grave-faced doctor going his rounds, the dentist who bore the bloodthirsty name of Mr Gore, the coal-merchant, the draper, the ironmonger, the butcher, the baker, the landlords of the various pubs, the neighbouring squires and the farmers who came in from the country. We knew an astonishing amount about what went on in the town: who was 'walking out' with whom, who drank at which pub, who had quarrelled with whom, and so on. I have a strong impression that in those days people were less ashamed of their emotions than they are now; they wore their hearts upon their sleeves and when they quarrelled they often quarrelled *coram populo*. They were not at all ashamed of making scenes in the street. At any rate there was a farmer who had an obscure and long-standing quarrel with the parson; and whenever by chance they met they always quarrelled in the street.

The farmer, whose name was Mr Jeffs, looked a bit like the pictures of old Cobbett, with his red face and white hair atop 'like snow on a berry'. He was a huge and florid man who always wore a flower in his buttonhole even at midwinter, whose breeches were always spotless and whose turnout was the smartest in the county. As he drove along behind his shining chestnut cob, he beamed at acquaintances to right and left; but if he saw the Vicar he scowled and shook his whip. It seemed that his grand old headpiece contained like Cobbett's some unreasonable dislikes; and that he shared with Cobbett an abhorrence of parsons because he objected to having to pay tithe.

The Vicar, as a matter of fact, was a most generous man, who'd have given back to Mr Jeffs double the value of the tithe if he had asked for it. Indeed the Vicar's generosity amounted to a mania; he gave away everything he possessed, including large sums of money, and then innocently borrowed from money-lenders in order that he might still be able to give things away. But we did not know this at the time; we merely thought that he must be immensely rich; and Mr Jeffs also thought that he was immensely rich, and that he waxed and grew fat at the expense of agriculture, out of the tithe. So, whenever he met him, Mr Jeffs would shake his whip angrily and cry out in a loud voice: 'Let them as wants Parsons pay for them!' And the Vicar, who was also a hot-tempered man, would engage Mr Jeffs in argument. Soon they would begin shouting at each other, the chestnut cob would prance excitedly, the lash of Mr Jeffs' whip would flick ever closer to the Vicar's nose until at last a crowd began to collect and the two protagonists in sudden embarrassment hurried away.

The Mystery of Fred

Sitting in our window-seat, we got to know the habits of people; for the inhabitants of a small town, much more than city-dwellers or country-folk, are creatures of habit. Always at exactly one minute past six Mr Robertson the draper would pass our window on his way to the Swan; but he didn't take long over his drink, for always at twenty minutes past he was on his way back again. You could set your watch by him. Mr Williams the ironmonger took his wife for a walk, wet or fine, always in the same direction and presumably by the same route at half past two on early closing day. Mr Tanner, who kept a greengrocer's shop, neglected his business only on one day in the year, June 16th, when he let his cherries and strawberries rot and his customers go hang and went fishing; for June 16th was the first day of the season.

In particular was our cousin Fred addicted to invariable and apparently unalterable habits. He was a lawyer, and his office was a few hundred yards from Tudor House, on the opposite side. At nine-thirty, never a moment later, he entered his office; at twelve forty-five, never a moment early, he went home to lunch. Back again at two-fifteen, home for tea at five. He was a mild-mannered, unassuming little man of about thirty-five. In summer he wore a straw boater, in winter he wore a bowler hat; and the change was effected always upon the first of May and the first of October, irrespective of what the weather might be on those days.

We grew so used to the passage of Fred to and fro between his office and his home that when one day he failed to appear it was as if the clock had stopped. Next day he was still missing. 'Where was Fred?' we asked. 'Was he ill?' No. 'What has happened to him?' He had gone away. 'Where had he gone?' Tight-lipped silence.

There were whisperings between Old Nanny and the nursemaid. We knew that 'something was up'. We watched Fred's office and witnessed unusual goings and comings. The police-inspector entered at ten o'clock and didn't come out till lunchtime. We went into the kitchen and tried to find out the truth from Old Cookie; but she was sober and surly, she'd had no drink to loosen her gossiping tongue, and all we got from her was a dollop of uncooked cake mixture, the scrapings of the basin which was so much nicer than real cake, and the usual admonition: 'Ask no questions and you'll hear no lies.'

We never saw Fred again; and it was more than ten years before I heard the strange story – no, fifteen years, because it was told me, when I was old enough to drink beer, in the bar of the Swan Hotel by the old men who sat there after hours. My curiosity had to wait till then; and the story must wait too, until it falls into its proper place in this book. The only clue we children had was the word 'railway train'; Old Nanny, whispering about Fred, had been heard to say 'railway train'. This was very strange, for we had learned that the disappearance and disgrace of Clem, the clever one, the one who was 'too clever by half' for the solid respectable family, was also connected somehow with trains. Trains, therefore, became associated in my young mind with mystery and adventure. They were magic carpets. They puffed conventionally enough out of Elmbury's little station, but they carried you – whither, ah, whither?

Christmas Fair

There was one day that fell in early December, more exciting than Christmas itself; the day of Christmas market. Always on this occasion my father's firm provided sandwiches and drinks for all comers: dealers, smallholders, cowmen, shepherds, drovers. (The more substantial farmers were entertained to luncheon at the Swan.) Great were the preparations on the day before the market. Enormous joints sizzled in Old Cookie's oven; baskets of loaves lay everywhere about the kitchen, huge pats of yellow butter, tongues, sausages, pasties. Maids were busy all day cutting sandwiches, which were piled on dishes and covered with napkins. There was an air of bustle and festivity all over the house; but, alas, the festive spirit coupled with the near approach of Christmas was too much for Old Cookie; when the last joint was roasted, she got drunk. Lachrymose, incoherent, completely plastered, she confronted my mother and was given the sack. Next morning, sick and repentant, she was re-engaged.

Although the sale did not begin till half past eleven, the first beasts began to pass our window as early as half past nine. Thenceforward for two hours there passed down Elmbury High Street a procession such as might serve as a country counterpart of a Lord Mayor's Show. But here were no city financiers whose riches were scraps of paper locked in safes – riches which might disappear tomorrow if somebody else juggled with his shares more cunningly. Here was solid wealth, the real wealth of England, a sight that would have warmed old Cobbett's heart to see: fat oxen, sleek and ponderous, white-faced Herefords curly-haired between their straight horns, Shorthorns as rich-red as the fresh-turned loam, dark as the winter ploughland where the sweat stained their sides; flocks of sheep, broad and flat-backed so that the collies could run about on top of them, thick-woolled, black-faced Oxfords, whose multitudinous breaths in the frosty air made a mist which moved as their great flocks moved like rivers down the street; and huge fat waddling pigs, sows whose bellies had brought forth great litters and which now brushed the earth between their short legs, bacons, porkers, Large Whites, Large Blacks, Middle Whites, blue-mottled cross-breds, sandy Tamworths, and the ancient dappled breed of Gloster Spots.

Here was the annual harvest of the great stick-fattening farms which lay in the rich valleys of the two rivers; here was a season's consummation, the happy outcome of the marriage between English weather and English soil, delivered by the skill and patience of men whose grandfathers had owned their farms before them. To this end the turgid waters of last winter's floods had left their rich alluvial deposit in the meadows, so that the spring grass sprang more greenly; to this end in Elmbury Ham in June, and in a thousand such great hayfields, sweaty men with pitchforks had built a village of sweet-smelling ricks; to this end swedes and turnips and mangel-wurzels, plump roots nearly as big as a football, had alternated in their proper rotations with golden corn and brown fallow on the slopes of the gentle hills which rose from the valleys. And now the purpose of all these labours was manifest. Down the street towards the market on slow hoofs waddled the Champion Beast, great-shouldered, broad-sided, deep-flanked; and a hundred more that were nearly his match. No man so poor that he would not taste a steak on Sunday; no family in such straits that they would not see a joint on their table on Christmas Day.

Just as the Lord Mayor's Show provides its moments of comic relief, so did this splendid progress towards the Christmas market. The calf that planted its legs four-square and flatly refused to budge, though one man heaved at its halter and another pulled its tail; the fat goodwife with a couple of cackling geese under her arms; the bull which entered Double Alley and rampaged about there, so that even the Hooks made common cause against it: all these events were matters for mirth and jesting. And later in the day, when the market was over and the farmers with bulging pockets rollicked home – when the drovers rich with Christmas tips began their Christmas pub crawl – when the butcher who had bought the Champion Beast paraded him through the town with rosettes upon his horns, a mighty fat butcher with a mighty fat beast – what merry greetings passed, what practical joking went on! I shall never forget the butcher's face wreathed in smiles as he met Mr Jeffs who had bred and fattened the champion; beaming at each other, they shook hands, and the crowd in the street cheered and shouted. I shall never forget the butcher's obvious pride that he had paid the highest price for the best animal. Nowadays, it seems to me, too many people take pride in having bought something cheap; but the butcher was proud because he had bought something good, and had paid well for it.

And so dusk fell, and the lamplighter went round with his long pole, the gas lamps glowed yellow, even that wan, cloudy nebulus that burned at the entrance to Double Alley, and the last of the country people went home. Only a few belated drovers still hung about the pubs; and the first carol-singers gathered round our front door to tell their old tale of peace on earth and good-will among men.

Elmbury Goes to War

But peace on earth had ended when I was seven. Already the Volunteers, re-named Territorials, had marched out of their dark and dusty creeper-clad Drill Hall, and the citizens who had always laughed at them for playing soldiers cheered them all the way to the station. Those farmers' sons, small tradesmen, keepers, poachers and hobbledehoys thereafter played soldiers in Flanders for the

better part of five years. They were maimed, blinded, and
slain; and they added proud battle-honours to the colours of
a regiment which already possessed more battle-honours
than most. Two of my cousins marched at the head of them;
one was killed in 1915, the other lasted until the Somme,
when company officers could not expect to last any longer.

But after the soldiers had gone, it was a long time before
the war began to have any visible effect upon the life of
Elmbury. My mother collected vegetables for the Navy; and
I remember the garden looking like a harvest festival, with
piles of cabbages, cauliflowers, lettuces, beets and marrows
on their way to Scapa Flow; but how they got there, and
what state they were in when they arrived, we never knew.
A big house nearby was turned into a military hospital,
and convoys of ambulances occasionally passed our window.
Men in blue uniform, on crutches or in bathchairs, became
a familiar sight in the street. Christmas markets were less
festive, perhaps because there was less to drink; and
Nobbler Price became more sober. Mr Hook sought
sanctuary from his wife in the Army.

And a stranger thing occurred in Double Alley. There
was a barrel of a man, some twenty stone of him, called
Dick Perkins, a genial rogue with mischievous and watery
blue eyes, a drover turned cattle-dealer, who lived there
presumably because it amused him to live there – for he was
prosperous enough to live elsewhere if he had liked. He had
two buxom daughters; and one morning these young
women dressed themselves up in green jerseys and tight
breeches and went off to work on the land. Double Alley,
which had witnessed many shocking things, was never so
shocked as by this tomboyish gesture. Where indecency
was commonplace, the trousers were regarded as the height
of indecency. The outraged neighbours came out in a
bunch to stare.

'The hussies!' exclaimed Old Nanny, as we too stared
from our window. 'They'll never dare to go back there!'
she added; and of course they never did. You wouldn't
go back if you'd lived in a farmhouse and worked in the

green fields. The emancipation of the Misses Perkins had consequences, as we shall see. It was a break with Double Alley's tradition; and it was the beginning of the end of Double Alley itself.

That must have been about 1916. Thereafter the war grew sterner. Officers who were billeted on us from time to time stayed for shorter periods, and always it seemed only a few weeks after they left us that we heard they had been killed. My father, aged fifty, and sick unto death, put on a red armlet and drilled twice a week with a Boer War rifle, or guarded railway bridges against imaginary and ubiquitous 'spies'. Recruiting posters became more frequent and began to betray a slightly hysterical note. Recruiting marches took place in the town.

Even Pistol, Bardolph and Nym were caught up in the maelstrom. These battered veterans of forgotten and possibly apocryphal skirmishes always went about together and generally got into trouble at the same time. They drank, begged and stole as a trio; recently the tall thin one, Pistol, abetted by the others, had knocked a policeman's helmet off, in private spite, while the policeman innocently stood directing traffic at Elmbury Cross. They were still tolerated, although they were such a nuisance, because of their humour, or I suppose I should say 'humours' in the Elizabethan sense; they were 'characters'.

Now one day, as we watched a military band marching bravely down the High Street, on one of the frequent recruiting parades, with a smart squad of carefully-picked soldiers behind it, and behind them a rag-tag-and-bobtail of sheepish-looking civilians who had taken the King's shilling, we were astonished to see Pistol, Bardolph and Nym bringing up the rear. It must have been almost the last time we looked through the Tudor House window; my father had died, and the lovely house was to be sold. Already the auctioneer was busy cataloguing the furniture, posters advertising the 'desirable residence' were stuck up on the walls.

It was high summer, the last summer of the war. The

band blared, and the soldiers marched stiffly at attention, left, right, left, right, never a foot wrong; then came the newly-recruited rabble, shuffling, out of step, looking curiously ashamed, not, I think, because they had joined up, but because they had held back for so long. Somebody from the entrance of Double Alley called out: 'There goes young Bert – at last!' and there was a ripple of laughter. Then came Pistol, Bardolph and Nym. They wore their medals; and they looked like soldiers. They threw their shoulders back, and they cast away all the infirmities which their flesh had inherited from their folly, and they marched. A passing policeman stared at them in astonishment and they shouted some piece of merry rudeness at him. We couldn't hear it, but he roared with laughter and shouted back: 'Now we shall have a bit of peace for a change!'

I suppose they were the dregs of England's manpower. Nym was lame from a wound he got at Mafeking; Bardolph suffered from rheumatics; and Pistol was lame also, but this was not, as he asserted, from the thrust of an assegai, but through falling off a fence, and breaking his leg, while trying to escape from a keeper who had caught him poaching. Crippled though they were, by God they could march. Somebody shouted in jest: 'We must be in a bad way if we've come down to that!' Black Sal came suddenly out of the dark entrance and ran into the middle of the street, pirouetted there screeching and fell in behind them, doing a sort of goose-step. Then suddenly the band stopped blazing, the order was given: 'March-at-ease!' and the soldiers slinging their rifles broke into song with *Tipperary*.

> 'Goodbye—
> Double Alley!'

improvised the three old warriors; and Double Alley cheered them as they went off to their last war.

PART TWO

BACKGROUND TO BOYHOOD

(1919–24)

Country Prep School – Entomology and Port – A Liberal Education – The Scholar Fisherman – The Young Alchymist – Anarchic Interlude – The Facts of Life – Business Man

Country Prep School

SHORTLY after this I was sent to school, underwent certain metamorphoses, and was transformed from a pampered and coddled brat into an extremely tough little ruffian. This was largely due to the glorious prep school, a gracious Georgian house in its own grounds about ten miles from Elmbury, where I learned to tickle trout and to read Virgil; to swim a length underwater and to enjoy English history; all about catapults, and a little about Attic Greek.

The poaching, the swimming, and the catapult-shooting I acquired partly by the light of nature and partly through the companionship of three other boys, Dick, Donald and Ted, who had the reputation of stopping at nothing short of murder. The Latin and Greek I learned from a man who loved the classics and knew how to teach them. One day, when I had been consistently slow at finding the verb in my Latin unseen, he sent me to the Headmaster with a note. The note was folded but conveniently unsealed. Naturally I wanted to find out what had been written about me and what was my probable fate. I hid in the lavatory and tried to read it. But the sentence was in Latin. For the first time in my life it seemed really important to construe a Latin sentence. My mind worked at three times its usual pace, I found the verb more quickly than I had ever found the verb before, and when I had the hang of the sentence I was encouraged to continue on my journey towards the Headmaster's study; for it said: 'Do not beat him with too many stripes.'

This wise scholar, Mr Chorlton, had a cottage at Elmbury where he spent the holidays. He was a link with home, and for this reason I never felt exiled. The school was such a civilized place that terms passed quickly; and in the holidays I never wanted to go to the seaside, but always returned to Elmbury, where Dick, Donald and Ted were near neighbours.

And now with my new-found freedom and my awakened intelligence I began to find out more about Elmbury than I had ever known before. I explored the rivers and the brooks, the field-paths and the woodlands; discovered one by one the villages and hamlets; made friends of poachers and foes of keepers; and enjoyed a kind of Richard Jeffries boyhood in which holidays coincided with seasons and each season had its special delights. Easter holidays were birds'-nesting holidays (curlews and redshanks on the Ham; plovers on the ploughed land; finches in the hedgerows; whitethroats in the nettles; magpies and hawks in the highwood on the hill!) Summer holidays, long and leisurely, were divided between fishing and butterfly-hunting, swimming and 'messing about in boats'. At Christmas we followed the hounds on foot, skated on the frozen floods, learned to shoot rabbits (and other game) with ·22 rifles, went ferreting with farmers, fished for pike.

I never minded going back to school; because school, too, was fun. But always, even at school, Elmbury was the background, its rivers, meadows and lanes were unforgotten, and with Dick, Donald and Ted in the dormitory at night I would plan next holiday's expeditions. We must make another attempt to catch the big carp in Brensham Pond; after that we'd hunt the old willows for Puss Moth caterpillars and Red Underwings; and when it grew dark we'd light lanterns and 'sugar' the trees in the rides for moths. We must tar the bottom of our old boat and make it watertight; we must go cub-hunting in September, and we must ask Keeper Smith if he'd let us beat when Squire started partridge-shooting; we must camp at the Hill Farm and help Farmer Jeffs with his harvest.

Elmbury and its green-and-brown countryside were always the stuff of our dreams. I was getting to know the place as Highlanders know their deer-forests: 'every stick and stone'. I was growing my roots.

Entomology and Port

One evening in the summer holidays we were up in the larch plantation above Mr Chorlton's cottage. Donald and Dick were searching for caterpillars and I was trying to stalk some fallow-deer which had escaped from a neighbouring park and which dwelt there as shyly as fauns in the thickest part of the plantation. Dick found a huge grey Hawk Moth sitting on a larch trunk, and hearing his yelp of delight we gathered round him, admiring the unfamiliar monster, while he stood at the ready with the net. At that moment along came Mr Chorlton, out for his evening stroll.

'Hallo, you rascals,' he said. 'What's the excitement?'

'Big moth, sir. Looks like a funny sort of Hawk.'

Mr Chorlton took one look over Dick's shoulder. 'Good God,' he said.

'Sir?'

'*Sphinx convolvuli*,' said Mr Chorlton, 'come all the way from Africa; and you three rascals pounce on him as soon as he arrives.' He put his hand in his pocket and brought out a large glass-bottomed pill-box. We should not have been more surprised if he had produced a white rabbit or a cage of singing canaries; for although we were aware that Mr Chorlton knew all about Greek accents we didn't expect him to know anything about moths. 'Now listen,' he said.

'If Dick nets him in his rugger-forward fashion he'll spoil him as sure as eggs is eggs. I'll box him for you. But in case I muff it Dick with his net must stand in the slips and you others at point and long stop.'

We watched breathlessly while Mr Chorlton with miraculous calm persuaded the great moth into the pill-box. He handed it to Dick. 'Lucky beggar,' he said. 'In thirty long years *I've* never found one.'

'But, sir, we didn't know *you* were a bughunter!' It was as if Zeus himself had come down to earth and we mortals, discovering his divinity, had exclaimed in awe: 'We didn't know *you* were a god!'

'Come back to the cottage,' he said, 'and I'll show you.'

The cottage lay among shrubberies of rhododendrons and its garden was full of flowers, pentstemon and tobacco-flower and valerian, which we were sure had been planted specially for the moths. He took us inside and sat us down in a room which was lined with books from ceiling to floor. We had never seen so many books in a room before. They mostly had Latin and Greek titles, and it seemed to us that all the wisdom in the world was enclosed between those four walls. Mr Chorlton said: 'I'll go and get the key of the cabinet,' and he left us free to explore the wonderful room. There was a net standing in the corner; and next to it a fishing-rod. In a jar on the windowsill some caterpillars which none of us could recognize nibbled a sprig of birch. And Dick, wandering round the room, discovered a photograph entitled 'Somerset C.C., 1895,' with Mr Chorlton, in flannels and cricket cap, sitting in the front row.

He came back and opened the cabinet doors. The glass-topped drawers slid out silently one by one while we stood and gasped. There long rows of Swallow-tails, Clouded Yellows, tawny Fritillaries in infinite variety; Blues in every shade from pale azure to the kingfisher's own colour: hundreds of little Skippers; and then the Hawks, a whole row of Death's Heads, olive-shaded Limes, Poplars ranging from palest grey to burnt sienna, Eyed Hawks with sunset-flushed hindwings, exquisite pink elephants (not those that topers see!) Bee Hawks and Humming Birds. But there was a gap above the label '*Sphinx convolvuli*'; and Dick, gulping hard and trembling with the ecstasy of glorious martyrdom said suddenly: '*You* have him, sir! Put him in that space!'

'No,' said Mr Chorlton; but hesitantly.

'*Please*,' begged Dick; as a man might offer up his one, his only ewe-lamb as a burnt offering to a god, and yet the cry escapes him, 'Please, *please* take it quickly, lest I repent!'

Mr Chorlton, who was infinitely wise and who knew all this, didn't hesitate any longer. He said: 'I'll keep him, then, because I've got a cabinet to keep him in; but he's still yours and you can come and see him whenever you want to. And now,' he added, 'we'll celebrate the capture of the first living Convolvulus Hawk Moth I've ever seen.' He went to the sideboard and fetched glasses and bottles. For himself he poured out a glass of port; for us, fizzy lemonade, into which he tipped enough port to make it pink. 'This wine,' he said, 'is Mr Cockburn's rarest and most precious; and it's the last bottle; and a great many people would have fits if they knew I poured it into fizzy lemonade. But Convolvulus Hawks are rarer even than rare wine, and deserve a proper libation when they appear.'

We drank to the moth ceremonially; then we sat down, and there was a moment's silence, and suddenly we all three asked questions simultaneously:

'Sir, have you read *all* the books in this room?'

'Sir, are you really a fisherman as well?'

'Sir, did you play cricket for Somerset?'

Mr Chorlton poured himself out another glass of port.

'I've read most of the books; not quite all; but I've still got a few years, I hope, to go on reading. Yes, I am a fisherman, and one day I'll teach you how to catch chub with a fly. And I did play for Somerset, and fielded against Archie Maclaren's 424, which as you know is the highest score in county cricket. Look it up in Wisden, and you'll find out roughly how old I am; if you can do the sum, which is doubtful.'

It was dark before we left. We made Mr Chorlton show

us the caterpillars – which turned out to be Kentish Glories – and then he tied us each a chub-fly out of a starling's feather and a brown hen's hackle, and finally we persuaded him to read us the Frogs' chorus from Aristophanes which always delighted us with its deep-throated 'Brekekoex-koex-koex'. He said goodbye to us, and added:

'Now for an hour I am going to contemplate *Sphinx Convolvuli* and finish the port.'

'The whole bottle?' asked Donald, full of awe.

'The whole bottle,' he said firmly.

As we went down the drive between the dark rhododendrons Dick put into words what we were all thinking. 'He can read a Latin book as if he were reading the paper,' he said, 'and Greek as easy as English. And he knows every moth that flies. And he's a fisherman. And he's played county cricket. What a mixture of things he can do!'

'And the port,' we said. 'Don't forget the port. He's going to drink the whole bottle!'

I think we all resolved that when we grew up we'd be like Mr Chorlton; and it wasn't a bad resolution, for I've never met another who could so beautifully walk the tightrope between the *bios praktikos* and the *bios theoretikos* and get so much pleasure out of the two kinds of life which lie on either side.

A Liberal Education

We had other schoolmasters.

Pistol, Bardolph and Nym were back from the war, unchanged and unreformed. Pistol claimed that the damp trenches had touched up his sciatickee, Nym had a new wound, this one in his backside, Bardolph had seen no Germans, for he had spent most of the time in jail. These three musketeers, to the great alarm of our parents, now took us under their distinguished patronage, and taught us how to set wires for hares, how to caulk a leaking boat, how to cook moorhens on a camp fire, and how to look innocent when we had our pockets full of things which shouldn't be there. Others contributed their knowledge and experience to make sure that we had a liberal education. A man called Jim Meadows, who was a porter and billposter employed by my uncle's firm, showed us how to make bird-lime out of boiled holly-bark and, with a decoy, to catch linnets and larks on Brockeridge Common. I don't know whether the Wild Birds' Protection Act was in existence at that time; I think it was; but it made no difference to Jim Meadows, who went about openly carrying clap-nets with which he cleverly swept goldfinches off the thistle-heads. He lived in an alley – not Double Alley, but one nearly as bad – where he kept in a home-made aviary canaries, bullfinches, jackdaws, magpies and even owls; he also kept, uncaged, somebody else's wife.

Old Jim introduced us to the dawn and the dusk, taught us much about walking in the woods at night, about traps and nets and ferrets, and above all about birds. For although he caught and caged them, inflicting great cruelty without even understanding that he was being cruel, he loved birds and knew more about their songs, their nests, and their habits than many naturalists who write books. Jim couldn't write at all; in my uncle's office, if it were necessary for him to sign anything, he would explain, 'I'm no scholard,' and make a cross on the paper: Jim Meadows, his mark. Yet he made a lot of money, partly out of the canaries, which were famous songsters, and partly out of antique furniture, which he could price more surely than most dealers. Whatever he made he drank; and when he was drunk he would go off and commit an assault upon the pusillanimous husband of his mistress, adding injury to insult.

A professional fisherman called Bassett was another of our holiday schoolmasters. He got well paid by the gentry for taking them out in his boat and showing them the likeliest places for sport, yet he would often sacrifice the chance of earning ten shillings to spend the afternoon with us and to teach us what he knew. He taught us one thing that nobody else could: he taught us to be quiet. Chatter and sudden

movement he abominated; he was the *stillest* person I have
ever known, as still as the cat waiting for the mouse, as the
stilt-legged heron fishing in the shallows. When he rowed
the boat you could not hear the splash of the oars nor the
creaking of the rowlocks; whenever he moved his action was
slow, calculated and completely silent. He was a hard
taskmaster; he would never let us rest our rods on the side of
the boat – 'Birmigum fishing,' he called that: the city-
dwellers' Sunday afternoon out. Always we must hold them,
although they were much too heavy for us, in aching arms
until we got a bite. If the float bobbed, there must be no
exclamation, no schoolboy's yelp of delight when the fish
was hooked. And when we caught one it must be killed
silently and swiftly – 'kill it as if you were a murderer,' was
his grim and blood-chilling instruction – lest it flap about on
the floor boards and drive the others away. He had never
read *The Compleat Angler* but old Izaak's motto, 'Study to be
quiet' was his also.

When fishing was over, he would take us home to tea. His
house smelled strongly of napthaline; for whereas Jim
Meadows' was full of live birds – there you might share
your bread-and-butter with a pecking magpie – Bassett's
birds were all stuffed. He was the local taxidermist; and he
had a strange limitation for although he could skin a bird or
an animal both quickly and cleverly – he taught us the trick
of it – he was absolutely incapable of stuffing them in a life-
like way. To sit for long among the birds and beasts in
Bassett's back room was to indulge in a palaeontologist's
nightmare; those finches, gulls, hawks, kingfishers, jays did
not belong to the present, but to some dark and remote past,
they were the prototypes, the remote amorphous ancestors
of our birds, those badgers, squirrels and stoats had a lizard
quality, they belonged to the forests of the Coal Age rather
than to our English woodland. They all suffered from the
same kind of distortion, as if you looked at them in a concave
mirror – for they were all to a ridiculous degree attenuated.
They looked as if they had been starved for months and then
for weeks painfully extended on a rack. In particular the

stoats and weasels, by nature tenuous, at Bassett's hands became almost eel-like; they were dreadful. And there was a heron with its long thin neck stretched out so that it looked like a pterodactyl.

Yet Bassett was proud of these creatures of his fantasy. He never tired of showing them off to us. In particular he was proud of a peregrine falcon which he had shot himself. If you have ever seen a peregrine, or any other kind of hawk, you will know that the most striking thing about it is the beauty of its eyes. But the artificial eyes which Bassett had seen fit to insert in his peregrine's head could not by any stretch of the imagination be said to resemble a hawk's; they might perhaps have looked realistic in a stuffed goose. The effect was too terrible for words. Bassett had a box of 'assorted eyes' which he had bought from a dealer; and he pulled them out at random, without respect for the size or nature of the creature he was stuffing. In consequence most of his birds had the appearance of bleary drunkards or squint-eyed lechers.

But we always enjoyed having tea at his house, although to Mrs Bassett the parlour must have seemed a Chamber of Horrors indeed. There were fishing-rods everywhere, with hooks dangling down haphazard so that they were likely to catch you as you passed by. A damp fishing-net smelling of waterweed leaned against the table. A bucket of live bait provided a hazard in the doorway. On the floor lay a basket with half a dozen moribund eels. A side-table was littered with scalpels, scissors, skulls, skins, and cakes of arsenical soap, to say nothing of a stick of cyanide for taking wasps' nests. (Yet Bassett's six grubby children all survived.) There were sure to be wasps' grubs, maggots, and worms in tins, and pike-spinners with more random hooks to catch the unwary.

And elsewhere, all over the room, on the mantelpiece, on bookshelves, wherever there was space, the frightful creatures of Bassett's myth extended snake-like necks and stared with glazed and terrible and dissipated eyes. On the hearth two parodies of badgers sat up and begged. In a glass case were squirrels on a tree-trunk, a kind of set piece which one might describe as an extravaganza on the theme of squirrels. Over the fireplace a crested grebe, with outspread wings like a Phoenix, looked backwards from its tortured neck and gaped with open beak at the wall.

The Scholar Fisherman

Bassett taught us the hard discipline of angling; Mr Chorlton soon taught us its beauty, when he took us up the river on calm summer evenings and showed us how to throw a fly. He was careful not to suggest to us that this method of fishing was necessarily superior to any other, so we grew up without any silly snobbery about floats and worms; instead we took the sensible view that the purpose of fishing is to have fun. We were equally happy, therefore, whether we were catching bleak with houseflies, or watching the long black porcupine quill when we fished for tench and bream, trolling for pike in winter, or sitting, oh! so quietly, in the stern-sheets of Mr Chorlton's boat while with exquisite grace he swished his shining split-cane rod and sent out the cobwebby line towards the dark eddy under the overhanging willows.

It was Mr Chorlton's custom (anathema to Bassett) while fishing to talk. He would chide the reluctant fishes with a quotation from Shakespeare, ask the favour of the immortal gods in Latin, curse a broken cast in Homeric Greek. He never talked down to us. If we didn't understand what he said we could always ask the meaning of it. And so we did, with the result that we learned a great many wise sayings in a far more pleasant way than if we had been sitting at a schoolroom desk.

The Young Alchymist

I left prep school in a blaze of glory. Illicitly and in secret, like an alchymist of old, I was conducting a complicated chemical experiment in an empty form-room when the bell rang for chapel. The experiment was somewhat empirical; it consisted of mixing together a number of different substances to see if they would explode. The chapel was next door to the form-room, and boys and masters had to pass through the form-room in order to get to it. Panic-stricken, I hid my concoctions in the grate, wiped my hands on the seat of my trousers, and wearing an expression of great piety went in to my prayers. The Headmaster entered, we knelt down, and he began to pray. He had got as far as 'Forgive us our trespasses' when a tremendous explosion rent the air. The whole building shuddered; bits of plaster fell off the ceiling; and soon wisps of smoke drifted across the aisle, smelling acridly of phosphorus. The Headmaster finished the prayer and led us out in silence through the shattered form-room. The grate was blown clean out, and with it most of the chimney. Even in my terror of the consequences I could not help reflecting with justifiable pride that my experiment had succeeded.

But it was the end of term, and my last term, so the consequences were not very serious. I stuffed my trousers with brown paper, but the precaution was unnecessary. The Headmaster had delegated my punishment to Mr Chorlton, who looked at me sternly and asked: 'When you mixed those chemicals together were you trying to prove anything or were you just hoping they'd explode?'

I thought it safest to be honest. 'Hoping they'd explode, sir.'

'Good. I was afraid you might have had some serious scientific purpose. If so I'd have beaten you. The educational value of chemistry is almost exactly equal to that of a jigsaw puzzle. Make stinks for fun, but if you want to *learn* things, stick to Virgil. You can go.'

Next day I had to see the Headmaster himself, to say goodbye. This was a ceremony at which, it was understood, we should be told the Facts of Life. We who were leaving all waited anxiously outside the Head's door and went in one by one. It was terrifying; we vaguely expected some sort of a revelation. What appalling mystery was about to be revealed to us? A boy came out snivelling. Our terror increased. What dreadful initiation went on behind that closed door? But when I got inside the Headmaster merely delivered a dissertation on the subject of dirty jokes. I didn't know any dirty jokes, so this rather missed its mark. However, I pretended to snivel when I came out; it seemed to be expected; and upon the face of the boy whose turn it was to enter I was pleased to see the appropriate expression of fear.

Anarchic Interlude

From the glorious free-and-easy prep school I went to a hateful public school where I found I was expected in summer to play a regimented kind of cricket instead of collecting butterflies and in winter to go for compulsory runs, curiously termed 'Voluntaries', instead of watching birds. I discovered that my form was still reading Ovid's *Metamorphoses* and Caesar's *De Bello Gallico*, which I knew practically by heart; so I decided to do no work until the tasks set for preparation became more interesting.

Unfortunately Mr Chorlton, who had instilled into me a love of the classics, had also communicated to me his own contempt for mathematics; so I decided to give up all mathematical studies also. I remained in the same form, called Upper Shell B, for three years, which was a record for the school.

But when I was not engaged in avoiding work or in escaping the consequences of having done none (exercises which required more application and ingenuity than I should have expended on the work itself) I read everything I could lay hands on, from Kipling to Shelley, from Surtees to Keats. I read all the plays of Shakespeare, including *Timon of Athens*; the poetry of Meredith and the prose of Thomas Love Peacock; the whole of *Man and Superman*, and *Tristram Shandy* four times. I even read *The Golden Asse*; it was discovered in my desk and confiscated as 'indecent literature'. Two Elephant Hawk caterpillars, and a lot of Burnet moth cocoons, were also found in the desk and confiscated at the same time.

I became a kind of anarchist. On OTC field days I deserted, hid in trees, and looked for birds' nests. I refused to play football, and went fishing for perch in a farmer's pond instead. As a punishment I was sent for long runs; this pleased me, because instead of running I concealed myself in a chalk quarry and looked for fossils. In form I never even attempted to solve the problems of Euclid, but instead decorated the foolscap sheet with maps of Elmbury, its confluent streams and rivers, its rabbit-warren back-streets, its roads and lanes which led to a dozen delightful villages, all infallibly drawn from memory. And on another sheet I made a calendar of all the dreary days, and blacked them out one by one, and counted daily the remainder, until the holidays came round again.

Release from this anarchic and unhappy existence came unexpectedly before I was seventeen. My uncle was old and likely soon to retire; his promising sons had been killed in the war; the 'family tradition' would be broken unless I joined the firm. It was suggested to me that if I liked to go into his office I could leave school at once. I wasn't enthusiastic about the office; but I passionately hated school, and I left it immediately, unregretful and unregretted.

The Facts of Life

During my last summer holidays a second attempt was made to teach me the Facts of Life. The Vicar, who was still borrowing wildly in order that he might be still more wildly generous, presented me with three expensive books and a spinning-reel and unexpectedly asked me to go fishing with him. This surprised me, for I didn't know he was an angler; and I didn't want to go, because it was the day of Elmbury Mop Fair. This was Elmbury's annual saturnalia, round-abouts were set up in the streets, and stalls which sold sticky gingerbread, and booths where you could have your fortune told, or see the Fattest Woman in the World, and the Hairiest, and the smallest Pigmy, and the Web-footed Man; and the Nameless Delights of Paris. I should have liked to have spent the afternoon at the Fair, visiting these marvels and shying at coconuts; but it would be impolite to refuse the parson's invitation, so I rigged him up a rod, dug some worms, and we set out. It was soon apparent that the man had never fished before; because he could not bring himself to impale his worm, and I had to do it for him. We sat in silence and watched our motionless floats. It began to rain. He cleared his throat. I had a terrible premonition that he was going to ask me if I knew the Facts of Life; and sure enough a moment later he began:

'Forgive me asking, dear boy . . . but your father being dead . . . as a great friend of your mother . . . and your parish priest . . . I feel it my responsibility . . .'

I was sorry for the poor man in his embarrassment, so I told him airily, yes, I knew all: my schoolmasters, before I left, had told me all the Facts of Life. He appeared relieved; and a moment later he suggested that as the fish weren't biting we might as well go home.

I had my revenge for my wasted afternoon. I made him take off his own worm; and he was nearly sick. That evening with Dick, Donald and Ted, I went to the Fair. We saw the Fat and the Hairy Women, the Pigmy, the Web-footed Man, and the Nameless Delights, which were so unimpressive that I have forgotten what they consisted of. We won armfuls of coconuts. We rode on the roundabouts and the swings and the cakewalk, we slid down the chute, and then stood at the bottom to watch three little wenches, with their skirts up to their middles, come tumbling down after us. We lifted them to their feet and took them on the swings. We bought them gingerbreads and sticky sweets. One was blonde, one was brunette, and one was red-headed; and later, when we left the crowded noisy streets and the weird white light of the naphtha flares, she taught me much more about Life than the parson had suceeded in doing.

Business Man

The time had come now for me to be articled to my uncle and to go into his office.

I was a lanky youth of seventeen. I had an astonishing store of knowledge about a number of things which were scarcely relevant to a commercial career. I could read the New Testament in Greek and recite much of the Georgics from memory. I knew the names of most wild flowers, could recognize most butterflies and moths and tell you their life histories, knew the birds' songs, their nests, and eggs, and had read the whole of Geikie's *Geology*. I could sometimes catch fish when wise old anglers couldn't; could shoot, ride a horse, sail a boat. I had read without discrimination every novel, play or biography I could lay my hands on, and I swallowed poetry with the voracity of a sealion swallowing fish. My method (which makes me shudder to think of it now) was to obtain from the Public Library the collected works of some poet, Tennyson or Browning or Longfellow, and read the whole lot, slap through, from page one to the end. In this fashion I had read the whole of *The Dynasts* when I was sixteen.

With these qualifications I set out to become an auctioneer.

PART THREE

GOING, GOING

(1924–7)

Grandstand for Sociologists

THE PROFESSION is not very highly regarded, as professions go; but if any earnest young student with a BSc and little experience of life asks me the best way to begin the study of sociology I shall suggest at least two years in the office of an auctioneer.

Consider the opportunities provided by such a course. The auctioneer's job brings him in touch with every class and person; we are all, at some time in our lives, landlords or tenants, buyers or sellers. It gives him the entry, from time to time, into every house in his district, great or small. So does the doctor's profession, or the parson's; but the doctor sees people only when they are ill, or when they think they are ill, and when the parson visits people they are either on their best behaviour or on the defensive. The auctioneer sees them at their best and worst; and usually at the time when some crisis, financial or otherwise, has disrupted their lives. He sees them when the head of the house has died; when their little business has gone smash; when they are in arrears with their rent; when the landlord has given them notice to quit; when the bum-bailie is seizing their furniture for debt; when they go bankrupt. He sees them when they are compelled by circumstances to sell their most precious possessions, and when they are covetous to buy the possessions of their neighbour. He sees homes set up, and homes broken; he sees poor men get rich and rich men ruined. He meets man in all his moods and all his manifestations: in sorrow, in avarice, in courage, in greed, in good fortune and bad, in the shadow of death itself.

Yes; the student of social science could do worse than become a clerk for a year or two in some such office as my uncle's. But this is very much of an afterthought; for I myself was nothing of the kind. I was a tough young rascal with my head full of poetry and the rest of my interest divided pretty equally between horses, fishes, motor-bikes and girls.

The Office

The office stood in the High Street, quite close to Tudor House; by squinting sideways you could still see Double Alley out of its big plate-glass window.

It needed a coat of paint outside and a thoroughly good clean-up inside. It was shabby with the shabbiness of enormous respectability. A coat of paint might have suggested that it needed (like a tart) to advertise its presence. Such a notion would have been abhorrent to my uncle. As for cleaning it within, there were documents and shelves of books on which the dust had lain since 1750. In the course of a spring-clean papers would be disturbed, books no doubt would be mislaid, it would be difficult to find things afterwards. That notion was abhorrent to my uncle also.

If the place was drab and dusty, then the very drabness and dustiness were earnests of its integrity. Cheapjacks and bucket-shops, no doubt, had to look smart; we could afford to be shabby, as a gentleman can afford to wear shabby clothes.

Although the building was large, with plenty of rooms to spare on the first and second floors, everybody who worked there crowded together on the ground floor. This was either because nobody had ever been able to face the task of clearing the junk from the upstairs rooms or because none of the partners would move up there for fear of being left out of whatever was going on. Instead my uncle and his two partners sat together in a very small office so full of maps and papers that if a fat farmer should visit them there was literally no room to turn round.

A slightly bigger office – the one with the plate-glass window – accommodated the articled clerks, who perched like monkeys on high stools at a long polished desk. In a corner of this room, hidden away and surrounded by a sort of barricade, as if we were ashamed of them (as indeed so old-fashioned a firm might be) reposed our only typewriter and an astonishingly pretty typist.

The walls of this office – and indeed of every room in the building – were lined with books: books in red morocco bindings, several thousand of them, which contained the 'Particulars of Sale' of every property that had passed through the firm's hands – almost every dwelling-house, in fact, every farm, smallholding, shop, pub, orchard and meadow within six miles of Elmbury. Out of these dreary-looking books, if you shook off the dust and opened them at random, sometimes there would leap out at you names that were pieces of poetry: the ancient country names of wood and field; names like Poppies' Parlour, Salley Furlong, Coneygree, Hungry Harbour, Merry-come-Sorrow.

There were other books, rows of great ledgers, which con-

tained a record of all the firm's transactions since its founda-
tion in 1750. If somebody could have translated the contents
of those books into terms of flesh-and-blood – of human
prosperity and human catastrophe – he would have been
able to read the complete social history of a county during a
period of one and a half centuries. Indeed, he would have
found, within the stout leather covers of those books, a
microcosm of English life and history. He would have
learned how good times had alternated with bad: how poor
men had risen to wealth and power and how rich men had
come down into the gutter; how the great farming families
had prospered, generation after generation, until some elder
son, by his folly or his drunkenness or his bad luck, had
brought them to bankruptcy and their patriarchal acres
under the hammer; how little tradesmen and smallholders
had struggled in vain against periodic 'depressions', against
the flow of economic tides which they were as powerless as
Canute to stem. It would be a tale of great manors and little
country pubs; of deer-parks and jerry-built housing estates;
of pheasant shoots and workmen's cottages; of bloodstock
and the poor man's pig.

Written here, in the neat impersonal handwriting of nine-
teenth-century clerks, you might read how John Smith in a
lucky year received two hundred pounds for the fruit in his
orchards on High Perry Hill; how he took a pub with the
proceeds; and how, four years later, when he had drunk
away all his capital, the miserable remnants of his estate were
sold by order of the Official Receiver in Bankruptcy: one
kitchen table; two Windsor chairs; pony trap; bay gelding,
aged. You might read how a June flood ruined a dozen
farmers whose hayfields lay along the banks of the river;
how a man was saved from disaster by a sudden miraculous
crop of mushrooms which appeared like manna from heaven
in his barren fields; how a great estate was broken up because
the son who should have inherited it married a barmaid
against the wishes of his father; how another was sold because its owner fell at Bloemfontein.

England's wars would cast their shadows over the pages of

the books and Stock Exchange crashes have their reflection there. They would reflect faithfully how successive Acts of Parliament had prospered some fortunes and caused others to decline. The clerks' cold copper-plate would record in brief undramatic entries, as Gabriel himself, the inevitable consequences of human frailty and human passion. And the old story of Naboth's vineyard would be told again there.

But the dust lay thick on the firm's old ledgers, and nobody took them down off the cobwebby shelves.

Words

The duties of an articled clerk were not very arduous. We were expected to learn the value of things, and the way to do that was to see things sold. We went to all the sales, of farming-stock, of horses, of growing fruit, of furniture, and stood beside the auctioneers, writing down the price and the purchaser's name in one of the red morocco-bound books. (Modern firms use tear-off sheets for this purpose. These would have seemed shockingly impermanent to my uncle, who believed that if a man bought Lot 224 Bedroom Utensil and sundries for two shillings the fact should be recorded for two hundred years.)

We also accompanied the partners when they made farm valuations, or took inventories, or valued a publican out of his old pub or into a new one. Thus we learned the huge and strange vocabulary of the auctioneer's catalogue; and we learned also those old and curious systems of weights and measures which are used to describe quantities of the various things men buy and sell – we got to know the precise meaning of such terms as a pipe of cider, a pot of plums, a bundle of osiers, a foot of timber, a bag of peas, a boltin of straw.

Even as a child I had loved words and the bright or sombre patterns which are made of them; and the new vast vocabulary delighted me. Nobody, surely, employs in his everyday work a greater number of unfamiliar nouns than the auctioneer. Each trade and business has its own extensive vocabulary; but the auctioneer must know them all. Each of his catalogues is addressed to the expert; and when he gets up in his rostrum to sell he must be prepared to speak as an expert. In the stock market he must talk of down-calving heifers, tegs, tups, wethers, ewes in yean, large white bacons, and so on. At the farm sales he will have to offer such things as a half-legged gelding, a Massey-Harris binder, GO lines, a scuffle, and a set of badikins, whipple-trees, swiveltrees or suppletrees (the term varies according to the district). And he must know the terms, not only of the farmers' and the horse-copers' trade, but of the timber-merchants', the builders', the market-gardeners', the publicans', and many more. Moreover, he must pay tribute in the proper form to the Lares and Penates by cataloguing correctly the thousand-and-one household possessions of all kinds and conditions of people; the mahogany tallboy, the Welsh cheese-cupboard, the whatnot, the oak refectory table, the Windsor chairs, the Wedgwood plates, the copper-lustre jug, the Worcester teaset; the glass, the brass, the pewter, the linen; the pictures and books; the kitchen utensils; the garden tools. And if by chance it falls to his lot to make a valuation or hold a sale in a factory, he must accustom his tongue to the outlandish new words which men use who speak of machines.

If nouns were gold, he would be richer than Midas; yet in curious contrast his adjectives are as beggarly, as threadbare, as out-at-elbow and down-at-heel as you would expect them to be after having been overworked for nearly two hundred years. The Desirable Freehold Residence; the Capital Farming Stock; the Sound Pasture Land; the Commodious Premises; and the Old-world Cottage: the adjectives never vary. But perhaps after all it is not for lack of epithets that the auctioneer always uses the same one; there is a con-vention in the matter, as strict as that which bound great Homer himself. The Residence must be Desirable; just as the dawn was always rosy-fingered.

Foot-and-mouth

During that winter of 1923–4 there was a widespread epidemic of foot-and-mouth disease. It passed like a blight from end to end of our green vale, striking at random the smallholder's little piggery and the dairy farmer's pedigree herd. Nobody knew where it would appear next; some farms escaped although surrounded on all sides by the infection, others remote from any outbreak were suddenly stricken.

The weekly markets were closed, except for the sale of fat stock to be killed immediately; and the auctioneer's painful job was to value the affected herds for purposes of compensation. Thus I had a grim introduction to agricultural life. There was no work to do in the office; we just sat and listened for the telephone. It rang almost every day to summon us to another valuation: the disease had been confirmed on a small farm near the Leigh; Guilding had it at Dykeham; Loveridge had it at Hardwicke; the vet had been called to investigate a suspicious case at Coombe Hill.

It was like the plague that walketh at noonday; and the farmers feared it almost as much as Londoners once feared the plague. Mr Jeffs, driving down Elmbury High Street behind his high-stepping chestnut, encountered the Vicar and demanded in a loud voice why he didn't pray. 'If thee be any good,' said Mr Jeffs rudely, 'get down on thy knees; for that's what we pay thee for, out of the Tithe.' Shaking his whip threateningly, as Cobbett once shook his whip at the Botley Parson, *Earn thy keep*, roared Mr Jeffs; and with that he flicked his mare, and her bright-shod hoofs struck sparks out of the cobbles as she set off at a good spanking pace towards Hill Farm.

But when he got home – 'twas a judgement on him, said old Jabez Jones who worked for the Vicar and believed in an old-fashioned, implacable and hard-smiting Jehovah – when Mr Jeffs got home his cowman asked him to have a look at a calf which was drooling saliva and going a bit hoppy on its off hind. Early next morning our telephone rang; and it summoned us to Hill Farm. It was a still, misty day; and as we drove along the brown dripping lanes we could see here and there the smoke rising from funeral pyres, and we could smell the sickening smell of burning flesh and hide.

For although only a single beast on a farm might be affected, all the rest of the stock had to be slain. This was the decree of the Ministry of Agriculture; and it was probably a wise decree. But the carrying-out of it was painful and often tragic. Because of one sick beast – such as Mr Jeffs' drooling calf – a whole healthy herd of valuable dairy cows might have to be killed; and not the cattle only, but also the sheep and the pigs. When that was done, and the bodies had been burned, the farm would be 'shut-up' for weeks. The farmer must not restock his land until the mysterious infection had been given time to die out. He was not allowed to buy or sell; and in any case he had nothing left to sell. Even though he was paid compensation for the slaughtered beasts, he suffered a loss which was always crippling and in some cases ruinous.

When we arrived at Mr Jeffs' farm we found a printed notice on the gate – 'Foot-and-mouth Disease – Road Closed', and the village policeman already standing guard. The Ministry's man and the slaughterers were waiting for us; we all put on rubber thigh boots and rubber gloves and smocks to cover our clothes, and went up to the farmhouse to meet Mr Jeffs. He took us through the wet November fields, through the Home Orchard and the rough ground called Starveall, to the meadows where the cattle were peacefully grazing: a herd of more than fifty pedigree Dairy Shorthorns which represented, perhaps, half of Mr Jeffs' working capital.

'Took twenty years to build up that herd,' he said. He looked at the Ministry's man, as if he pleaded, 'Surely there's some way out, surely you won't kill my beautiful cows?' He went up to one and ran his hand over her sleek side. 'Brockeridge Bountiful,' he said. 'I bred her on the farm. Refused seventy-five for her only last week.' We all tried not to look at Mr Jeffs; it didn't make any difference, we knew, whether the cow was Brockeridge Bountiful worth seventy-five guineas or just Blossom or Daisy or Old White-face, gone in two quarters and worth a tenner for fattening. Pedigree Shorthorn or old screw, it must be slaughtered all the same.

Mr Jeffs, usually so jovial, looked grey and old. 'My father never used to take no note of foot-and-mouth,' he said. 'Nine times out of ten he'd cure it with a bit of rocksalt and a dab of Stockholm tar.' He couldn't understand the necessity for wholesale massacre; couldn't understand the new scientific methods, the careful statistical surveys, which had proved to the Ministry of Agriculture that it was better to slay ten thousand beasts than to risk the infection of a million: a million which might recover but would be useless for milk or fattening for a year. Mr Jeffs didn't realize that if the epidemic was allowed to spread it might ruin the whole industry of stock-rearing for a generation. He only looked back into his long memory and remembered what his father and his father's father had done. 'Rocksalt and a dab of Stockholm tar . . . If they'd killed off grandfather's herd for foot-and-mouth he'd have shot 'isself.'

My old uncle, silver-haired and courtly, sympathetically shook his head.

'It's a bad job, Mr Jeffs, a bad job.'

'Aye, 'tis a bad job'; and Mr Jeffs shrugged his shoulders and accepted it, as he accepted bad seasons, floods in hay-time, or thunderstorms at harvest which cost him five hundred pounds. But he did not wait to see the slaughterer begin his grim business; he turned away suddenly, muttered something we could not hear, and with bowed head made his way back towards the house.

The Invisible Invasion

The cause of the disease was a virus; but nobody knew how the virus was spread. There was one theory that foreign straw, used in the packing of imported goods, brought it to the farms; another that it came on the feet of starlings and other small birds which in the autumn conduct mass migrations from Holland and Belgium across the North Sea to Britain. Once the virus was planted in the soil or grass any one of a dozen agents might bear it elsewhere and spread it about the countryside: rooks, stray dogs, night-prowling foxes, far-wandering hedgehogs, the tyres of the corn-merchant's lorry and, of course, man himself – the farmer when he went to market, the cattle-dealer travelling from farm to farm, the poacher who knew no boundaries, the squire's guests at the shoot, even the vet himself.

Therefore, as soon as an outbreak was confirmed, the Ministry's experts must carry out a very thorough piece of detective work. What stock had been bought or sold recently, and where had it come from? Who had visited the farmer during the previous week? – A commercial traveller selling cake? Good; his movements would be investigated. Farmer Jackson from The Mythe? – We must keep an eye on his cattle. The squire's agent, looking at the gates? – We must find out where he went afterwards. And so on.

Sometimes these inquiries had embarrassing or comic consequences. The son of a farmer whose cattle got the plague had been secretly courting a neighbouring yeoman's daughter whom his parents disapproved of. Torn between fear of the Ministry's inspector, fear of his own father, and fear of the girl's father (whose cattle he might have infected) he eventually confessed; and, thinking that he might as well be hung for a sheep as a lamb, married the girl into the bargain.

But there was precious little comedy during that dark depressing winter, which in memory smells of disinfectant and burning flesh. The post-war prosperity which had made our farmers rich now suddenly ended; there had been two bad seasons in succession, followed by this plague of foot-and-mouth. The closing of the markets froze whatever assets the farmers had; and private dealing ceased too, for no stock could be moved on the roads unless it was going straight to the butcher. Moreover, for the first time perhaps, farmers were not as a matter of course welcomed on each other's farms; who can tell, each thought, but that *he* has the scourge, unbeknownst, and brings it on to me upon his boots? So the flow of money ceased and soon the people of Elmbury found themselves face to face with a severe local depression. Tradesmen had bad debts, the first since the war; bank managers wore long faces; dealers, having nothing to deal in, took to drink. Even my uncle's firm, which had stood like a rock through many economic storms, began to feel the effects of this one. Our turnover at markets had been two or three thousand pounds a week; there wasn't much profit in the foot-and-mouth valuations, and there was certainly no pleasure as we went upon our grim errands through the muddy lanes, with the stench of burning always in the air, and always in the evening the glowing ashes of the fires dotted along the horizon, like beacons warning of invasion.

But this invasion came stealthily, invisible, unheard, unheralded, as random as the winds. That wheeling flock of starlings drooping to roost in Towbury Wood might be the carriers of it. The red fox slinking down the hedgerow as he set out upon a mating prowl might take the virus twenty miles in a night on his soft pads or between his toes. Even Poor Tom, the half-wit who was trying to empty our rivers, might bear it upon his feet as he shuffled with his leaky bucket towards some distant brook.

The Wind Blows Cold

Partly as a result of this epidemic, partly through national and world causes which we knew nothing of, a cold wind of economic depression began to blow through the vale; Elmbury felt it too, the townspeople as well as the country-folk turned up their collars, put their hands in their pockets – and found nothing there. Elmbury had no independent industries; it was simply a market or clearing-house for the produce of the farmers on the one hand and the goods of the industrial cities on the other. It bought corn, cattle, sheep, pigs, eggs, butter and garden produce, consumed them, or distributed them to the big towns; it sold in return agricultural machinery, cars, lorries, cattle-cake and the various domestic goods which its tradesmen obtained from the manufacturers. But eighty per cent of these goods were bought by the farmers and others who got their living from the soil; theirs was the only real purchasing power, because they were the only real producers. In fact Elmbury was a perfect example of a 'country town'; because without the country it would have perished.

As we have seen, it had no industries that were not directly connected (eg, flour-milling) with agriculture; it had no considerable population of rentiers, for it was not a residential town, and the retired colonels and rich widows preferred to live in more fashionable places; and it had not yet discovered its one valuable and 'invisible' asset, the traffic in tourists, nor was it selfconscious enough, in 1924, to exploit it.

So when the farmers lacked ready money, there was scarcely a man or woman in Elmbury whose livelihood was not affected. The doctors, the dentists, the vet found that their bills were not being paid; the publicans sold less beer; the ironmonger's premises remained overstocked with tools and implements which he could not sell; the draper was the poorer because farmers' wives bought fewer new clothes; grocer, tobacconist, butcher, took less money and had less to spend in their turn; and Mr Tempest the bank manager received anxious letters from his head office inquiring why so many of his clients' accounts showed balances in red.

'Twas all the fault of the foot-and-mouth, people said; and blamed, as usual, the Ministry of Agriculture. We did not know, then, that there were other and more profound causes of the trade depression, connected with sterling and the gold standard and international markets; we did not know that the wind of which we felt the sharp edge already was a mere zephyr compared with the blast which would soon wither us. We were blissfully unaware of the storm that was brewing in London and New York and Amsterdam; so we put all our troubles down to the autumn epidemic of foot-and-mouth, and looked hopefully to the spring.

The Idle Apprentices

Though my uncle and his partners went about with grave faces, and shook their heads over their December balance-sheet, we clerks were nothing loath to be idle, and spent the time very pleasantly sowing a winter crop of wild oats.

There were two other youths articled to my uncle, tough and happy-go-lucky fellows who mistrusted me at first because it had been reported to them that I had been to a public school, was probably lahdidah and sissy, didn't drink beer, and wore plus-fours instead of the conventional breeches and gaiters. Sure enough I arrived in the hateful plus-fours; and it was also true that at the age of seventeen I wasn't very familiar with pubs. Both matters were soon put right. I bought some breeches which were even yellower, and some gaiters which were even shinier, than theirs; and to match both breeches and gaiters a horse (eight pound ten from a friendly dealer) which although spavined and gone in the wind was possessed of a flashy and exhibitionist nature, and bucked me through the plate-glass window of Mr Tanner the greengrocer the first time I rode it.

As for pubs, by Christmas-time there were very few in Elmbury or in the neighbouring villages which I didn't know. On Boxing Day we drank our way from the office to a dance at Brensham Village Hall which involved stops at the George, the Shakespeare, the Black Bear, the White Bear, the Trumpet, the Cross-Keys, the Fox and Hounds, the Royal Oak and the Railway.

It was a useful apprenticeship which I served with these two merry ruffians; for I am sure it is a good thing to learn about drinking when you are young. At seventeen you are an experimentalist; and your methods are empirical. You learn by trial and error, you make yourself sick, you make yourself sozzled, but you're very unlikely to make yourself a drunkard. Not so the man who has remained a teetotaller until he is thirty. He has been brought up in the belief that drink is an evil, and that it is only tolerable if taken 'as a medicine' or 'in strict moderation'. So at some time when the winds of the world blow unkindly about him, chilling his thin teetotaller's blood, he takes a drop 'as medicine' and perhaps he takes two or three drops because after all that is 'strict moderation'; but – mark this carefully – he is too old and too set in his ways to undertake empirical experiments, he hasn't the guts to get roaring drunk to see what happens. Instead he applies reason to the matter, and takes each day just as much as he thinks will 'do him good' (biologically the right amount to do him the maximum harm). He's afraid of the stuff; and the man who is afraid of it is already halfway to a toper's grave. He discovers that it takes a little more 'to do him good' every month or every week; and down he goes to his dreary end, without even having had his money's worth of fun.

So I thank the good god Dionysus for the company of Stan and Geoff, those rip-roaring sons of yeomen who taught me the rights of the matter when I was seventeen. The worst consequence that happened was a spill off the back of a motor-bike when we skidded at forty round a sharp corner slick with frost. I was thrown slap into some milk-churns which were standing on the grass verge; and I daresay I should have hurt myself if I had been sober.

Come Lassies and Lads

Village dances were minor Bacchanalia, and would probably have shocked the Bright Young Things of Mayfair who at that time were very much in the news. It is a fallacy that country boys and girls dance the polka and sing folk songs; the favourite dance of the 1924 season was the Charleston, and Ern, the leader of the band, who also played centre forward in the football team, sang hot jazz. As for drink, there was the pub next door; and our village virgins weren't too finicky to enter its little bar nor too unsophisticated to drink gin and Italian.

My memory of the affairs is made up of noise, kisses, and warm sticky hands. But they weren't just village hops; a dance was an occasion, and the farmers' sons wore tails and white waistcoats, the girls wore their best and most exiguous frocks. It was the accepted custom towards the end of the evening to lead your heart's fancy outside, snow or fine, and to walk with her down the dark lane where you might or might not find a car to sit in. (For most of the young men came on motor-bikes, nor was it very unconventional to ride to the dance on horseback, as I did before I'd saved up enough money to buy an old Triumph.) The astonishing thing, remembered in tranquillity, is the fortitude of those village maidens, who would face frost and blizzard in a thin scrap of a dress all for the sake of a little inept and rough-and-tumble love-making.

Satellite Villages

The dozen or so little villages that lay in a circle about Elmbury were as planets to her sun. Economically, they were sub-markets, smaller distributing centres for goods, smaller receiving centres for produce; but each was a social entity nevertheless, each had built around its church, pub, shop, and village hall a local tradition. All shared the common tradition of Elmbury; each possessed its own individuality and character, as the different sons of one mother.

Thus Brensham was the cricket-village. As long as men could remember its village green had been rolled and mown till it looked every summer like a billiard cloth. If you passed through Brensham after work in the spring you'd scarcely fail to see old Briggs the blacksmith rolling the pitch, and some of the village boys loosening up their bowling-arms or knocking a ball about the nets. Each Brensham generation gave one or two professionals to the county team; and often you would see a Harlequin cap on the village green, as Mr Chorlton, standing behind the net, taught the yokels how to slam a loose ball round to leg.

Yet the neighbouring village, Kinderton, had no cricket team and was noted for darts and drunkenness, which it practised simultaneously. The Men of Overfield had a tradition of poaching; there was a permanent gipsy camp on their common, and a gipsy admixture in their blood – dark and sombre men, they were, who would never tell you whither they were going nor whence they had come. Dykeham folk were fishermen and liars, to a man; they had a stuffed pike in their village pub which they said weighed twenty pounds and had been caught on a minnow; yet it was common knowledge, outside Dykeham, that the creature had weighed just twelve and a half pounds and had been picked up dead after the draining of Dykeham Pond thirty years ago.

The Tirley people were famous boatmen; as indeed they must needs be, for their low-lying village was half-flooded for three months of the year; they were Rough Islanders indeed. At Tredington, which was river-rounded too, the people grew osiers and were handy at making baskets and wickerware. The village of Warren was noted for fair women and also for promiscuity; its illegitimate birth-rate was the highest in the county, a fact of which it was proud and boastful. Flensham was well known for its footballers; Marsham by reason of the fact that every cottager possessed a pig; Oxton for wheelwrights; Lower Hampton for woodmen; and Adam's Norton for singing – everybody sang in Adam's Norton, its church choir often came to Elmbury and sang in the Abbey, while in the Salutation Inn (which was the curious name of the Adam's Norton pub) you could hardly hear yourself speak for the hollering of old songs and new songs and particularly of bawdy songs, which the wicked old men of the village had invented and matched to hymn tunes and handed down to their sons.

There was only one of the satellite villages which seemed

to have no individuality or character of its own. This was Partingdon, which possessed a rich and generous squire. He ran the cricket club, the football, the village whist drives and had built the cricket pavilion and the village hall. His wife organized the Women's Institute and the Mothers' Union. His gardeners mowed the cricket-field.

In Partingdon every well-behaved person was certain of employment; because the squire employed everybody on his estate. He also housed them, arranged their recreation, and pensioned them when they were old.

There were no ill-behaved persons in Partingdon.

Yet this ideal village, where nobody ever got drunk or had illegitimate babies or sang bawdy songs or made revolutionary statements in the pub, seemed somehow unnatural and we always felt vaguely uncomfortable if we went there to play cricket or darts. It was the same kind of uncomfortable feeling which one has when one visits a hospital; Partingdon was a sterilized sort of place. ''Twould give a man the willies to live in Partingdon,' was the kind of remark one heard afterwards. The well-meaning paternalism had somehow emasculated it; and to go from thence to Adam's Norton just three miles away was like passing from a prim chintzy drawing-room tea party into the company of merry men at a good pub.

Songs at the Salutation

The landlord of the Salutation Inn at Adam's Norton was a small merry man who reminded you sometimes of a towelled fox-terrier and sometimes, in his less decorous moments, of a minor and mischievous imp. His pub was noted not only for singing but for huge fires, which on winter nights he stoked continually so that people remarked that he was getting into practice. His reply was always the same: 'I believes in being comfortable. You're here today and tomorrow you're bloody dyud!'

He had a moronic cousin who helped him in the bar, a

good-natured oaf with a tremendous body and a tremendous voice for singing. This oaf was called Herb; and the landlord tells how once he went off to a Licensed Victuallers' Dinner at Elmbury and foolishly left Herb in sole charge. When he got back he asked him how he'd got on. 'Fine,' said Herb, with a great grin. 'They were all drunk by closing-time.' It began to be apparent to the landlord that Herb also was drunk. 'How much money did you take?' he asked. Herb went to the till and counted it out laboriously. 'Three and tuppence.'

Herb, though his voice was so powerful, knew only one song, which was called Dumbledumdollakin. It was a wonderful thing to watch Herb's enormous chest working like a blacksmith's bellows as he roared the chorus:

'Dumbledumdollakin,
Dumbledumderry!'

and I often thought it was the only cheerful song they sang at Adam's Norton. All the rest were either sad, sardonic, mystical or obscure. They delighted most in those in which bawdiness and irony were mixed in equal proportion with a mournful nihilism, or in those which were mystical and almost meaningless like 'Green Grow the Rashes O!'

'Two and two for the lilywhite boys,
Clothe them all in green-O!'

This they sang exquisitely and with a sort of reverential air, as if they knew it was strong magic, which indeed it is.

Market Day

In the early spring the epidemic of foot-and-mouth disease gradually died out and the stock markets were reopened at last. Like flood water when a dam bursts the stock poured down the vale and off the neighbouring hills to the weekly fair at Elmbury. The sheep indeed were like a flood flowing down Elmbury High Street, up Station Street, and into the market, where their dammed stream widened and flooded into a great pool as the separate floods, white woolled, dirty-grey woolled, ochreous and chrome yellow (for some had been recently dipped), joined together in one flock a thousand strong and belonging to fifty different owners. Their owners, their shepherds and their yelping collies added to the confusion as each tried to sort out his own. We clerks were called in to help; we rolled up our sleeves and plunged into the bleating flood, tackling, heaving, pulling this way and that, until our arms were greasy with lanoline off the fleeces and our breeches were covered with muck from the backsides of the nervous ewes. My uncle, seeing me at work, patted me on the shoulder and said: 'That's the way, my boy: I believe in young men starting at the bottom'; and never realized that he had made a joke.

On market days we always had about three jobs to do at once. We stood beside the auctioneer and took down the prices and the purchaser's name as each lot was sold; then dashed across to the little office at the market entrance and made out the purchaser's bills, took their money, gave them their receipts and strove to keep our books accurately: a job that would have taxed the arithmetic of a bookmaker's clerk.

It is a great wonder to me that we ever succeeded in balancing the books when market was over. The record of a multitude of transactions, involving two or three thousand pounds, was scribbled in pencil on a greasy or rain-soaked sheet smeared probably with marking-paint or sheep-raddle. Sums as difficult as '69 tegs at 56/6' had to be done 'in our heads' among all the distractions of the crowded market: squealing pigs, cursing drovers, dealers shouting their bids, cows running amok, greetings and badinage flying hither and thither. The little 'market office' where the purchasers paid their bills was always filled with an assortment of noisy, angry, disputatious or drunken people. There were always half a dozen arguments going on which he had to settle. An old woman had lost the hamper in which she had brought her ducks to market. Somebody else had taken the wrong lot of pigs. A drunken dealer angrily denied that he had bought 12 heifers at £17 10s. Two farmers were having a political argument. A man in a hurry to catch a train emphasized his urgency by banging with a stick upon the rickety table.

Conversation Piece

' 'A didn' 'ave no call to take th' 'amper as well . . .'

'Walked off with they under my very nose, 'e did, twelve little weaners, an' there was one screwey one amongst 'em, an' I said to our Alfie, I said, Mark 'em on the arse with blue crosses, and so 'e did, and I'll 'ave the law on 'im as took what 'e'd got no right to . . .'

'Never looked at the auctioneer, never so much as blinked me eyelid. As a matter of fack when they was knocked down I was 'avin' a pint at the Red Lion . . .'

'Wot I thinks is this, there be three pestses us has to contend with, rooks and wireworms and Ministers of Agriculture . . .'

'Nah then, *nah* then, bloody fine clurk you are, bin waitin' ten minutes, got to ketch me trine to Bairmigum . . .'

Market-peartness and Illiteracy

We learned the virtue of patience in a hard school; for everything had to be explained very slowly and carefully to people who were partially illiterate or partially drunk or both. We have a term in Elmbury which is used mainly by wives to describe the state in which their menfolk return from the fair: the term is 'market-peart'. 'Peart' signifies sharp, like rough cider or an unkind word. The man who is market-peart is raw and ultra-sensitive; his women know that they must feed him and let him be, and avoid the provocative word.

This was our maxim too. We must humour them. Dealers who could appraise the exact value of a bunch of heifers or a close-packed penful of ewes were incapable of doing the simplest sum of addition or subtraction. They scarcely ever wrote out their own cheques. They would sign them (usually with a blunt indelible pencil, which they first sucked, so that the signature was a blue smudge) and then they tossed us the cheque so that we could fill in the amount they owed. Once, when I was very hard-pressed, I lost my temper and snapped 'For God's sake, write it out yourself – can't you see I'm busy?' There was no answer. I threw the cheque back. Still no answer. I looked up, surprised that I had got no angry reply. Instead of the red-faced infuriated bully I expected to see, a man with gentle and timid eyes glanced furtively over his shoulder at the impatient crowd behind him, then swiftly leaned down towards me and whispered: 'Scribble it out for me, mister, please, it won't take a minute. I never had no schooling. Except to sign my name I can't manage writing.'

I still remember my embarrassment and shame, and I remember also the amount of the cheque – it was three hundred and seventy-two pounds ten. The dealer who couldn't write was a far richer man than my uncle, or any of the Elmbury doctors, or the manager of the bank.

Not only were we subject to these numerous distractions while we dealt in happy-go-lucky fashion with several hundreds of pounds but we were extremely haphazard ourselves. We had been told that it was part of our duties 'to get to know the farmers'; we interpreted this – correctly, for it was the only way – as 'to have drinks with the farmers'. So we would frequently dodge backwards and forwards between the market and the Red Lion, with our pockets stuffed with cheques and notes, and perhaps would borrow five bob from the takings to buy a round of drinks. Yet we were hardly ever short when we came to balance at the end of the day. Bank clerks would have been scandalized by our conduct; because they have a worshipful attitude towards money. They see money in terms of respectability; because respectability means credit balances and cheques that are always honoured. We, who never in those days had more than a few shillings of our own, saw money made and spent by feckless farmers as if they were lords; and we crammed the crumpled notes into our pockets as casually and contemptuously as if we had been lords and millionaires too.

Economics of Farming

'Getting to know the farmers' took me some time. The first step was to know their names; for it was regarded as elementary good manners to address a man by his correct name when you greeted him and shook him by the hand. City-dwellers, conscious of their unimportance, aren't so particular. They know there are so many people like them; they don't expect to be remembered. But a farmer is used to being known on the roads, in the shops, in the pubs, for twenty miles around. He is aware of his own personality. He is Mr Jeffs of the Hill Farm or Mr Nixon of Downend, and he expects everybody to know it.

There were no short cuts to this knowledge, as I discovered when I greeted a fierce red-bearded man as Mr Trewin on the strength of the name on his dray; but his name was Mr Yarnall, he had bought the dray at a sale, and Mr Trewin – it seemed – was his deadliest enemy.

The next step was to visit the farmers in their own houses. Encouraged by my uncle, who abominated motor-bikes, I bought a new horse and rode him from farm to farm, visiting perhaps half a dozen villages in a day, Brensham, Kinderton and Overfield in the morning, Dykeham, Tirley and Tredington in the afternoon. Farmers, who on the whole live isolated and solitary lives, are always glad to see a visitor. They always asked me in to have a drink, and if by rare chance they were teetotallers they offered me cider which was often more potent than whisky. Their lovely rambling farmhouses were always cool in summer and warm in winter when a great open fire burned in the living-room. These farmhouses were very gracious places. The furniture had been passed down from generation to generation; it was generally good and sometimes rare. And how well appointed the kitchens were; what an array of dishes, saucepans, coppers, ladles, kettles, all spotless and shining bright, how well stocked were the larders, what variety of herbs and spices were there, what great hams hung from the ceiling! The farmers had been brought up to know what was good and to abhor the cheap and the shoddy. The gun standing up against the wall was generally a Green or a Purdey; it was never a cheap foreign make. The farmer's boots were always good boots (the sticky ploughland would have found them out if they weren't!), his breeches and his jacket were made by a good country tailor out of the best cloth he could buy. He had learned – as he of all men should learn – that it pays best to buy the best.

I often wondered how much money these successful farmers made. They were certainly not rich in the sense of having a lot of capital behind them; they didn't have much money to spare to invest in property or securities, though their farming-stock and cultivation alone locked up perpetually a capital amounting to thousands of pounds on a big acreage. Mr Tempest the bank manager once told me that I would have been surprised how small in relation to their capital their incomes actually were: £800–£1,000 per annum was the average for a 350-acre farm in a good year. But of course this only represented what went through the banking account and was shown in the Income Tax return; lots of transactions would be conducted in cash, and probably the whole of the *personal* expenses of the farmer – drinks and meals on market day and so on – would be paid for in cash out of money that properly belonged to the farm. Moreover, the farmer and his wife, and the whole of his usually large family, would live off the farm to a great extent; they wouldn't need to buy milk, butter, bacon, eggs, chickens,

vegetables or fruit, so their cost of living would be at any
rate halved. Probably the real income of these men was
nearer £1,500 a year; and they had very little to spend it on.
Clothes lasted them till they wore out; neither they nor their
womenfolk were much concerned with fashions. Hunting
was free, or indeed showed a profit, because they would
often buy young horses at the beginning of the season and
sell them as 'made hunters' in the spring. Shooting cost no
more than the cartridges (and the sale of rabbits balanced
even that cost). Doctor's bills were infrequent. The car and
most of the cost of running it were a charge upon the farm.
The only other expense was the education of children; but
this was not heavy, for the boys went to Elmbury Grammar
School, and the girls to the High School, where the fees were
fairly low. In any case the girls, by helping in the house, and
the boys, by working on the farm, more than paid the whole
cost of their own education; the wages of the equivalent
hired labour would have come to much more.

To Be a Farmer's Boy

They had fine upstanding sons; and they practised among
themselves, whether consciously or unconsciously I am not
sure, an admirable form of artificial selection. Indeed, I
believe that the farming community is the only one, in
England, which still breeds at a sufficient rate and yet
manages to keep its stock sound by the inbreeding of good
qualities. Modern biologists believe that not only ability,
but specific kinds of ability, can be transmitted from generation to generation. In the Elmbury district the farmer's sons,
a boisterous rip-roaring breed, had their young flirtations
with the local barmaid; but in the end, almost to a man, they
married farmer's daughters. The offspring were likely to be
homozygous – they would carry a double dose of the good
dominant tendency; and so the stock improved itself by
selection. Unfortunately England's wars imposed a different
sort of selection, and killed off a high percentage of this good

stock as soon as it became bullet-worthy, but before it had had time to breed.

For they were not the sort who would hold back. They went to the Great War with the yeomanry, riding their own horses which they refused to leave behind; about twenty of them from the Elmbury district alone. Somebody decided that the time had come to 'exploit a break-through' and ordered the cavalry into the gap. But there hadn't been a break-through, and there wasn't a gap. The young men settled down in their saddles and rode as they would ride a Point-to-Point into the enemy lines. Both of Mr Jeffs' fine sons fell that day; and after four years, out of the twenty, only seven came home.

It was these seven, and some younger ones just out of school, whom I met first at markets and got to know later out hunting and at shooting-parties and Point-to-Points. They were strong as lions, merry as crickets, and proud as Lucifer. There was no game or country sport which they did not excel in, with the exception of fishing; this they considered 'too tame'. (Curiously enough, you hardly ever find a farmer who is a fisherman.) But they were grand free-hitting cricketers, good shots, and remarkable horsemen. They raced and rode to hounds with the recklessness of John Myttons. They sometimes broke their bones, but horses couldn't kill them, it took motor-bikes to do that. When they turned their attention to motor-bikes terror came to the quiet country lanes. Previously their recklessness had been limited to some extent by respect and pity for horse-flesh; but for internal combustion engines they had neither respect nor pity, and since fear was unknown to them it was inevitable that some of them should break their necks.

The Grammar School had given them as much schooling as they were prepared to take; they could do simple sums (and even a few complicated ones, for they kept their father's books and practised the usual ingenuous deceptions upon His Majesty's Inspector of Taxes), they could read, and actually did read the poems of Whyte-Melville, and they could write (though they could not spell) in that large, round, schoolgirlish script which is due to lack of practice. Their big hands were unfamiliar with pens; but they could do most other things with them, they knew how to hold the reins when the four-year-old started bucking; how to chuck the gun when the pheasants streamed over down-wind, how to set the ploughshare at the right angle, how to use a scythe with beautiful and rhythmic grace, how to lay a hedge, how to carpenter a gate, how to hold a new-born lamb, how to snap a rabbit's neck, and how to take an engine to pieces -- although they despised engines.

You would meet them at market, fresh from a nine-mile walk leading the bull which was 'so bad-tempered they didn't trust the man with it'; and if you walked round with them you'd find out that even at twenty they could price a pen of sheep to within a few shillings, a milking cow to the nearest pound. Most of them kept pigs, which are on most farms the sons' perquisites, as poultry are their mothers', and they would drive a hard bargain till the dealers cried out for mercy and said, 'When you boys step into your fathers' shoes, we'll all be ruined!' You would meet them again in the bar at the Shakespeare (for their fathers went to the Swan) drinking quarts of beer and flirting outrageously with Millie and Effie, the two blonde barmaids.

These two merry wantons, whose favours were famous for miles, were at once generous, fickle, careful, and utterly amoral, yet they did not lack either tenderness or humour. They were therefore the very thing for awkward young men between the ages of eighteen and twenty-one; and in Heaven it shall be accounted to them for virtue that they never broke a home nor a heart beyond mending, that they never spent more of a young man's money than he could afford, and that they endured the amateurish embraces of hobbledehoys and sent those hobbledehoys away, in the fullness of time, wiser and better and tenderer men.

Midnight Steeplechase

And you would meet the farmers' sons at village dances, with scrubbed and shining faces, very stiff and uncomfortable-looking in their white waistcoats and. tails. On one occasion – it was just after Ted Norris had broken his neck in a motor-bike accident – no less than six of them arrived at Brensham Village Hall on horseback. It seemed that a sort of Trades Union of fathers, alarmed at the increasing mortality among their sons, had gone on strike: Not a penny of pocket-money unless you give up your motor-bikes. They stabled their horses at the Bell Inn, danced till one o'clock in the morning, and then sat drinking with the landlord at the Bell in a private room until nearly three. When they saddled up their horses it was bright moonlight; and this reminded them of the old engravings of 'The Midnight Steeplechase' which hung in the Shakespeare bar. I believe it was Jerry Nixon from Downend Farm who actually had the idea; he was generally the ringleader of their mischief. 'I'll race you all to Elmbury Cross for a fiver,' he said, 'and the Devil take the hindmost!'

They agreed that the landlord should be starter. Each could choose his own route, either cross-country or along the road. It was four and a half miles to Elmbury Cross: just the right distance for a Point-to-Point. They shortened their stirrups and prepared to start.

But there was a girl, Dorrie Monks, who had somehow got left behind after the dance. There had been a muddle about who was to take her home; or more likely, for she was a great tomboy and very much in love with Jerry, she had deliberately given her partner the slip in order that she might have a drink with the boys at the Bell. They had arranged with the landlord to put her up there; but goodness knows what her father would have to say in the morning, for he was the sternest and strictest of all those farmers who had banded themselves together against motor-bikes and wild behaviour. Now Dorrie went up to Jerry as he prepared to mount his great horse Demon, and whispered something in his ear. He grinned. 'Damn it,' he said, 'you're right. Demon won three races last spring; he must carry a penalty!' – and he lifted her up and perched her on the saddle in front of him, one hand round her waist, the other holding the reins.

'Now, Mister Landlord,' he said, 'we're ready when you are. Give us a start.'

They went down the village street with an appalling clatter, waking half the inhabitants including the policeman, who pursued them ineffectually on his bicycle. At the end of the village they began to scatter, each taking his own route. Denis Woodbridge stuck to the road, which luckily was not tarmac'd in those days. Derek Surman chose the road too; but he preferred to gallop down the grass verge where he soon encountered a heap of stones into which his mare neatly pitched him. Pat and Ray Loveridge went across country and were doing well until they came to the Carrant Brook, which was in flood. Their horses couldn't jump it, so they swam across; but the delay beat them. Tom Spry also went across country, but he suffered from two handicaps: he was drunk, and his horse was one of those fortunately rare and perverted beasts which from time to time elect to lie down without respect for their rider's wishes and roll in the mud. When he was sober, Tom could usually prevent this; but he was far from sober. The horse rolled to its heart's content and trotted home, leaving him incapable in a Slough of Despond.

Jerry and Dorrie left the road early, took a bridle path along the river bank, and found the going very easy; they would have won had not Dorrie remembered a short cut across her father's farm but forgotten that the vital gate had been padlocked on account of a troublesome bull. Finding their way barred, they tried another short cut through the garden; but here again the gate was locked – Dorrie's father was a careful man – and Jerry decided to put Demon at the fence. They cantered up to it through Mr Monks' asparagus bed; and Demon would have managed it easily, even with the double load, if he had not slipped on the soft ground just as he was taking off.

Dorrie fell clear; but Jerry was pinned to the ground by Demon's heavy quarters, and as the horse got up its off-hind hoof struck him on the head. It wasn't a serious injury; but it knocked him out, and it caused a great flow of blood. Dorrie, meanwhile, was smothered with mud and scratched by the thorn hedge, and her dress was practically torn off her.

This, then, was the tableau which confronted the amazed Mr Monks, who had a cow calving and therefore happened to be about early: a great horse careering over his asparagus; a seemingly moribund young man whose white shirt and waistcoat were smothered with blood; and a half-naked daughter.

It took him about a week to see the joke. Meanwhile Jerry was put to bed in his house and anxiously nursed by Dorrie. Jerry's father arrived in a great rage determined 'to give the boy a good talking to'. But Jerry, looking very pale and with his forehead full of stitches, disarmed him altogether by saying:

'Well, Dad, you might just as well have let us ride our motor-bikes!'

He then called Dorrie, who was shamelessly listening outside the door, and before Mr Nixon could get in a word they'd confessed to him that they were going to get married.

'Well, I'll be beggared!' was all Mr Nixon could say; and having suitably blessed them he went downstairs and discussed the matter with Mr Monks, who brought out a bottle of whisky, so that they sat together drinking all the afternoon and on into the evening. From shaking their heads over the irresponsibility of their offspring they got to shaking their heads over their own youthful follies, and to wishing they too were young again and congratulating each other that their children were none of your namby-pamby modern brats but chips of the old block, young rips to be proud of.

And then they each had another drink, the last in the bottle, to celebrate the engagement.

The Long View

Jerry took a small farm of about eighty acres; it was an uneconomic size, being much too small, but as his father said, 'It'll do for him to practise on.' Mr Monks added gloomily that 'It'd learn the young folk that farmers lose money, but 'tweren't big enough for them to lose too much.'

It happened, however, that by sheer good luck Jerry made more profit, in his first year, than either his father or his father-in-law. The little farm had two orchards of very good Bon Chrétien pears. The trees were bearing well, whereas on the whole it was a bad fruit season. Jerry asked my uncle to sell the growing fruit by auction. Three dealers bid against each other for the Bon Chrétiens and ran them up to two hundred and fifty pounds.

The two old men, stocking up their land after foot-and-mouth, faced a loss on their year's trading. After the sale they congratulated Jerry on his good fortune, but they spoke wise words of warning also. Mr Nixon said:

'Average it out, my boy. Average it out over ten years and then you'll see what the orchard's really worth. Gold doesn't grow on pear trees.'

And Mr Monks said:

'Don't let it go to your head. I've seen more young men ruined by a good first season than by a bad one!'

Both had been farming for forty years. They took the long view. They knew that any fool, given a bit of luck, could make a profit on a single season; but it took a good farmer to tide over the bad seasons which would follow as sure as the leaves would fall.

Orchards

These sales of growing fruit were a pleasant contrast to the bustle and noise and worry of markets. They took place on summer evenings in the leafy orchard country around Brensham Hill. We would meet the buyers at the farm gates and lead them through the orchards; they would see the fruit half-formed already though the late snow of fallen petals still sprinkled the grass between the trees; and they would calculate in their wisdom how many pots of plums or apples or pears or cherries were a-growing there among the green leaves, safe and sure save for the slight risk of a June frost or a July blight, waiting only for St Swithin's rain to christen them and the midsummer sun to paint them purple or yellow or red. At the gates of each orchard we would pause, and wait for the oldest and slowest of the buyers to catch up with us; and then my uncle would ask them what they would bid for the season's prospects, how much for the apples which as yet were knobbly and green, how much for the cherries which were so small you could hardly see them and to which the last reluctant petals still stubbornly clung.

The Blow a-Blowing

Blossom-time was always a period of anxiety in the neighbourhood of Elmbury where big areas were given over entirely to fruit-growing. For the market-gardeners and fruit-farmers it was a time of hoping and fearing, praying and cursing, rejoicing and grieving. How anxiously they read the weather forecasts (if they had faith in meteorology) or consulted the wet-and-dry thermometer at their back door (if they understood it) or more likely prognosticated country-fashion on the basis of the behaviour of birds and animals, the colour of a sunset, or the remembered jingle of an old weather rhyme!

We didn't like the blossom to come too early. In forward seasons the plum orchards would get their first sprinkling of snow at the end of March, with the cherry – 'loveliest of trees' – breaking into full bloom a few days later. The growers would shake their heads gravely. 'Hast seen the blow a-blowin' at Brensham? ... If we should get two-

three sharp frosses now . . .' That would mean the ruin of
their crop; in some cases, where 'little men' depended on a
few acres for their livelihood, it might mean their own ruin.
They dreaded the brief white frosts of middle spring which
crept with the early-morning mists up the valley; but worst
of all were hailstorms followed by keen nights:

> 'If the drop do freeze in the cup of the blum
> We shall have neither cherry nor plum!'

And yet if the season were too kind there would almost
always be a glut of fruit so that the crop was practically
worthless. The weather, and the law of supply and demand,
worked hand-in-hand with a crazy capitalism to frustrate
the fruit-farmer; so that his best hope of making money was
that a hard frost should blight the trees of his neighbours
and, as sometimes happened, leave his own unharmed.
Given such a stroke of luck, a man whose average profit was
two hundred pounds might make two thousand. Thus was
fruit-farming conducted in a state of anarchy and disorder;
with that old and disorderly anarch, the weather, turning
things topsy-turvy each year.

Timber

All manner of things came our way for sale or valuation from
time to time: shop-fittings, the machinery of a flour-mill,
builders' materials, standing timber, the stock-in-trade at
public houses. Timber was an expert's job and we used to
call in the help of a wonderful old man called Charlie
Hewlett, who was over eighty, yet he could walk all day
through woods and parkland, and when he had stared at a
tree for a few seconds through his old and bleary eyes he
could tell you its height and girth and its cubic content when
reduced to timber. Although he was the judge condemning
them to death, a hundred great trees in a day, he loved them
and would shake his head sadly over the fate of each. ' 'Tis

a fine sound oak,' he would moralize, 'and three hundred years if it's a day, and all sprung from one little acorn. 'Twould thrive for another three hundred if 'twere let be. Pity, pity.' And he would pick up a sprouting acorn and plant it in the soil. 'Please God make that grow another oak as fine.' Alas, I doubt if any of Charlie Hewlett's acorns are saplings now; for you can't plant a tree like that. Rabbits nip off the green cotyledons; cattle and horses eat the young sprout down to the ground. But there was something in the idea; England would be a lovelier place if landlords were compelled by law to plant a tree, and to tend it, for every proud spreading oak or tall elm their woodmen chop down.

It was my humble task, at these valuations, to chip off a piece of bark with a hatchet and paint a number on the smooth piece of wood; which was like signing the tree's death warrant, for next season the timber-feller would come with his axe and saw, and read that number upon the paper his master had given him, and set to work upon its great bole.

Pubs

Public-house valuations were also matters for a specialist; but we had an expert of our own in one of the partners who knew all the esoteric customs of the trade. He carried a curious little instrument in a box, with which he performed experiments upon samples of whisky and gin. He was inclined at first to be rather secretive about it; I think he liked to be thought a bit of a witch-doctor; and he was disappointed when I demonstrated that I could use the little instrument too and carry out the simple experiment for determining specific gravity. 'Do they teach you *that* sort of thing at school?' He was rather shocked. 'Waste of money,' he said; and I remembered Mr Chorlton's advice: 'Stick to your classics,' and agreed with him; though I daresay he'd have thought Latin and Greek were a waste of money too.

These pub valuations, in contrast to those of Tenant Right

and farming-stock, were rather sordid affairs. Death or
disaster was almost always the occasion of them, for inn-
keeping is rarely a lifetime's profession like farming and a
man takes a pub when he retires in order to ensure him
company and a small income during his declining years.
He stays in the same pub, as a rule, until he dies or until the
brewers kick him out. Therefore our clients on these occasions were generally either distressed widows or men
broken by drink or – curiously enough, most frequently of
all – men broken by their wives' drinking. I remember one
meek little man who hadn't a vice in the world, nor a five-
pound note, who flitted about nervously while we valued
what little was left of the spirits and confided to us tolerantly:
'It's the missus, you see, bless her, she likes her little nip
from time to time!' Another inn-keeper, ruined by horse-
racing, was far less interested in the price he would get for
his few remaining assets than he was in a peak-faced menial
wearing a battered bowler hat who crept in and out of the
bar furtively bearing betting-slips to Mr Benjamin, the local
bookie. A seafaring man, whose arms and neck were tattooed
with landscapes showing the seafronts of Yokohama and
Singapore, and with dragons from China and wondrous
beasts from all the jungles of the world, accompanied our
deliberations with song. He was suffering from delirium
tremens, and the words of his song, endlessly repeated were:

> 'O for the wings of a—
> *Soda-water-bottle!*'

and each time he came to the words 'soda-water-bottle' he
made the appropriate gurgling and sizzling noise.

Sometimes neither drink nor women nor betting were the
ruin of the publicans, but just sheer financial folly or bad
luck. There were certain small dingy pubs in depopulated
villages where it was impossible in any circumstances to
make a living. These, of course, were the ones we got to
know best: the tenancy changed every two or three years.
There was one in particular which stood in a small village

opposite another, and larger, pub called the Angel. It was always a wonder to me that anybody ever went to the little pub at all, so dreary and dismal was it both inside and out; and indeed, scarcely anybody did, except on the occasion of the installation of a new landlord, when it was likely that there would be free drinks all round. The old men of the village sombrely accepted these, drank them rapidly, wished the newcomer luck in much the same tone as one would use in wishing luck to a man suffering from an incurable disease, and took themselves off, shaking their heads and declaring gloomily: ' 'E seems a nice fellow enough, but 'e'll never do any good there 'cause 'e's got the Angel up agin 'im!'

The last owner of this pub, which was a free house* and was known throughout the village as The Landlord's Ruin, had more money to spend than his predecessors. He soon realized that there was no profit to be made out of the old men, so he decided to try to attract the custom of the town. 'I'm going all out for the Better Trade,' he said; by which he meant young men in sports cars and girls who drank gin. To the great wonder of his neighbours he installed a chromium-plated cocktail bar and a shelf full of unfamiliar bottles bearing unfamiliar names. He had a card printed and placed it in a glass frame outside; the village came to read it and lo! the first title in the long list was:

BOSOM CARESSER

The village went away dismayed; but the landlord stood happily in his cocktail bar experimentally compounding many-coloured drinks and waiting for the crowds of rich young men and attractive young women who, no doubt, would drive out from Elmbury as soon as they heard that the new cocktail bar was open.

Night after night he waited; but the customers never came. Possibly one or two started out to try to find the place; but it's pretty certain that they got lost on the way. For you have to take the third turning on the left, off the main road, and

* One not tied to a brewery.

then the right-hand fork at the bottom of the muddy lane –
if you take the wrong one you fetch up in Farmer Guilding's
duck-pond – and then you have to keep left down a winding
cart track with many turnings, and then you go down a
drive with four gates which swing against the car unless
you've got somebody to hold them open; and finally a very
sharp right turn brings you to the pub – but if, as is most
likely, you miss it and go straight on you drive down a steep
slope into the river.

Now I come to think of it, there was a young man drowned
in such a fashion just about that time; and perhaps he was
the first customer on his way to the little pub. There were
no more; and the landlord waited and waited, until at long
last a car drove up to the front door and he prepared to shake
a Bosom Caresser; but alas, it was no customer, but a dun
employed by the Wine and Spirit Merchant, come to demand payment of their bill.

Roadhouse and Bar Parlour

In Elmbury itself there were twenty-eight pubs to serve a
population of less than five thousand. Of course on market
days this population was swelled enormously by people
coming in from the country, and in the summer there were
'outings' and visitors from cities as well. On the other hand,
there must have been among Elmbury's five thousand, if no
teetotallers at least two thousand five hundred women,
children, and sick people who drank rarely or not at all. That
leaves one hundred persons to a pub. I don't understand the
economics of the business but I confess that if I wanted to be
a rich man I should think twice before I took a pub in
Elmbury.

The Nonconformist Ministers and the few militant teetotallers who troubled us and wrote letters to the local paper
regretting 'the drinking habits of Elmbury's population',
always made this point about the great number of pubs in
proportion to the inhabitants, and seemed to think it was a

very lamentable state of affairs. But this was great nonsense. A man doesn't drink ten drinks because there are ten pubs in his street; and if he is in the habit of drinking ten drinks he usually drinks them all in one pub. In fact almost every man has his own 'local' where the beer, the company, the darts, the landlord or the barmaid happen to be to his taste; and since men are conservative in their habits he rarely makes a change.

However, at every session of the Licensing Justices there was much talk of 'redundant' licences; and from time to time they would refuse to renew the licence of some small pub, and some poor man's 'local' ceased to exist. The brewers who owned most of the pubs were partly to blame for this. They were only too glad to exchange two old licences – perhaps of pleasant but unprofitable little pubs – for one new licence, promising to build a roadhouse 'with large commodious bars and every modern amenity'. The Justices, and oddly enough especially the teetotal justices, seemed to believe that there was some special virtue in large and commodious bars, catering for people who came in cars and charabancs, and some special wickedness in small cosy bars where old friends got together for their evening drink. But for my part I always regretted the passing of the little pubs. I'd rather sit round the fire with half a dozen good fellows in the Wheatsheaf or the Barrel and drink beer from the wood than perch myself on a high stool at a long bar in a roadhouse and be served by refained and supercilious young women with stuff called beer which comes sizzling out of a tap having been pumped through miles of chromium-plated pipes by hundreds of pounds' worth of machinery. Nor is this just my old-fashioned obscurantism; the majority of the population, it seems, likes the little pubs also and people from the cities drive twenty miles on Sunday morning to crowd us out of our local because they hate the big road-houses too. A pub, after all, is not just a place for convenient drinking; if it were these modern palaces with their ceaseless fountains of beer would serve the purpose very well. But a pub is primarily a meeting-place for friends; where friends as well as drinking may talk, argue, play games, or just sit and think according to their mood. The personal relationship with the landlord is important too, it is good that there should be a 'host', for thus good manners are observed. I would rather that my host was the landlord of a little pub, a poor man drinking with his fellows, than a 'manager' who has no more in common with his customers than the manager of a chain store; which is exactly what he is.

Nevertheless, the Licensing Justices who were appointed because they were teetotallers (and therefore best qualified to arrange things for the comfort of people who drink) got their way, and Elmbury lost the Three Tuns and the Cross Keys and got its 'roadhouse' instead. And it doesn't matter much; for we've still got the Shakespeare, nobly named, where the farmers' sons talk about horses and never tire of admiring the engravings of 'The Midnight Steeplechase' upon the wall. We've still got the Swan, of which I shall have more to write later; the George, the Black Bear, the White Bear, the Railway; the Anchor, where Pistol, Bardolph and Nym will come up to you hopefully and, if you buy them a drink, will tell you a tale of arms and the man; the Goat and Compasses, which seems to be built around its enormous landlord, so that if he wants to go out he must edge sideways through the door; the Barrel, the Wheatsheaf, the Coventry Arms which has a little back-parlour where grave old citizens like to sit in semi-darkness and sip their beer and talk of old times while the shadows close in upon them; the Plough, the Wagon and Horses, and the Red Lion where the drovers gather after market.

These endure; but the brewers and the teetotallers, strange and ominous partnership, have plans for another of their great, shining drinking-palaces on the new by-pass road just outside the town. They have established a curious and illogical principle that no new licence will be granted unless an old one is surrendered; and this time it will be the Goat and Compasses, or perhaps the Coventry Arms, which is sacrificed to Moloch.

Furniture Sales

But much as I delight in pubs, I didn't much like the valuations; the ruin of their landlords was a dreary tale too often repeated, and since it was inseparable from the auctioneer's profession that he should be in at the kill each time I found the business depressing. There was another aspect of my profession which I heartily loathed; and that was the job of conducting furniture sales. These, too, were generally the consequence of somebody's death; and I was a bit squeamish about them. People's possessions are sharp reminders of their personality; and I couldn't help feeling that it was an insult to the Household Gods when the chair in which Mr So-and-So had sat by the fire each evening, his pipe-rack, his favourite books, were offered for the comments of a noisy and cynical crowd, usually to the accompaniment of appalling jokes. There was a kind of convention about these jokes. They were traditional. 'Who'd sleep on the floor when he could buy a bed at this price?' the auctioneer would say. He'd said it a thousand times; other auctioneers had said it a million times; but the crowd always laughed. It was a formality and it was harmless, but it always made me squirm. He had his set, conventional jokes for almost everything he sold: the mattress, the mirror, the hearthrug, the chamber-pot, even for that rather useless article which almost everybody possesses yet nobody really knows what it is until he sees it described in the auctioneer's catalogue: the jardinière.

There was something, to me, unutterably depressing in the atmosphere of a house where a furniture sale was being held. The carpetless rooms and staircases; the bare dingy walls with brighter patches where the pictures had hung; the accumulation of trivial bric-à-brac routed out of forgotten cupboards; the dust-sheets like shrouds; the books, once loved, heaped on the floor in lots which would be sold for a shilling apiece; the muddy footmarks everywhere. It was as if the house too were dead; the spirit gone, one saw only the husk which had contained it, trivial, ridiculous, irrelevant.

I was glad indeed when the auctioneer came to the end of his long pilgrimage which generally began in a top-floor bedroom ('Iron bedstead with spring mattress') and finished in the outhouse or garden-shed ('Two dozen flowerpots and a bundle of raffia'). Game to the end, he still churned out his ancient and traditional joke when he offered for sale the very last lot of all. 'This is the one the cobbler threw at his wife.' And the crowd, unflagging, laughed at the final joke which they had heard a hundred times before.

Two classes of people, as a rule, attended these sales: women and dealers. The women were awful. Ordinary decent housewives suffered a terrible metamorphosis as soon as they entered the sale room, and became predatory, acquisitive, utterly ruthless, and at times even dishonest. Dealers, compared with them, were upright citizens; which is a measure of the behaviour of women at a furniture sale.

The dealers, of course, couldn't afford to be honest. It is the job and the livelihood of a dealer to buy cheap and to sell dear; if he fails to do that he goes bankrupt. In order to buy cheap he must either take pains to discredit the article he wants to buy, declaring in the presence of the whole company that it is a fake, its legs are broken, it isn't worth a pound, he bought one like it last week for five bob, etcetera, etcetera, meanwhile arranging with a friend to buy it on his behalf; or alternatively he must arrange with the other dealers present to form a 'ring', ie, not to bid against each other, and to share out their purchases equally after the sale. Neither practice could be considered ethically sound; but if you are at dealer in anything you can't afford to consider ethics.

However, I suppose by a stretch of imagination you might call these tricks negatively honest rather than positively dishonest. The positive malpractices of the dealers are varied and ingenious. Elmbury had two firms of dealers who carried on business in the town. The one was Smith Brothers, the other Percy Parfitt. Mr Parfitt was a craftsman as well as a crook; and later in this book I shall have occasion to pay him the tribute which is a craftsman's due. The Smith Brothers were altogether different. Albert was tall and flashy, Eric was squat and scruffy-looking. They preyed mainly upon country cottages and the inhabitants of the villages. Eric, riding upon a bicycle, would make the first reconnaissance, calling at the cottages and inquiring 'whether the missus had any odd bits of furniture to sell'. If he was asked in and allowed to rout round he would deliberately fix his attention upon something trivial and worthless, declaring 'That's a very nice engraving,' or 'That's a very interesting little table – might be worth a lot of money if it's genuine.' Meanwhile he would perhaps discover something, let us say an antique oak chest, which was really valuable; but he would appear to take no notice of it or would dismiss it as being worthless. Instead he would return again and again to the little table, shaking his head over it gravely: 'Wish I knew more about antiques, missus, I'm not much better than an old junk merchant myself. But I've got a hunch about this little table. Might be real Queen Anne. Might be worth a tenner. But I couldn't risk a tenner on it myself. Now I've got a friend in London who knows about these things. I do a bit of business with him – just junk, you know – and if ever he's down in these parts I'll bring him along to have a look at that little table of yourn.'

So saying, Mr Eric Smith would depart upon his rickety bicycle. The cottager, being no fool, took the earliest opportunity to find out the real worth of the table; and found out that it was worth about ten bob. Guileless old women are rare in country cottages; and the Smith Brothers and their kind had long ago discovered and fleeced the last of them. Eric and Albert relied now on making their profit not out of the guileless but out of the most cunning: the ones who would take the trouble to get the local connoisseur's opinion on the value of the table and who, finding it worthless, would eagerly await the coming of that mug who was Mr Eric Smith's friend from London.

In due course the friend from London arrived. This was

Albert, dressed in fearful plus-fours and driving a respectable motor-car. 'My friend, Mr Smith,' said Albert, 'told me you might let me have a look at your little table . . .'

Having examined it, shaken his head over it, turned it upside down and looked at the worm-holes through a magnifying glass, Albert would inform the delighted cottager that it might – it might just possibly – be genuine Queen Anne; and he'd be prepared to take a risk and offer fifteen pounds for it. The cottager, knowing the thing was worth ten shillings, would promptly accept the offer; and then Albert would count up his money and find that he only had five pounds.

'I could write you a cheque,' he would say doubtfully, 'but I couldn't expect you to trust me, could I, being a stranger?'

The cottager, wise in the ways of crooks from London, would indicate politely that he preferred to receive cash.

'Quite right,' said Albert cheerfully. 'No offence taken, I assure you. But I'll tell you what I'll do. I'll be passing this way tomorrow and I'll bring the cash then. Meanwhile you'll keep the table for me?'

That sounded fair and honest enough. Albert shook hands with his victim and prepared to leave; but as he was putting on his coat his glance fell upon that valuable oak chest which brother Eric had told him of. He took a casual look at it and said: 'It's not a bad little chest; but there's not much sale for such things today. If you like – since I'm buying the table – I'll give you another ten bob and take the chest as well.'

Now the cottager, probably, didn't know the value of the chest; but even if she thought that it was worth two or three pounds, she felt inclined to let it go, in view of the huge price she was getting for the table. Perhaps she haggled a bit, then said:

'Very well, you can have it for a pound.'

'Done,' said Albert, 'and since I've got the cash I'll pay you for the chest straight away. I shan't have room in the car for both chest and table when I call tomorrow.'

So Albert went off with the chest, having bought it for a pound, whereas it was worth twenty. 'See you tomorrow,' he called out from the car. 'Don't sell the table to anyone else, mind, before I come back!'

But of course he never came back. He never meant to come back. The cottager was left with her worthless table; and it was generally quite a long time before she realized that Mr Smith's friend from London had cheated her out of nineteen pounds.

And when she did realize it, she had no remedy; for Albert hadn't committed any offence for which she could prosecute him. He had simply changed his mind about buying the table; and a chap couldn't be punished for changing his mind.

Forty years in business, said the Smith Brothers, and a tricky business at that; and never broke the law once save when Albert forgot to renew his driving licence and when an interfering bobby copped Eric for bicycling without a light: things that might happen to anybody. Virtuous citizens of Elmbury were the Smith Brothers, and great respecters of the Law; unlike some people they might name but wouldn't, who stooped to practices abominable in the eyes of Albert and Eric and all upright men – practices, for example, such as those of Mister P. P. (no names, no pack-drill) who had a workshop behind his business premises, and what went on in that workshop, in the way of faking and fiddling and turning modern junk into genuine antiques – well, the Smith Brothers would blush to tell you.

The Crooked Craftsman

For my part I liked Mr Parfitt a great deal better than I liked the Smiths. I liked him for his merry crinkled smile, for his craftsman's love of his trade (even though it was a dishonest trade), and for the fact that he never cheated anybody who didn't deserve to be cheated; which was more than you could say of Albert and Eric.

He had a shop in the unfashionable part of the High Street. Over the door hung the simple, austere and untruthful sign, 'ANTIQUES'. You went into a small low room which was always very dark (it was necessary that it should be dark) and out of the shadows, himself like a Shade, there came shuffling towards you the small, wizened form of Mr Parfitt. He peered at you with bright, inquisitive eyes and asked you rather tersely what you wanted. He was never obsequious to his customers; he always seemed reluctant to sell anything; and indeed he had been known to weep at parting with a fine old Welsh dresser which, he said, was his proudest possession. His tears weren't faked; though the dresser was. He was indeed proud of it, and he grieved to part with it, for he had spent long days and nights fashioning it, with skill and ingenuity and loving care, out of some odd bits of old, dark oak which he'd picked up at a sale.

Mr Parfitt was probably the best carpenter in three counties, and he had a right to be proud of his job, which was the most difficult in all the carpenter's trade. It was much more difficult for example, for Mr Parfitt to fake a Chippendale chair than it had been for Thomas Chippendale to make the original; but I assure you that Mr Parfitt would make you a very passable Chippendale chair for about ten guineas. An expert could detect the forgery; but he would have to be a real expert, for Mr Parfitt knew all the old tricks, and had a few new ones of his own. For instance, if you bought, in his shop, one of those convex mirrors, period about 1800, which are much sought after, and you took the precaution of taking out the glass, you would find behind it, separating it from the frame, a sheet from a newspaper bearing the correct date. And if you were an old junk merchant you would be aware that you could always get a few shillings from Mr Parfitt for a bundle of newspapers dated round about 1800.

Not only was Mr Parfitt a fine craftsman, but he was also something of a pioneer. He discovered, long before anybody else, the enormous possibilities of Elmbury's tourist trade. Here was El Dorado, lying at every tradesman's doorstep;

but nobody realized it until Mr Parfitt began to sell curios which had 'local associations' to the visitors who came in summer to see the Abbey. Soon others imitated him, and there grew up a brisk trade in guidebooks, picture postcards, drinking mugs inscribed 'A Present from Elmbury', and even in pink sticks of Elmbury rock. But Mr Parfitt, as befitted the discoverer of this El Dorado, continued to reap the greatest riches from it, ever mining deeper into the tourists' pockets and finding new deposits of gold. It was he, for example, who started a new archaeological legend concerning the existence of the Long Man of Elmbury. Spending a summer holiday in Dorset, he happened to visit Cerne Abbas where he duly marvelled at the huge phallic giant whose chalky outline sprawls across the hill. It appears that somebody in the village turned the tables on him – the biter bit indeed! – by selling him a curio; it was a rough-carved model of the Long Man, and it cost a pound. The carving itself was only worth a few shillings; but you paid extra for the magic: the thing was supposed to be a charm for child-bearing, and Mr Parfitt, whose wife was barren, greatly desired a child.

He brought it home, and what Mrs Parfitt said about it we cannot know; she was probably very shocked indeed, for the Long Man, as you must know if you have seen him, has very little respect for the modesty of middle-aged ladies who run the Women's Quiet Hour for the Methodist Church.

Whatever the reason, the thing didn't work. Priapus refused to take the hint; and Mr Parfitt remained childless. Doubtless he cursed the crafty carpenter of Cerne Abbas, who had thus cheated him out of a pound; and doubtless he reflected that here would be a profitable sideline for himself if only the ancients of Elmbury had had the sense to delineate a phallic symbol upon the side of the nearest hill.

From this speculation it wasn't very far – it was no farther than the distance to Mr Parfitt's workshop with its chisels and saws – to experimental attempts to remedy the ancients' custom. Before long Mr Parfitt had manufactured with very great skill and artistry a Long Man, in a sense indeed an even longer man, which he placed in the darkest corner of his shop to await the coming of an archaeologist.

Heaven sent one that very summer: an earnest curate on a bicycling tour who had stopped to take some brass-rubbings in the Abbey. He went into Mr Parfitt's shop with the innocent intention of buying a picture postcard of the West Window to send to his vicar. He came out with the Long Man of Elmbury discreetly wrapped up in three thicknesses of brown paper.

We may suppose that the curate mentioned the matter to a fellow student one night over a glass of port. ('Deplorable, of course, these pagan superstitions, but their survival in the countryside is not without interest.') At any rate, next season there was no lack of customers, clerical, professorial and otherwise, who furtively entered Mr Parfitt's dark shop and whispered to him when he came sidling out of the shadows that they'd heard tell of certain – er – primitive statues which were carved in the district and were associated with certain rites of interest only to anthropologists. And there were plenty of little statues to be had, for Mr Parfitt had occupied himself during the long winter evenings in carving them.

Folk-lorists, as Mr Parfitt had long ago discovered, are singularly gullible people. They will believe any old wives' tale, give credence to the wandering wits of any old gaffer in a pub. Folk-lore, in fact, is made up of old wives' and old gaffers' tales. So there wasn't much difficulty in answering their questions about the Long Man. 'Where was the original figure?' 'On the side of Brensham Hill, some say; but others have it that 'twas at Towbury.' 'What happened to it?' 'The parson had it filled in long, long ago; set twelve men to work, he did, and promised them each a gallon of ale in addition to their wages so long as no mortal trace of it should remain. So my grandfather told me; and he had the story from one of the men who did the digging. When was that, Mister? 'Tis hard to say. My granfer was a boy at the time and the man a greybeard ... Granfer used to tell us that parson got rid of it because he said it set a bad

example to the maids. But there still be a few as remembers
how to carve the likeness of it.'

Oh, innocent folk-lorists! There is a very learned book by
a great professor, I have forgotten the title but you will find
it in the British Museum catalogue; and on page 561 or
thereabouts you will read this paragraph:

> '. . . An equally remarkable figure, differing only in
> degree, existed until *c* 1720 on a hillside in the neighbour-
> hood of Elmbury. It is stated by Maffikins (*op cit* p 301)
> that this figure was destroyed by the orders of the incum-
> bent in that year: a piece of gross vandalism inspired no
> doubt by concern for the morals of his villagers . . .'

Thus even so humble a person as Mr Parfitt may contri-
bute his quota of knowledge to our Island Story.

You've Got to Leave the Bed

I shall have more to say about this mischievous little man,
whose presence at Furniture Sales (where he obtained the
odds and ends of table legs, panels, and worm-eaten wood
which were the raw materials of his trade) did much to en-
liven those dreary and often dreadful events. I say 'dreadful'
advisedly; for there was a certain kind of sale which did
indeed fill me with dread and horror and which, in the end,
proved the determining factor which made me decide to
throw up my job. These were sales held under what is called
Distraint. If a tenant fails to pay his rent the landlord is
entitled, having given due notice, to 'distrain' upon his
possessions. A bailiff enters the house and remains there to
see that the tenant's goods are not taken away; and after a
certain interval, if the rent is still unpaid, the goods are sold
by auction and the arrears of rent are paid to the landlord
out of the proceeds of the sale.

I do not suggest that this is necessarily unjust; while
private landlords exist they must clearly have the right to

protect their interests. But the practice never failed to shock me and I hated having to participate in it. Almost always the smallest and meanest cottages provided the scene; almost always the amount involved was only a few pounds; almost always the defaulting tenant was less to blame, in my view, than the social system which had in many cases denied him the means of making a livelihood.

Whenever I could I made some excuse or discovered some urgent job in order to avoid taking part in these dreary little ceremonies. Sometimes I could not get out of it; and I remember in particular – because it was the last and the decisive occasion – one such sale in the village of Tirley on a drizzly miserable November day.

Tirley, being set in the midst of low-lying meadows, surrounded by dykes, and shrouded for most of the year in mists and miasmas, is never a very cheerful place. On this day it was almost islanded by dirty brown floods dimpled by innumerable raindrops. The cottage stood in its own little garden; pools of water lay in the potato-patch and the single flowerbed. Outside were the usual half-dozen prams belonging to village women who could neither resist the sale nor leave their babies unattended, Mr Eric Smith's unmistakable bicycle, and Mr Parfitt's pony-and-cart. Inside I found Reuben Bowles, the bailiff, a salmon-fisherman by trade who performed this grisly function in the close season. Reuben was a very gloomy man, as befitted one whose chosen task was so unenjoyable; he was sitting in the only comfortable chair in the only downstairs room, and he addressed me sombrely, shaking his head several times as if he reported a great catastrophe:

'There ain't fifteen quid's worth 'ere, mister. You'll be lucky if you makes two.'

The distraint was for about fifteen pounds.

'In this room,' Reuben went on, 'there's one chair wot I'm sittin' on, and one that's bust. There's a table worth seven and sixpence and a carpet full of holes and a kettle that leaks and a teapot without a spout and some cracked crockery, and a lot of wot you calls bric-à-brac that I wouldn't 'ave for a gift. Upstairs there's a washstand and a towel rail and a busted jerry and a bed; but by law you've got to leave him a bed.'

That was so; the Law is just so merciful. Not even the landlord may take a man's bed in order to sell it for the rent.

I felt sick and I said to Reuben:

'Is the tenant anywhere about?'

'He's down at the police-station. Tried to commit suicide this morning,' said Reuben, as if it were the most natural thing in the world.

'*What?*'

'Cut 'is wrist wiv a safety razor blade,' said Reuben, gloomily enjoying himself. 'Then come cryin' down to me wiv 'is hand all bloody. Fair turned me up it did. I bound it for 'im; but it was bleeding something 'orrible and I couldn't stop it, so I sent for the policeman, and 'e took 'im away. 'E'll look after 'im and stop 'im doing any 'arm to 'isself. Then 'e'll let 'im go; though there ought to be a charge rightly.'

Yes, I supposed there ought to be a charge rightly. We contrive our world in such a fashion that a desperate man prefers to take his leave of it; and we are so shocked at his dislike of our beautiful world that we call him a criminal. I asked Reuben what the trouble was and he said: 'Football pools.' Off the shaky table he picked up an exercise book full of calculations about the number of goals the Arsenal and West Bromwich Albion might kick next Saturday.

''E was ill,' said Reuben, 'and 'e couldn't get work, so 'e took to football pools. Could never see the sense in 'em myself. But that's where the rent went. Two or three bob a week, and always 'oping to make a fortune.'

There was the familiar, trivial, undramatic story. He fell ill and he couldn't get work, because employers don't want sick labourers. He could have gone to hospital? Not unless he was an urgent case; the hospital has no beds for 'chronics' who are also paupers. He could get help from the Parish? from Public Assistance? from some charity? No doubt; but men – even the meanest, idlest, most ineffectual men – often have an absurd pride. He preferred the romantic dream; he preferred Football Pools. What was two bob a week after all? – when he might wake up any Monday morning the possessor of a thousand pounds? Thus he could get his own back on the world that had used him badly; thus he could establish himself again, in his own esteem and others', as a proper citizen, who'd got the better of ill-fortune and made himself master of his fate . . . After all, it *did* happen sometimes. It happened to somebody every week.

But it didn't happen to him. Perhaps he wasn't very good at Football Pools. He wasn't very good at anything: not even at committing suicide.

'Reuben,' I said, 'can't anything be done? Must we go through with it?'

'Can't stop it now,' said Reuben inexorably, nodding towards the poster on the wall: The Sale will commence at twelve o'clock promptly. (Why do auctioneers always write commence instead of 'begin'?) 'Can't stop a Distress,' said Reuben indignantly, 'just because a bloke tries to commit suicide.'

He didn't mean to be funny, I'm sure he didn't mean to be funny, but I'll swear he added, 'or we'll have everybody else doing it.'

And now indeed it was too late; for the time was twelve-fifteen, and two women with babies in their arms, and Mr Parfitt, and the unpleasing Mr Eric Smith, had come into the room. Others were on their way down the creaking stairs. Eric Smith said cheekily:

'Come along, mister, we ain't got all day. Can't wait all morning for a few sticks of furniture which ain't much more than firewood.'

So I began; I commenced. I felt as if I was committing some appalling indecency, but there was no escape and I sold the bric-à-brac and the ornaments and the cooking utensils and the only comfortable chair. Reuben continued to occupy it, and I couldn't even bring myself to laugh when one of the women called out:

'Are you selling Reuben as well, mister?' and another one said coarsely:

'From what 'is missus tells me 'e ain't worth as much as the chair!'

Then I went upstairs and sold the rubbish in the bedroom; and in the end I made eight pounds seventeen and sixpence for the landlord and according to the law I left the bed.

I got in my car and drove away from the damp, dreadful cottage and the miserable village of Tirley where the rain still dimpled a hundred acres of flood water and made a sound like a soft sigh. I was angry and bitter and I asked myself whose fault it all was: not the tenant's, who'd never had a chance; not the Football Pools promoter's, who provided quite honestly a few hours' cheap entertainment each week for millions of people who had little entertainment in their lives; not even the landlord's, perhaps, who for all I know may have been himself a poor man to whom fifteen pounds was desperately important. Who, then, was to blame? I didn't know the answer then, and I am not sure that I know it now. But at least I determined, as I drove back to Elmbury, that I would take no further part in a business of which some aspects were so unpleasant and distasteful. I walked into my old uncle's office and to his great astonishment told him I was going to chuck up my job.

Farewell to the Office

This action of mine was not so quixotic and impetuous as I have perhaps made it out to be. There were other reasons as well as my genuine distaste for the 'distress' sales which decided me to take leave of my uncle's dusty office. There was the matter of trigonometry. It was deemed necessary that I should pass an examination for a Fellowship of the Surveyors' Institution; and in order to do so I must know both the theory and practice of surveying. Mr Chorlton, good classicist, while teaching me to love Latin had also taught me to hate mathematics. Moreover, he had very improperly taught me that it was a good and gentlemanly thing to despise mathematics, unless they were of the Higher kind when a philosopher might take note of them. I therefore despised mathematics at school and in my uncle's office; and when I went up to London for the examination I despised trigonometry so successfully that I got nought for my paper on that subject. However, I got 100 for Forestry and 100 for Agricultural Botany and nearly 100 for a curious subject, about which I have now forgotten everything, called Agricultural Chemistry. I might have scraped through; but unfortunately there was also a practical exam in the course of which I was confronted with an instrument called a theodolite. I knew that the purpose of the thing was to measure angles; and indeed there were two striped posts some distance away and I was requested to find the angle between the instrument and those two posts. I pointed the telescope in the direction of the first post and looked through the eyepiece but could see nothing. I therefore resolved to bluff. I swung it slowly in what I thought was the direction of the second post, looked hard through the eyepiece, frowned, calculated, and made a guess. The angle, I said, was thirty-one degrees. The examiner looked surprised. 'As a matter of fact,' he told me, 'you are very nearly right; but I can't give you any marks for your guess, because you omitted to take off the cap from the end of the telescope.'

Naturally enough, I did not pass the exam; and I was very unwilling to try again. For I had discovered, while sitting on the high stool in my uncle's office, a passionate and painful pastime, that of writing stories. With my uncle's foolscap paper and my uncle's scratchy office pen, and for dissemblance's sake a copy of some such book as *The Law of Landlord and Tenant* open on the desk in front of me, I wrote with fierce delight two whole novels. The first was very properly rejected by seven publishers; the second was accepted by the first I sent it to. Its subsequent fortune has nothing to do with this book; but at least it provided me with an answer when my astonished uncle, shaken for once out of his quiet courtesy, almost shouted at me:

'But what the devil are you going to do instead?'

'Write,' I said.

'Write! That's a hobby, my boy, not a profession!'

So I showed him the publisher's letter, and a cheque for a hundred pounds.

Turkey Trouble

However, I did not leave his office at once; for it was late autumn, a season when auctioneers are generally busy, and I volunteered to stay on until the Christmas markets were over. I therefore took part in one more Grand Christmas Fat Stock Show and Sale at Elmbury; and I unwittingly enlivened the occasion with a great comedy.

I had graduated, during three years, from sticking labels on the behinds of cattle to selling cattle myself. At Christmas Market, however, it was my uncle's custom to mount the rostrum and with due dignity auction the finest fat beasts; when he grew tired one of the partners took on the job. So I was relegated to that part of the market occupied by the poultry. Fat turkeys, geese, ducks, cockerels and the like, even rabbits, guinea-pigs, and ferrets were my humble merchandise that day.

I must explain that all this miscellaneous livestock was housed in little pens or hutches arranged in tiers along a wall, and numbered from 1 to 200. As each lot arrived before the sale it was taken out of its hamper and placed in one of the pens. That curious old man, Fred Pullin, who had been my grandfather's coachman, had the job of doing this and also of writing down, on a sheet, the owner's name, the description of the lot, and the reserve price, if any, thus:

Lot 7. Mrs Trotwood. Fat Turkey. Reserve 22/-

That meant, of course, that I mustn't sell Mrs Trotwood's turkey under twenty-two shillings; if less was offered I must buy it in on her behalf. Unfortunately old Fred, who was half-blind and couldn't see the lines on the foolscap paper, wrote this particular reserve price in the wrong place; so I sold Mrs Trotwood's fat turkey to an old woman called Mrs Peel for seventeen and sixpence.

Mrs Trotwood, however, was unaware of this; for auctioneers often use false names when they 'buy in' a lot that has failed to reach the reserve. Mrs Trotwood had faith in me and remarkable faith in Fred, and finding Pen 20 unoccupied she carried her turkey thither in order that I might try again.

When I came to Pen 20, there was a turkey of which I had no record in my book. I asked whom it belonged to. 'Mrs Trotwood'. I assumed that Mrs Trotwood was the possessor of more than one turkey; and I knocked it down to a farmer's wife called Mrs Doe for nineteen shillings.

The name Doe is said to be legal fiction; Mrs Trotwood certainly thought so, for she lifted her turkey again to Pen 36, where I sold it to the warrior wife of that old warrior Pistol for nineteen and six. The trade in turkeys improved somewhat as I came towards the end of them. Mrs Trotwood hopefully removed her turkey successively to Pens 42, 49 and 55, where I sold it successively to a Mrs Attwood, a Mrs Phillpots and a Mrs Holmes for prices ranging from nineteen shillings to a guinea. Mrs Trotwood then lost hope and went to fetch her hamper in order to take the turkey home. In blissful ignorance of the storm which was about to burst over my head I went on to sell the geese, ducks, cockerels, the little boys' rabbits and guinea-pigs, the ferrets, the bunches of mistletoe and all the other odds and ends which were somewhat oddly lumped together under the heading of 'Poultry'.

I had nearly finished when I became aware of a disturbance in the region of Pen 55. Mrs Trotwood, Mrs Holmes, and a turkey seemed to be engaged in a noisy flurry. I fondly imagined the matter had nothing to do with me, and went on selling.

The row got worse; for Mrs Phillpots and Mrs Attwood had now joined in. I sent Fred Pullin to see what it was about; but Fred was excessively stupid and only succeeded in setting the four women more fiercely at loggerheads.

Moreover Mrs Pistol had now blown into the battle like a tornado. Fred retired discomfited.

I had now finished selling, so I went across to see what was the matter. The row was appalling: five women – and a turkey – all cackling at once. There must have been something, a distinguishing mark or label perhaps, which made it possible to recognize the turkey; for Mrs Doe and Mrs Peel arrived on the scene and hastened to claim it. Mrs Doe, far from being a legal fiction, turned out to be a most ferocious and belligerent woman with an umbrella which she waved recklessly to emphasize her claim. This provoked the anger of that Volumnia, Mrs Pistol, who called up the whole clan to her aid: Pistol, Bardolph and Nym were always to be found hanging about the market on the chance of earning a tip, begging a drink, or finding something they could scrounge. They eagerly joined the noisy crowd which surrounded Mrs Trotwood's wretched turkey.

A brief glance at Fred Pullin's ill-written sheet told me what had happened: I had sold the turkey six times, but each time for less than the reserve; there were therefore seven claimants for it, since Mrs Trotwood insisted on taking it back. I tried to explain the situation to the impassioned women. I might as well have tried to reason with a thunderstorm, to seek compromise with a cloudburst, to still the north wind with soft words. Mrs Trotwood was easily squared; I promised to pay her twenty-two shillings for the turkey, which was what she wanted for it, and she went away satisfied. But there remained seven other women who all had an equal claim to the creature; who all complained that it was the only turkey they had been able to buy; who all protested that unless they took it home their husbands and their loving children would have to go without their Christmas dinner.

'Seven children,' said Mrs Pistol, 'looking forward to the turkey I promised 'em three months ago.'

'No Christmas dinner,' echoed Pistol, Bardolph and Nym ominously.

Mrs Doe, Mrs Phillpots, Mrs Attwood, Mrs Peel **and Mrs**

Holmes all had a similar tale to tell. On sentimental as well as purely ethical grounds none had a better right to the turkey than the rest; legally, it seemed to me, each one of them owned it. Solomon, who solved an analogous but simpler problem, would, I felt sure, have been confounded by this one; and I was no Solomon. Tired of abusing each other, all six of the women now started to abuse me. There was no remedy but in flight. I therefore winked at Pistol, whom I knew would do anything for a drink, and suggested that he and I should discuss the matter in the market office. Bardolph and Nym, of course, followed us. As soon as we were out of hearing of the women, I said: 'Let's leave them to settle it. We shall find it quieter in the Red Lion,' and thither we hastened, where Pistol told me a lengthy and fantastic and probably untrue story about some long-forgotten campaign in Baluchistan, so that I never knew what happened in the end to Mrs Trotwood's turkey, nor which one of the six belligerent women triumphed over the rest. I heard tell of Mrs Doe prodding Mrs Pistol with her umbrella; and of Mrs Holmes fetching a policeman; and of Mrs Pistol pulling the bird's tail-feathers out in handfuls when Mrs Attwood tried by force to bear it away. But all that is hearsay; for as I have said I was leaning comfortably upon the Red Lion bar with Pistol, Bardolph and Nym and hearing them confess that though they feared neither shot nor shell, nor cannon's roar, nor sniper's bullet, nor tribesman's knife, nor Zulu's assegai, yet a pack of angry old women struck terror into their hearts. Uhlans were lambs, the fuzzywuzzy was a kitten, the wily Pathan was a cooing dove, said Pistol, by comparison with a woman in a temper. And he should have known.

We Be Getting Old

For reasons other than this comic one I remember my last Christmas market. It was the last time my uncle sold the champion beast and the last time the great fat butcher bought it; for my uncle was growing deaf, he could no longer hear the bids, and the butcher was sick of some mortal malady from which a few weeks later he died. I remember my uncle inclining his silvery head towards the bidders with his hand up to his ear. 'Come, come, gentlemen! Only fifty-seven pounds ten for Mr Parker's champion beast! Only fifty-seven pounds ten I'm bid. Shall I make it sixty?' My uncle never shouted or swore or got excited when he was selling; he never mitigated his old-fashioned courtesy to match it to the rowdy, boisterous dealers, who stood round him now with their fat red shining faces rather like beeves themselves (for it always seemed to me that dealers grew to resemble the beasts they dealt in, that horse-dealers had a horse-like countenance, sheep-dealers were inclined to baa and bleat, pig-dealers had little piggy eyes, and the cattle-men were generally rubicund and bull-like).

'Come, come, gentlemen!' said my uncle. In his little way he was himself a great gentleman; there was pomp and ceremony, dignity and good manners, whenever he mounted the rostrum, and his company always behaved as gentlemen, being treated so.

He looked towards the great fat butcher. 'Come, offer me sixty,' he said.

The fat butcher hesitated, then nodded his head.

'Sixty it is. Sixty I'm offered. I'm going to sell this fine beast for sixty. You know where it comes from, gentlemen. Mr Parker's of The Reddings. Mr Parker, who's won the championship four years out of the last seven. At sixty. I'm selling at sixty. Going, going, gone.'

The fat butcher smiled.

''Tis a lot of money, Mr Moore,' he said.

''Tis a lot of good meat,' said my uncle. 'Congratulations. Let me see, it's twelve years running, isn't it, that you've bought the champion beast? And this is the highest price you've ever paid, and this is the best beast, in my opinion. Congratulations to you and to Mr Parker.'

There was a sudden burst of clapping. Somebody shouted

out, 'And congratulations to you, mister! It's thirty-five years you've been selling here.'

'Is it? Thirty-five years! Well, well. One doesn't like being reminded of the years at my age. Dear, dear! Thirty-five years!'

'Aye. We be getting old, Mr Moore,' said the butcher. (I wonder if he had some queer premonition, a flash of fore-knowledge?) 'We be getting old, you and I. We be going going, gone!'

Falstaff He Is Dead

Three weeks later he fell ill, the great fat butcher with the fire-red cherubim's face. He bore his great mountain of flesh up to bed, and lay there for three days, and then he died. I went into the shop next week and his wife was there, carrying on as best she could (for she had no sons). The rosettes of the champion beasts still hung on the wall behind her: twelve rosettes in a row. I told her I was sorry; and she said surprisingly:

'He went very quiet, for a man of his size. As quiet as a little child, he lay. But once or twice he cried out, and once or twice he groaned; and I tried to hear what he was saying, but 'twas only a whisper. "What a job it is, missus," he said to me. "What a job it is, what a job!"'

I felt a little shiver run down my spine; for although the words were different, I could hear an echo more than three hundred years old: a faint far echo of what Mistress Quickly said when Falstaff died.

Tempora Mutantur

That year, for the first time, we had sold no fat beast for Mr Jeffs. He was at the market; and I watched him standing beside the ring while my uncle was selling; but he, who had always been larger than life, seemed suddenly to have grown smaller. A month or two before he had left his great farm on the hill; he was growing old, he said, and he could no longer get round it. He had bought 'a little place' in which to spend his last days, and somehow he seemed to have shrunk as his lands had shrunk. He still wore the flower in his buttonhole, the well-cut tweeds, the grey bowler hat; but he was no longer distinguished-looking, he was no longer Mr Jeffs of the Hill. You would scarcely have noticed him, you would scarcely have picked him out from the lesser men crowding about the ring.

But he was wise, I think, to get out of the business when he did. He knew which way the wind was blowing; and he knew it was going to be a cold wind for farmers. Stock prices were beginning to sag; wheat at seven shillings a bushel was scarcely worth growing; many of his friends, who had less capital than he, were giving up their farms not because they chose to but because they must. The bank was beginning to call in its mortgages; mortgages which had been taken up in the prosperous times just after the Great War, when land was selling for twice its real value. My uncle's firm had sustained within a month three bad debts each amounting to more than a hundred pounds. 'Dear, dear!' said my uncle, shaking his courtly old head. 'Poor old So-and-So – and I've known him for thirty years!' He thought of the debtors' misfortune before he thought of his own. My uncle in his declining years had a theory that if only he had known a man sufficiently long, there could be nothing wrong with the man; and this was associated with a still more dangerous theory, that if the man could afford to owe the firm a sum as large as a hundred pounds, he must be financially stable. Both notions did great credit to my uncle's heart, but great harm to his pocket.

'Don't press him!' he would say. 'Write him a nice letter, John. I wouldn't hurt the old fellow's feelings for worlds!'

Property Sale

Mr Jeffs' farm had been sold by my uncle at Michaelmas, in the long market room at the Swan Hotel. In contrast to the bustle and noise and boisterous fun of stock markets there was always a pleasant quiet dignity about property sales. The presence of lawyers, who always like things to be done according to the form and the tradition, lent to the occasion something of the air of dusty respectability which hangs about their offices. There was no badinage or shouting; for the sale of several hundred acres of green English land was a solemn occasion and out of respect for the owner who was like a tree about to be uprooted the company seated themselves in hushed silence. There was a rustle of papers as they re-read the Particulars of Sale which they already knew by heart. Then my uncle got up, stroked his silvery hair, and began in his silvery voice to describe the property. 'It is not very often, gentlemen, even in my experience – fifty-two years of it: it was fifty-two years last month that I joined my late father's firm – it is not very often that I have the pleasure (a pleasure, though, mixed with regret) of offering for sale by auction a farm such as this. Four hundred and forty-two acres, two roods, five perches of rich, loamy, easily-worked arable land and sound old pasture; its orchards well planted with mature fruit trees in full bearing, including the choicest cherries, Early Prolific plums, Blenheim, Russet, and Cox's Orange Pippin apples, and Bon Chrétien pears. (Only two years ago I sold the fruit in these orchards for more than three hundred pounds.) The farmhouse, whose hospitality many of you have known' – a few respectful handclaps – 'was well and solidly built in the time of Queen Anne; the byres and buildings are modern and commodious; I don't need to describe the place to you, you know it well. As I say, it is very rarely, even in a long life such as mine, that one sees such a property come under the hammer. Such places remain – as they should remain, as we all would wish them to remain – in the hands of our old farming families, passed down from father to son, from generation to generation. But I do not need to remind you of the sad circumstances, which we all most deeply regret, which have caused this valuable, this unique and valuable possession, to come into the open market and to be offered for sale by auction this day.'

My uncle was referring to the death of Mr Jeffs' sons in the Great War. If they had lived, they would, of course, have taken on the farm from their father.

'Now, gentlemen,' my uncle went on, adjusting the little hour-glass which he always had before him when he sold property – an old-fashioned affectation, for if there was a chance of another bid he took no notice of the sands running out inside it – 'Now, gentlemen, I have taken up too much of your valuable time already. What are you going to offer me for this splendid farm, with its beautiful house, its dairies and outbuildings, its arable land, pastures, well-watered meadows, orchards and coppices – the timber alone is valued at four hundred and fifty pounds – and its four labourers' cottages all in good repair? What shall I say for a start, what will you give me – come, come, gentlemen, surely you will not remain silent for long with one of the best and most famous farms in all the county going a-begging?'

Live and Dead Farming Stock

The farm was sold to Jerry, Mr Nixon's son of Downend, he who rode in the Midnight Steeplechase and married Dorrie Monks in consequence; and that pleased everybody, including Mr Jeffs, who saw in him, perhaps, a shadow of those two sons of his own who fell with the Yeomanry.

Early in October the farming-stock was sold. The sale was a great occasion. There was a marquee, and the landlord of the Swan got a licence to sell drinks and sandwiches; farmers came from forty miles away, and it was a day out for all the neighbours.

The first part of the sale took place in the farmyard. I remember Mr Jeffs sitting on the gate and watching, with young Jerry beside him, and Jerry putting his hand on the old man's shoulder, as if to say, 'I know it's hard to watch them go,' as a son might do to his father. The horses, with beribboned manes and tails and coats polished till they shone like horse-chestnuts glossy-new out of their shells, were trotted up and down so that knowledgeable dealers standing behind them could criticize their action. Then the milking cows were sold, the cows with calves, the proud imperious bull, and the store-cattle; the sheep; and lastly the pigs. Now the men who had come to buy stock could retire to the marquee or set off home with their purchases; and the auctioneer, with the crowd following him wherever he went like rats behind the Pied Piper, made his way to the Home Field – the pasture nearest the house – where the wagons, carts, and implements were set out in a long irregular line which looked from the distance like the reconstructed back-bone of a dinosaur. The posters advertising a farm sale always began:

THE WHOLE
OF THE
LIVE AND DEAD FARMING STOCK

and since there were never any carcasses I suppose the wagons, binders, rakes and mowing-machines were 'dead' within the convention of auctioneers' English.

As I stood beside the auctioneer – one of my uncle's partners – during his slow progress down the line of imple-ments, I realized for the first time the extraordinary com-plexity of the farmers' job. There was the binder and the threshing-machine,* each needing the frequent services of a mechanic to keep it in running order. There were the implements of haymaking: the mower, the tedder, the horserake, the haysweep; the implements of sowing and

* Today, of course, Jerry uses a combine-harvester.

cultivation – drills of different sorts, scuffles, ploughs, horse-hoes, harrows, and so on; and there were all the various tools which a man's hands must learn to use – which Mr Jeffs' hands during the long years had learned to use – such as spades, forks, hoes, pitching-forks, hayrakes, scythes, short curved bills for ditching and hedging, saws, hatchets, and so on. The good farmer must be handy with all these, he must possess the ancient knowledge of the ploughman and the new craftsmanship of the motor-mechanic for he will have to keep in order his petrol-engines, gas-engines, tractors and lorries. He must be a bit of a carpenter, a bit of a wheelwright, a bit of a blacksmith. He must know the old secrets of the dairy and the modern practice of chemical manuring. In a single morning he may be called upon to repair a gate, to clear a blocked drain, to cold-shoe a horse, to mend a pair of reins, to graft a young apple tree, and to clean the lorry's carburettor.

But besides this considerable technology, he must possess a kind of wisdom which is much more profound and much more difficult to acquire. He must know about land and about the use of land, how to match his stock to the pasture and his crops to the soil. This is something which cannot be described in terms of technology. It is true that he must be in a sense a botanist, a chemist, and a biologist, a good meteorologist, knowledgeable in genetics, and perhaps a horticulturist and a forester as well. But it is much more than that; it is much more than technique. There is strategy mixed up in it. His farm is the battlefield, upon which he deploys his crops and stock against his foes, which are sometimes visible, such as pests and blights and weather, and sometimes invisible such as economic blizzards and falling markets.

Unless he is a bad farmer, or a sort of farm-cum-dealer, his problem is hardly ever a short-term problem; it is not a matter of tactics. For he must look forward into the future, to next season and the season after that; and he must look back and seek wisdom out of the past. Always it is a strategist's battle; and the battle never ends.

Tenant Right

We saw something of the planning of the battle when we undertook Mr Jeffs' Tenant Right valuation about the same time as his sale. 'Tenant Right' means the cultivations and improvements which an outgoing farmer hands over to his successor and for which he is entitled to be paid: seeds sown, dressings of lime, manure, and phosphates, labour of harrowing, hoeing and so on. The incoming farmer will get the benefit of these Acts of Husbandry; so a valuation is made to settle the price he must pay.

The young wheat pricking the ploughed land in spring; the beans pushing their stout cotyledons through the dark brown earth; and in autumn the plough slashing the first red scars across the yellow stubble, the little heaps of burning squitch * in the fallow field, the pile of purple and bronze mangels earthed and thatched against the frost – all these are aspects of the farmer's long war. As we stood on the hill and looked down upon Mr Jeffs' farm, we could see most of his battleground spread out below us; we could read his plan of campaign, his blueprint of next summer's battles, written in the hieroglyph of hedge and headland, furrow and fallow, green pasture and seeded field.

It would have been unthinkable to Mr Jeffs, or to any good farmer, to skimp his labour in the summer because he knew he would be leaving the farm at Michaelmas. Seeds were planted, fields were hoed, with the same loving care though somebody else would reap the crops. There was more in this than mere professional pride; for a man who has farmed since boyhood sees himself, I think, as the servant of the soil and the seasons, he has a duty towards the land, he is not so much its owner as its High Priest. Ancient compulsions drive him on, though he can only hobble round his cattle and lean on the gate to watch the wheat growing.

* Squitch – couch-grass.

Ave Atque Vale

When the valuation was done we went back to the farm-house and had tea while my uncle totted up his figures. Mr Jeffs and Jerry sat down to a bottle of whisky and talked about the farm.

'I was thinking I might fallow that long field next season,' I heard Jerry say.

Mr Jeffs shrugged his shoulders.

'Thee'll never do much with un. Starveall, 'tis called; Starveall by name and Starveall by nature. Nigh forty years I've strove with un. 'Tis the only blot on a fine farm.'

Then Jerry asked: 'What'd you say to puttin' Cheviots on those hill pastures?'

'Nay, nay! Take a tip from an old un, me boy, and stick to black-faced sheep. Cheviots are all right on the big hills where they can run free; you'd never keep 'em in here. You'd be chivvyin' 'em and chasin' 'em over half the county. They'd give you Midnight Steeplechases!'

Mr Jeffs poured out another whisky and the two men fell silent. Jerry, perhaps, in a daydream saw his acres peopled with the broad-backed Oxford sheep and the deep-flanked Shorthorn cattle, his wheat rippling like a golden sea, heard the murmur of bees about his beanflowers and the swish of the knives of the mowing-machine in the long grass; while Mr Jeffs looked back into the past, at his full barns and his sweet-smelling rickyards, at the fat cattle in the yard knee-deep in straw before the Christmas market, at the apple blossom in the Home Orchard and the cherry's snowdrift on the slope of the hill.

At last my uncle finished his complicated sum. He told them the amount, and there was no word of discussion about it, though the old man may have thought it too little and the young one thought it too much. The cheque was written out and accepted, there were handshakes and drinks all round. Mr Jeffs lifted his glass and said suddenly:

'Listen, Jerry. I've had a good life here and I wish you as

good fortune as me. But 'tain't going to be easy. I'm an old
man with an old man's headful of fancies. And I can smell
bad times coming. You know how a man goes out in the
morning with the barometer set fair and he wonders if he
shall cut his grass, but he smells change in the air? Well,
that's how I feel about the world. There's a storm brewing,
there's tempest in the sky. You mark my words, Jerry.
You've got a tougher job in front of you than I had.' He
paused, then laughed his great rumbling laugh. 'An old
man's fancies! Don't let 'em trouble you. We'll have
another drink all round; and I wish you good fortune with
all my heart.'

The Pattern

When it was time to go, Mr Jeffs came out into the garden to
see us off. Few farmhouses have flower gardens; but his was
ablaze with tawny chrysanthemums. Jerry had gone to the
stable to saddle his horse (he never drove anywhere that
was not too far to ride) and my uncle was having a last
word with Mr Jeffs about the valuation. I leaned on the
garden gate and looked down upon Elmbury.

It was a perfect autumn evening. There was mist like blue
smoke hanging about the little wood they called the Dogleg
Spinney and down in the vale you could see streaks of
whiter mist over the river. The sun was setting in a mass of
airy pink clouds like flying flamingoes and the Abbey
tower, catching the light, burned like a beacon. The chestnut trees in the churchyard, with brown and yellow leaves,
were incandescent also. Sprawled around the Abbey, half
in light and half in shadow, lay the lovely and haphazard
town.

I knew it so well that I could people the crooked streets in
my imagination, see the townsfolk passing to and fro, the
tradesmen locking up their shops for the night, Pistol,
Bardolph and Nym setting forth on an evening scrounge,
the alleys like anthills stirring suddenly into life as the men

came home from work and the housewives got the evening meal and rounded up their numerous children to put them to bed. Round the rim of the green bowl of the Ham the evening fishermen would be rigging up their rods and chucking in their ground-bait. The nightshift would be going to work at the flour-mill; the white-dusted men of the dayshift would be coming back into the town.

It was as if I could even see through the weathered roofs; watch Millie and Effie, those indefatigable blondes, lighting the first autumn fire in the Shakespeare bar, Mr Chorlton in his cottage boiling up his 'sugar' for a night's mothing, Mr Parfitt in his dark and secret workshop firing a dust-shot cartridge at ten yards' range into a mahogany chair to produce the necessary worm-holes, Jim Meadows feeding his canaries, Bassett stuffing an improbable squirrel, the regulars gathering in the Swan for their evening drink.

There was hardly a house there, great or small, which I hadn't been into; hardly a person whose life history I didn't partially know; hardly a man or woman who didn't know me by my Christian name. I belonged to the place as a limb belongs to the body.

I looked beyond the town at the villages which lay about it: Brensham with its smooth cricket-field, Tirley and Tredington misty in the hollow, Dykeham by the river where everybody owned a punt, Overfield in the deep woods, Flensham where already the lads would be kicking about a soccer-ball, Marsham with its allotments always smelling of pigs, Partingdon among its oaks with its great house and green parkland, Adam's Norton with its tall-spired church and crooked-chimneyed pub where all the men were singers. I looked, between the villages, at the great pastures and stubbles and the rootfields and rickyards of the rich land from which they and Elmbury drew their sustenance; at the byres and the barns and the labourers' cottages and a hundred farmhouses nearly as fine as Hill Farm. And I understood the inter-relation of all these good things, and how they wove themselves into a pattern, which was a microcosm of English life and history.

And now Jerry came back, on his great raw-boned Point-to-Pointer, Demon, and leaned down to shake hands with Mr Jeffs. 'I think I'll cut up along to the Stanks and into Dogleg Spinney,' I heard him say, 'then along Tomtit Lane and so to Downend.'

'You know your way about,' said Mr Jeffs, 'as if you'd been born here.'

I could guess what he was thinking. Jerry looked very splendid on Demon. He didn't look very different, I expect, from those two proud young men who had ridden away on their Point-to-Pointers in 1914. I believe Jerry guessed too; for once again he let his hand rest on the old man's shoulder in that typical, affectionate gesture of his. And so for a moment they were still against the landscape: the grand old man with his brave buttonhole, with his red face and white hair like snow on a berry, Cobbett come to life; and the young one magnificent upon his great horse. Behind them lay the big farmhouse, the background to their lives, with its orange-red bricks aglow, and the fields sloping down to Elmbury, and the deep-cut rutted lane between the hazels along which each season for hundreds of seasons the fine fat cattle had gone to market and the crops had gone to the mill.

They stood there, Mr Jeffs and Jerry against the flaming sky, and I saw them in that moment as part of the pattern; and Mr Jeffs' two sons, who had galloped their horses against a hundred guns, they made part of the pattern too; and my uncle, and his sons who fell with them, and the old ploughman in Starveall cutting his last furrow, and the labourers going home to tea, and the poacher who may have been Pistol shuffling along at the edge of Dogleg Spinney; and the Shorthorns grazing in the meadows, and the cart tracks in the lane leading down to Elmbury and the market and the mill and the barges and the boatmen and the Abbey and the alleys and the pubs.

There might be other patterns; and even this pattern would change; but it was all I knew, and I was part of it, and I found it very fair.

PART FOUR

THE UNEASY PEACE

(1931–5)

Homecoming – Hedges – Hearing the News – Grim and Gay – 'Hang Art, Madam, and Trust to Nature' – Mr Brunswick and the Chain Stores – Large as Life and Twice as Natural – The Unemployed – In Defence of Odd-job Men – Economics of Odd-jobbing – Farmer-cum-Dealer: A Moral Tale – Double or Quits – Anarchy in Scarlet – Sporting Encounter with the Colonel – Social Encounter with the Colonel – Regulars at the Swan – Miss Benedict – The River-god – 'A Rat! A Rat! Dead for a Ducat, Dead!' – Big Game – I'd Give a Hundred Pounds . . .

Homecoming

I CAME BACK to Elmbury on a frosty February afternoon just four years after leaving my uncle's office. Those four years, spent partly in London and partly abroad, are no concern of this book. It took me so long to discover that in order to practise the craft of a writer it isn't really necessary to spend most of one's time drinking gin with other writers and discussing each other's books.

But meanwhile my roots remained deep-dug in Elmbury soil; I was irrevocably bound to the place. It did not seem at all strange, it seemed predestinate and proper, when a remembered rhythm in the clatter of the train on a bridge stirred me out of drowsiness and I knew that we were crossing Brensham Bridge two miles from Elmbury.

I looked out of the carriage window. Hurray, I was home.

The black wood straggling over the hillside could be no other wood. Only sloe-bushes turn so deep a sepia, with purplish-black patches here and there, when the dusk falls in late winter; and that thicket at the bottom corner was unquestionably our prickly sloe-thicket where we used to find longtailed tits' nests and where the keeper's terriers used to scratch their little dewberry-noses when they went whimpering after rabbits. And there on the skyline was the tall elm we used to climb, with last year's rakish crow's nest still balanced in its fork. And there was the deep-cut lane winding down from Hill Farm to Elmbury, its hazels still decked with wisps of hay plucked from Jerry's laden wagons last year. I kept my eyes open for Jerry, but I had caught a glimpse of scarlet coats against Dogleg Spinney, and he would be down there on Demon, if Demon still galloped after the hounds.

Soon Hill Farm was out of sight and the slowcoach train was puffing along beside the main road. Now I knew every meadow, every hedgerow, almost every tree. There was the Tiddler Brook where as boys we slaughtered minnows; the rickyard where we sought red worms for fishing, among last season's rotting hay; the rabbit bury under the oak tree, the row of aspens where Mr Chorlton found rare caterpillars, the post-and-rails where I once took an awful toss out hunting, the favourite stile where I and many another lad used to flirt with the wenches and carve our names with penknives.

Now we puffed past Cowfield Mill, the Carrant Brook, the big feggy field called Bull Pates, the ferryman's cottage, Northway Back Lane. The country round Elmbury wasn't strikingly beautiful. It was higgledy-piggledy vale country, made up of small farms and small fields with various and haphazard cultivations: homely, unspectacular, neither too rich nor too poor. My people, I thought, were like that too: homely, unspectacular, neither too rich nor too poor. Their heads were full of common-sense mixed with a few foolish superstitions and salted with unexpected poetry. Their hearts were composed of kindliness and prejudice in almost equal proportions: just as their Ribston Pippin apples were both sweet and sour. They were a people whom you had to know well before you could love them; but if you belonged to them you were sure there was no people like them upon the face of the earth.

We drew slowly into the station. There were the allotments, cabbage-stalks, hen-houses, pigeon-cots, onions, withered chrysanthemums, various expressions of the individuality of the station-master and the landlord of the Wheatsheaf and the baker's vanman and the police-sergeant and the garage-hand, who cultivated each his little bit of private soil in his own private and haphazard way.

The short train stopped; and there was Perks the red-faced porter standing on the platform to welcome it, the third and probably the last train of the day, and shouting in a great voice although doubtless all the seven passengers were natives like myself:

'ULMBREE! ULMBREE! ALL CHANGE! ULM-BREE!'

Hedges

By the time I had talked with Perks and the station-master and seen to my luggage and arranged for the carrier to collect it, the swift dusk had fallen, and the little owls were calling in the trees as I walked into the town along Gander Lane. The hedges dividing the patchwork land were blurred and blackened as if they were drawn upon the landscape with a piece of blunt charcoal.

It occurred to me that one of the things I had missed most when I was abroad was the ordinary English hedge, which we take for granted, yet it is the very texture of our landscape, it is a theme which runs repetitive throughout the English countryside. The tall unkempt hedge of Gander

Lane was made of hazel mixed with hawthorn, but it had elm, sloe, bramble, elder, and spindle tree in it too; half a dozen shrubs composed it, yet it was homogeneous, it was a typical English hedge. In the spring the place was a great favourite of nightingales, which love hazels, of glow-worms, which like mossy hedgeroots, and of lovers, who take pleasure in quiet lanes.

Hearing the News

The first person I met in the High Street was Mr Chorlton, so I took him into the Swan bar, bought him a drink, and commanded him to tell me the local news.

'Well,' he said, as he settled himself down with a whisky-and-soda, 'as you know I have retired from schoolmastering. I couldn't stand the sons of gentlemen any longer; the latest generation was even worse than yours. How do I spend my retirement? I breed magpie-moths. I confine thousands of caterpillars in muslin sleeves upon my gooseberry bushes. I select each season the lightest-coloured moths and mate them, and my ambition is to produce one which is completely white. If I live for another ten years I shall do it; and die contented.'

'All those learned books on all your shelves—' I said. 'Does the sum total of all their wisdom teach you that there's nothing better to do than breed a white magpie-moth?'

'If I had read them all,' said Mr Chorlton cynically, 'they might well have driven me to the conclusion that there was nothing more important. But I must confess that I haven't read 'em all, and lacking the complete wisdom of Diogenes I still take an active part in affairs. Let me tell you, my boy, that I am now a very notable person in Elmbury. You must take care how you speak to me. You must show me proper respect. "Scipio is the soul of the Council; the rest are vain shadows."'

'Good Lord!' I said. '*You* among the Town Scoundrels!'

'Even I. I was elected last November. You find it surprising? It surprised me. I never thought they'd vote for an old dodderer with a butterfly-net. But they did. I topped the poll. I'm told that Double Alley voted for me solid. I bribed little boys with caterpillars and they went about on election day beating upon tin cans and singing

"Vote, vote, vote for Mr Chorlton!"

So now once again I wear a gown. And once again I try to drum elementary truths into stupid people's heads!'

He would be a disturbing presence among the Town Scoundrels, I thought: like Socrates among the Athenians. I asked him why he had got himself elected, and he said:

'That's exactly what my fellow Councillors ask. They can't understand what I hope to get out of it. But really, of course, it's the schoolmaster's ancient vice: his passion for instructing and improving his fellows. I ought to know better after thirty years of it. I taught you the rudiments of Latin and Greek and the only result, as far as I can see, is that you write extremely immoral novels. Well, I thought I'd have a go at teaching adults for a change; but I find the Council Chamber very little different from the Lower Fourth. The only difference is that I lack my old authority!'

Grim and Gay

I sat late in the Swan bar, while Mr Councillor Chorlton told me the news. Both comedy and tragedy had walked the streets of Elmbury during the previous few weeks. The tragedy overshadowed all. The Vicar, continuing to give away every penny he could borrow, at last faced bankruptcy. His creditors had carried off most of the furniture from the vicarage. It was said that during the coldest snap of the winter he hadn't been able to afford a fire. Even Mr Jeffs had taken pity on him and patched up the ancient quarrel, sending him a side of bacon as a token of peace.

Yet the Vicar, half-saint, half-profligate, possessing nothing save his mania of generosity, persisted in borrowing from the moneylenders in order that he might continue to give away what was not his to give. He shared his last bottle of port with the duns which were his only visitors.

Another piece of news was that Black Sal had at last been marched away to the workhouse. Comedy and tragedy accompanied her hand-in-hand. She went as to a wedding in all her dark and flapping finery, gaily and obscenely defiant, shouting an insolent rhyme:

> 'The silly old muckers
> Have sent I to the Wukkus!'

But now, said Mr Chorlton, she was dying. They had bathed her and sterilized her, and the shock had proved too great. In a cold, clean ward in that cold, cruel house she lay and babbled o' Double Alley.

'Hang Art, Madam, and Trust to Nature'

Double Alley, said Mr Chorlton, was in the news as usual. Last summer the inhabitants had pitched out into the street an earnest and blameless spinster, a holidaying water-colourist, who had dared to set up her easel in the vast midst of their rabbit-warren and started to paint the terrible and beautiful scene. A well-meaning policeman tried in vain to dissuade her, suggesting that there were other parts of the town, equally beautiful and far less smelly, where she would not be so liable to embarrassment and offence. She replied tartly: 'If I can look after myself in the slums of Naples I can look after myself in a sleepy little English country town.'

'Yes, Mum,' said the policeman. 'But begging your pardon, Naples ain't Double Alley, if you see what I mean.'

She didn't see what he meant. Indeed, she would have to belong to Elmbury to understand Double Alley. She intimated tactfully that she considered herself too old to be the object of any interference; that she was too widely-travelled to suffer any embarrassment; and as for offence, if he meant the smell she had some excellent aromatic lozenges. She added: 'Mark my words, young man, these quaint people and I will soon be on the best of terms.'

That was where she was wrong; for she failed to reckon with one very important characteristic of the Double Alley folk: their pride. They might be drunkards, ne'er-do-weels, wantons, sluts; they were indeed filthy, lewd, incestuous, the lowest of the low; but in spite of that and perhaps because of that they clung fiercely to certain absurd and apparently incompatible notions about the dignity of man.

They who in the past had bundled out many a prying welfare-worker and a district visitor and a curate's wife and the local Lady Bountiful for the same reason, now drove forth the water-colour painter, and chucked her easel after her, because it hurt their unreasonable pride that they should be regarded in the same light as animals at the zoo. Frightful indeed was their squalor; but it was their own business. Their sins cried out to Heaven; but that again was their business and Heaven's. Their poverty was shocking and shameful to see; all the more reason why it should be hidden from men's eyes.

The wretched woman, during the course of her ejection, was heard to remark that Double Alley was a public highway and that she had as much right there as anybody else; and this was certainly true. But in practice the Alley, because of its squalor, was never used as a thoroughfare, and the inhabitants had come to look upon it as their own. The woman's very entry into the place seemed to them an unwarrantable intrusion into their privacy; and *because* that privacy happened to be such a very unpleasant privacy they bitterly resented her sitting down upon her folding canvas stool in the middle of it. If you live in a pigstye you don't keep open house.

So the 'quaint' people, old wives, young sluts, and little guttersnipes – the men for the most part held aloof – chivvied the lady artist out of the Alley and went yelping at her heels down the High Street. And of course she was very angry indeed. She wrote a letter to the local paper in which she declared her opinion that 'these brutish creatures' – she could scarcely term them human beings – 'would be fitter subjects for the brush of Hogarth than for herself.'

Maybe, said Mr Chorlton drily; it was probable that the lady was not so good an artist as Hogarth. As for the 'brutish creatures', they had demonstrated by their actions that they were very human indeed. The pig, said Mr Chorlton, betrays neither pride nor shame in its style. The inhabitants of Double Alley had shown that they possessed a kind of pride and a kind of shame and even a kind of dignity, which is the property solely of mankind.

Mr Brunswick and the Chain Stores

Mr Chorlton told me one more story before dinner-time; and that was pure comedy. It concerned Mr Brunswick, who kept a small unprosperous haberdashery and who had been affronted recently by the erection on the opposite side of the street of a large shop belonging to one of the 'Chain Stores' which sold not only haberdashery but many other things in 'cheap lines' also. The particular group of plutocrats concerned had bought a fine half-timbered dwelling-house for conversion into their new shop. Let no one fear, they had said, lest the result should give offence. Far from it; the appearance of the street would actually be improved, for they would employ the best architect and instruct him to make sure that the building was in keeping with the architectural tradition of the town.

'God help them,' said Mr Chorlton, 'I believe they really think they have kept their promise. They wrote to the Council and asked if the Mayor would attend a formal opening; and they said they were sure the building was "one of which the town might feel justly proud".' What they did, of course, was to build something resembling their idea of Ye Olde Village Shoppe magnified five times.

Wherever they had removed the original half-timbering they had painted imitation half-timbering on the white walls. The name of the firm was displayed in enormous Gothic lettering; and beneath it the firm's motto, also in Gothic lettering, MENS SANA IN CORPORE SANO.

('Don't ask me,' said Mr Chorlton, 'why these extraordinary people, who sell mainly girls' cheap underwear, should have chosen that particular motto. If only they'd consulted me, I'd have thought cf lots of suitable ones!')

Poor Mr Brunswick, naturally, was very upset indeed. From the dark doorway of his dingy little shop he watched and brooded. The windows of the new store were filled with cheap lines at cut prices and Mr Brunswick, who like the people of Double Alley had his peculiar pride, didn't deal in cheap lines nor pretend to cut his prices. But he saw his late customers flocking into the store. Perhaps these fickle ones would come back to his shop when the shoddy things wore out; but meanwhile he was helpless, he could neither outbuy the opposition nor out-advertise it, his whole capital was a mere three hundred pounds matched against the Chain Stores' millions.

So Mr Brunswick shrugged his shoulders and went down the street to Mr Parfitt's furniture shop and persuaded Mr Parfitt to write him, in Gothic lettering, a new sign. Mr Brunswick didn't know any Latin; but he had an original sense of humour; for the new sign, hung over his shop next day, declared defiantly:

MEN'S AND WOMEN'S SANA IN CORPORE SANO

The great plutocrat who owned the Chain Stores might quote that, if he liked, as an example of the ignorance and stupidity of his rivals the country tradesmen. He was welcome to dine out on the story if it amused him; for Elmbury humour is not for strangers and certainly not for such strangers as he.

Large as Life and Twice as Natural

At last I said goodnight to Mr Chorlton and walked home through the crooked streets between the crooked, crazy houses. Out of the dark entrance to an alley a long spidery figure came sidling up to me and I recognized Ancient Pistol. He touched his cap and said he was pleased to see me again. I gave him a shilling. He leaned conspiratorially towards me and asked if I would like a salmon. If so I must take a walk down Gander Lane after dark tomorrow night and I should find it in the ditch on the left-hand side just by the stile into Margaret's Meadow. It would be covered with dead leaves. I could settle up later . . . Pistol touched his cap again and vanished into the shadows.

My way home was punctuated by encounters with old friends, and by fragments of local gossip and local politics which, because I had been so long away, I only half understood. It seemed that there was a great row going on between the Operatic Society and the Dramatic Society which until recently had been one. The Operatics were Lowbrows who wanted Gilbert and Sullivan; the Dramatics were Highbrows who wanted Shaw; and both wanted (at the same time it seemed) the same stage, the same scenery, the same stage manager and the same leading lady. There was another fine row going on in the Council; it was very obscure and it was something to do with the appointment of a rat-catcher. Bardolph had been sent to prison for stealing the bicycle of the police-constable who came to arrest him for some other offence. There was fierce controversy about the Abbey services, which some deemed too High and others too Low. The whole Committee of the local Farmers' Union, partaking of a drink called Plum Jerkum to fortify themselves against hecklers at their annual meeting, had appeared scandalously drunk upon the platform. And Mr Parfitt was in trouble over the sale of Indecent Literature: he had printed picture postcards of the Long Man.

And so on. It occurred to me that Elmbury was still a very lively and vigorous place; and when I recollected that one of my London friends had professed himself shocked at my intention 'to bury myself in a dead-alive country town' I nearly laughed out loud. This particular friend belonged to a school of writers which had its headquarters in Bloomsbury and prided itself on being very unconventional and free. Its adherents were always talking about 'the sacred right of self-expression', which served as a jolly good excuse for seducing your neighbour's wife or breaking up the furniture when you were drunk. Yet it seemed to me that they didn't know how to express themselves half as well as a great many of the Elmbury people did. Compared with some of our folks, they were positively hidebound; they were as conventional as the heroes and heroines of their novels, who always talked in the same conventional idiom at the same conventional cocktail parties. And as for Elmbury being dead, why, the guests at those cocktail parties were very shades compared with the full-blooded exuberant company at the Shakespeare or the Swan.

In fact, by comparison with Elmbury people, those daring intellectuals seemed rather colourless and dull. Their outlook seemed curiously limited. I wouldn't have hurt their feelings by telling them so, but they seemed to me to have a small-town mentality, somehow.

And so, as I walked home through the fantastic populous streets of Elmbury on that first night of my homecoming, I did not feel that I had exchanged a great world for a little one: I felt exactly the opposite.

Emotion seemed larger here, pleasures were keener, sorrows sharper, men's laughter was more boisterous, jokes were funnier, the tragedy was more profound and the comedy more riotous, the huge fantasy of life was altogether more fantastic. London, for all its street lights, was a twilit world; Elmbury, on a murky February evening, seemed as bright as a stage.

The Unemployed

It was a bright world, yes: but the glow which lights Elmbury in my memory shows up also the dark shadows. That was 1931, during which western civilization demonstrated for the first time that it could contrive a peace which was, for most of its citizens, nearly as uncomfortable as war. The storm which Mr Jeffs had sniffed in the balmy air four years ago had broken with a vengeance now. Already Elmbury had more than three hundred unemployed.

It was the first thing I noticed when I walked down the High Street by day; the crowd of idle men standing at the Cross. Of course there had always been men at the street-corners in Elmbury; but only a few and these the familiar ones, such as Pistol, Bardolph and Nym. Those had a purpose in standing about; they were on the look-out for whatever they could scrounge. Others of their kidney would often hang about deliberately on the chance of picking up an 'odd-job'; and if we wanted the garden tidied up, or extra help in the market, we would always send somebody to the Cross to find a man who wanted a job.

These hangers-about had been purposeful, they had had a very good reason for standing at the Cross, but now Elmbury saw something which it had never seen before, something very grim and terrible and shocking, it saw men loafing about *purposelessly*, men who had long ago given up the hope of finding a job but who stood at the street-corner out of habit, or perhaps because it was slightly more interesting, and not much colder, than sitting in their own house.

You could find a score any morning at the Cross; another little group outside the Anchor Inn; a third at the end of the town where the road bridge crosses the river. On Fridays the queue outside the Labour Exchange stretched for nearly a hundred yards down Church Street.

Most of the men were young, many were in their teens. The majority of the older men with regular jobs were still in employment. Elmbury was luckier in that respect than many another small town. Its own little industries – flour-milling, malting, boat-building – were not greatly affected by the depression and were able to carry on; and agriculture, though severely hit, could not cut down its labour beyond a certain indispensable minimum. Cows must be milked, stock reared, fields ploughed, and crops harvested, even though these operations resulted in a loss. The colliery and the factory could close down; but not the farm.

The bitter consequences of the depression, therefore, fell first upon the casual labourers and the semi-skilled odd-jobbers, of which Elmbury had a great number; and next upon the lads who had never had a job at all. Many of these boys, in normal times, would have gone away to learn a trade, the more adventurous would probably drift to the cities and would either remain there – adding good country stock to the urban populations – or return in due course to their home town bringing back new ideas and new ways to Elmbury. Both city and country town reaped benefits from this migration of labour. But now the cities had no jobs to offer. They themselves had an unemployment problem, not of hundreds, but of tens of thousands; and so our young men at the very time when they should have been learning a trade lost heart and hope at the street-corner.

In Defence of Odd-job Men

The casual labourer and the handyman, the odd-jobbers who could turn their hands to anything from making a rabbit hutch to picking plums, sprouts, or peas, from gardening to hay-trussing, from thatching to salmon-netting, now spent their days with the youths lounging on the pavement. Plums last season had fetched less than the cost of sending them by rail to Manchester; sprouts at a shilling a pot were best left to rot on the stalks; there was no sale for hay, and no job for the hay-trusser.

This was a local disaster, for the popular notion that the casual labourer doesn't matter (or at best is unimportant by comparison with the man in regular work) is a very mistaken notion. In Elmbury at any rate the class of odd-job man included some of the best elements in the community. These were the men with independent spirits who would bind themselves to no master. 'Better be a free man than have a full belly twice a day,' one of them said to me once. These were the adventurous and the imaginative men, whose restless minds and ingenious hands would scorn to perform the same set task day in, day out, through the long years. These were the jacks-of-all-trades. They might perhaps be masters of none; but they were the last free men in Elmbury.

England has always been lucky in her possession of such a class, bound to no trade and no employer, handy at many things, quick to learn, experimental and adventurous. When the agents of Drake and Raleigh looked for men for a voyage to the Americas it was among this class, I'll wager, that they first sought. It was not the men in regular jobs who'd leave hearth and home and the certainty of a weekly wage to follow a romantic captain to the ends of the earth. And it was this class too, the unstable and the adventurous, which gave the first volunteers to all our wars. The odd-job man makes a good soldier. He learns quickly to handle weapons as he has often learned to handle new tools. He is not set in his ways like the regular worker; he has a mind more easily moulded to the event. And best of all, he doesn't look to the future; the future, for him, has always looked after itself. Sufficient unto the day is the evil thereof is his watchword; and it serves for a soldier's watchword very well indeed.

However, these admirable men were the first to go to the wall when that strange, disastrous dislocation of trade and finance happened in 1931: they, and the young men, equally adventurous, who had not yet started to learn a trade. These two classes, containing some of the best of our manhood, were thrown upon the rubbish heap. In many places, of course, the skilled and regular workers were affected as well; but in Elmbury it was chiefly a problem of the youths and the casual labourers: about 150 youths, about 200 'odd-jobbers', for whom there was no work and no likelihood of work until this catastrophe of peace was solved by the catastrophe of war.

The Town Council did what it could. It published a most expensive brochure with the idea of persuading people to spend their holidays in 'unspoilt Elmbury'; and another expensive brochure for the purpose of persuading manufacturers to come and spoil it. But this ingenuous attempt to make the best of both worlds was doomed to failure. Money seemed to have dried up at its mysterious source. There were few visitors, and they had little to spend. Nobody contemplated building factories at such a time and if they had done so would have been unlikely to choose a site so far from coal, ports, or railway junctions.

'I will give you work,' was the easily-made, easily-broken promise of every candidate at the Council elections. Any ill-paid drudgery, in 1931, seemed utterly desirable. A man deemed himself fortunate indeed if he were taken on by a farmer to dig ditches at thirty shillings a week. And this, I think, was one of the worst aspects of the tragedy as far as Elmbury was concerned. Our people, who by lucky chance had escaped the defiling touch of Victorian industrialism, were now driven to accept the horrible heresies of Victorian industrialism, that the giving of work was a favour, that the doing of work was a virtue *per se*. While there was plenty of casual work to be had, the men of Elmbury had always been free to choose what work they should do and whom they should work for: for they could always go and pick sprouts or plums, fell timber or make hay. And because they had been able to do the work of their own choice, they had generally taken pleasure and pride in it. Now all that was changed. The industrial heresy, beloved of great capitalists, bemused even the rugged independent spirits of Elmbury. Hard and uninteresting work was something rare, desirable, and of itself virtuous. The man who had the privilege of working long hours at a dull job was a better man than his neighbour who worked as little as he need. The man who had work to offer was necessarily a good citizen; the man who refused a job because it was uninteresting was wicked – or mad. You didn't look for interest or pleasure in your work; the virtue lay in the doing of the work for the appointed number of hours, whether it was ill done or well done; in serving humbly and blindly the great capitalist god.

Thus the blight settled on men's minds during the depression. The gay, happy-go-lucky fellows who would do six different jobs on six different days, do them well, and enjoy doing them – and then, feeling prosperous, take three days off to go fishing – these men weren't wanted any more. They must toe the line, join the queue, think themselves lucky if they were found worthy to serve the god.

So the skill of the handyman went to waste at the street-corner; so the adventurous spirit was lost and the happy-go-lucky mood turned sour. The odd-job men and the pale-faced youths stood together at Elmbury Cross, hands in pockets, shoulders slumped, coat collars turned up against the cold wind. Our best manhood rotted alongside our best youth.

We should need them both in 1940.

Economics of Odd-jobbing

As an example of what I mean by the odd-jobber, I quote the typical case of Jim Fletcher, an alert and able-bodied man of about thirty, a jolly good worker when he wanted to work but also a devoted angler who was almost always to be found at the waterside when the weather was right and the fish were biting. I asked him how he contrived this, while supporting a wife and three children and how nevertheless he managed to have plenty of money to spend in the pub. I give his answer, which referred to the year 1925, in the form of a statement of his income such as he might have sent to the Inspector of Taxes if he had had to pay Income Tax.

JIM FLETCHER'S EARNINGS DURING 1925

	£	s	d
January.			
14 days' sprout-picking for Mr Jeffs at an average of 11/8 a day	8	3	4
(The pickers were paid 10*d* a pot and Jim could pick 14 pots a day. It was hard work and rough on the hands on frosty mornings; and the pickers worked from dawn to dusk.)			
6 days' trapping Mr Nixon's rabbits on Brensham Hill. For the whole job . .	5	0	0
About 2 days' work knocking together some dog-kennels for Mr Sparrow, for which he was paid over and above the cost of the timber	1	0	0
February.			
9 days' salmon-netting. The net caught 14 fish and Jim was paid a fifth share of the takings, which came to	5	12	0
He also patched up 2 old punts which he sold for £3 10/- each, having spent 10/- on tar and timber	6	10	0
2 days' beating at the Farmers' rabbit-shoot at 6/- a day	0	12	0
(He was also given a rabbit on each of these occasions.)			
March.			
10 days' sprout-picking at 11/- a day .	5	10	0
5 days' salmon-fishing at which he earned	3	10	0
Profit on feeding a bunch of pigs in his allotment	3	3	0
April.			
20 days' cutting osiers in the Marsh at 7*d* a bundle. A bundle measures 37 inches in circumference, and Jim would cut about 20 bundles a day, say 20 days at 12/- a day .	12	0	0
5 days' drovering to the sheep fairs, with tips, say 10/- a day	2	10	0

	£	s	d
May.			
Sand-dredging, 12 days, at 7/- a day . .	4	4	0
Elver-catching at night whenever the elvers were running. He could easily catch 20 lb of elvers in a couple of hours, and he sold them at 4*d* a lb. Say 15 nights at 6/8 a night	5	0	0
June.			
Haymaking whenever the weather was fit. Say 17 days at 7/- a day (plus a quart of cider)	5	19	0
The Coarse Fishing season opened on June 16th; and Jim supplied worms and gentles to visiting anglers out of which he made about	1	0	0
He also took some Birmingham gents fishing in his punt and acted as gillie. They paid him 10/- a day for 3 days . . .	1	10	0
Sale of produce from his allotment (April–June)	1	15	0
July			
5 days' haymaking at 7/- a day . . .	1	15	0
10 days' plum-picking at 9/- a day . .	4	10	0
Gillie-ing for the Birmingham gents, 4 days	2	0	0
(Jim also earned £1 in rather grisly fashion by fetching out of the river the corpse of a holiday-maker who'd been drowned.) .	1	0	0
During the summer he collected certain rare caterpillars for Mr Chorlton, which earned him usually about	0	15	0
August.			
6 days' plum-picking at 9/- a day . .	2	14	0
3 days' gillie-ing	1	10	0
Profit on pigs	3	5	0
Profit on pigeons which he kept in his backyard	0	15	0
Sale of produce from his allotment (July–Aug)	0	10	0

	£	s	d
(Jim also earned £4 by selling eel-putcheons which he'd made out of withies and another £2 by mending some old salmon nets)	6	0	0

September.

4 days' gillie-ing	2	0	0
Sale of worms and gentles to competitors in the angling competition	0	12	0
Taking 3 wasps' nests and sale of wasp grubs	0	12	6
Sale of mushrooms collected at dawn on various days	2	5	0
Sale of blackberries (about 3 days' picking)	2	0	0
12 days' timber-felling at 9/- a day . .	5	8	0
Sale of produce from his allotment . .	0	6	0

October.

Beating at partridge-shoots, 6 days at 6/- a day (plus free dinner, cider and a rabbit)	1	16	0
Eel-catching. This was simply a matter of laying the 'putcheons' in the river and later collecting them. Eels were fetching 6*d* a lb. Jim caught 68 lb and sold them for	1	14	0
Earth-stopping for the Hunt: occasional work at night which brought in . .	0	10	0
Mushrooms	1	0	0
Sale of baits to fishermen . . .	0	15	0
Tying flies on wet days, which he subsequently sold for	1	0	0
2 days' drovering	1	0	0
2 days' timber-felling at 9/- a day . .	0	18	0
Clipping Butcher Smith's pony . .	0	7	6

November.

14 days' work with the flour barges at 7/- a day	4	18	0
Sale of an otter-skin, shot on the river .	1	10	0
Sale of 8 wild duck, shot on the river .	0	16	0
3 days' timber-felling at 9/- a day . .	1	7	0

December.

7 days' rick-cutting at 8/- a day . .	2	16	0

	£	s	d
4 days' drovering to the Christmas markets with tips, say 10/- a day . . .	2	0	0
5 days' beating for the pheasant-shoots at 6/- a day (plus free dinner and cider) . .	1	10	0
Earth-stopping	0	15	0
Profit on pigs	4	0	0
7 days' trapping Mr Trewin's rabbits .	4	10	0

£143 18 4

You will see that although he earned £143 18s 4d in the year – an average of nearly £3 a week* – Jim Fletcher did little more than 200 full days' work, an average of less than 4 days a week. His work was almost always fun – except the sprout-picking, which he didn't enjoy. (But it happened at a time when odd-jobs were hard to come by.) He had no appearances to keep up, and spent practically nothing on clothes. His household was never short of food. He grew his own vegetables, brought home plenty of eels and other fish (including, I daresay, an occasional poached salmon), and could always lay his hands on a rabbit or even – though he wouldn't admit it – a hare. He killed a pig once a year, and was never short of bacon. He always had plenty of firing, for in flood-time he went out in his punt and collected logs from the river. The three days a week when he wasn't working he spent in fishing, 'mucking about in his boat', or running after the hounds.

In fact, Jim Fletcher lived like a lord.

Farmer-cum-Dealer: A Moral Tale

Apart from the growing queue outside the Labour Exchange ('This running sore in our body-politic,' as the Mayor, given to pomposity, frequently described it) I found Elmbury little changed. The farming community for the most part was still living on its fat; it hadn't yet felt the full blast

* Agricultural wages at this time for a 52-hour week were 30s.

of the depression and most of the farmers had respectable bank balances left over from the prosperous years. The cautious majority, anticipating that it would be a long time before conditions became normal, cut down their expenses and husbanded their resources, reckoning their capital would 'tidy them over' till trade improved. The feckless ones persisted in a belief that next season the topsy-turvy world would mysteriously right itself, and took comfort from some mystic saying of their grandfathers, 'Things always goes in threes; three bad years, and then three good ones.' These optimists overstocked their land on the principle, 'Now is the time to buy, when prices are at rock-bottom.' Unfortunately the economic waters were uncharted; no lead-line could find where rock-bottom lay. Six months later stock prices were lower still, and the farmers found that they had given free hospitality to a large number of beasts which they sold for less than they had paid for them.

Since common-sense appeared to fail them in the face of inexplicable disaster, other farmers discovered a belief in luck and took to dealing, in the frantic hope that they'd be lucky enough to catch the chancy unstable market at the right moment. Mr Tempest, the wise, tight-lipped little bank manager, would warn them in vain: 'When I hear of a farmer going in for dealing, I always expect that the next time I hear of him will be through the Official Receiver.' A farmer's job, said Mr Tempest, was to grow things; and mixing his metaphors a bit, he added, 'Let him stick to his last.'

It was good advice; and Mr Transome, for example, would have been wise to heed it. Jeremy Transome was a fairly successful farmer with an eye for a bargain. He knew a bit about cattle and had often been pretty lucky in the past. He farmed the Highwoods Farm at Lower Hampton: 280 acres of mixed pasture and arable, where for fifteen years he'd made a good living. When the Depression came he began to get into difficulties, and he thought he'd get out of them by doing a bit of dealing. He persuaded the reluctant Mr Tempest to increase the mortgage on the farm by five hundred pounds and he bought fifty yearlings for an average price of ten pounds each. On the whole he bought them well; he was a very good judge of beasts. He turned them out in his pastures and proceeded to 'watch the market'. This meant attending the stock sales in four different towns once a week. When he went to market he spent money. He spent about thirty shillings each time; it was mostly spent on drinks for potential customers, and he put it down quite fairly to 'expenses'; six pounds a week for expenses.

At last he decided to send twenty-five of his yearlings to market. They were looking well, for they'd had a month's good grazing; but the market happened to be a bad one, Mr Transome was dissatisfied with the prices and he bought them in at eleven pounds a head. Indeed the prices for yearlings at that sale were so low that Mr Transome thought it would be a golden opportunity missed if he didn't buy some more. He bought thirty at nine pounds each.

Next day it began to freeze and the grass stopped growing.

He was short of grazing, for he had grossly overstocked his land; and soon he had to start feeding the cattle with hay. He was short of hay too, and he had to buy a ten-ton rick at three pounds a ton. He would gladly have sold his cattle now, for eleven pounds; but during the hard weather they had gone back in condition, and even to his prejudiced eye they didn't look worth more than nine pounds ten.

Now he was on the slippery slope indeed. His dealing excursions, and his days at the markets, had caused him to neglect his farm. He was short of labour, for he'd sacked a couple of men when he decided to go in for dealing; and the few labourers he had were inclined to take things easy when the boss was out. The farm, which had been tidy and well kept, began to look neglected; there were broken gates and fences, and one day some yearlings got out and it cost him a day's work – and a couple of quid – to get them back again.

Ditching and draining had been put off too long; and when the thaw came, with heavy rain for three days, some fields flooded and Mr Transome was harder put to it than ever for grazing. He was compelled to keep one bunch of yearlings in a sloppy field where, as the neighbours said, 'they'd soon grow webbed-feet like ducks.'

And now the rumour began to spread about the countryside that Mr Transome was in a bad way. Perhaps he owed his hay dealer or his cake-merchant a larger sum than usual, and had left it longer unpaid. Perhaps Mr Tempest had even been compelled to return one of his cheques: 'Refer to Drawer'. At any rate the dangerous rumour went about, and the professional cattle-dealers, who had long ears for such tales, came to hear of it.

And so before long unasked visitors began to call at his farm. They came in cars; they came, very often, from a long way off. They were genial and friendly men, and business had brought them, they said, into the district. They'd heard by chance that Mr Transome might have a few yearlings for sale. Yes, thankee very much, they'd come in and have a drink and talk it over . . .

Their visits generally cost Mr Transome a bottle of whisky. That was only twelve and sixpence then, but it was another charge added to the cost of the yearlings.

The dealers offered nine pounds apiece for them. Mr Transome held out for nine pounds ten. The dealers politely refused; they'd had a look round the farm and noted its condition. They smiled to themselves and drove away.

But a fortnight later, by a curious coincidence, they would find themselves in the district again.

Meanwhile Mr Transome had to buy some more hay. The floods went down, but left the grass sour and muddy. Some of the cattle went sick, and Mr Transome had to call in the vet. Two of them died. He sold them in the end, desperately, foolishly, ruinously, at eight pounds fifteen apiece. He had to; his creditors were threatening to put him in court. The yearlings had cost him, in hay and grazing, drovering, travelling, vet's bills and whisky, about fifty shillings a head more than the purchase price. But they had cost him more than that; they had cost him Highwoods Farm. For the dealers' cheque went to pay the hay-dealer and the cake-merchant; and Mr Transome hadn't enough capital to restock his farm. The fields which had been over-stocked now lay empty; and there was no profit in that. The next season was a bad one, and it finished him.

'My Head Office deeply regrets,' wrote Mr Tempest, 'having to foreclose on the mortgage'; and as he dictated the letter he was thinking, in his favourite mixed metaphor: 'The cobbler should stick to his last.'

Double or Quits

Some of the farmers, especially the madcap, John Myttonish, Devil-take-the-hindmost crowd, decided to ignore the Depression and carry on as if that mysterious catastrophe hadn't happened. You would find them in the Shakespeare drinking damnation to the Ministry of Agriculture; you would see them out hunting, going as if the Devil indeed were at their heels. After market about a dozen of them would gather in the 'private' room at the Swan and play solo half the night; or an even sillier game, the silliest card game in the world, which is called Farmers' Glory. They lost and won a great deal, and paid their losses by cheque, adding to the complexity of their farm accounts. They also had a habit of tossing for everything. If they lost at cards they would say, 'Toss you double or quits'; if they wanted a round of drinks they'd toss to see who paid; if they bought a cow for twenty-five pounds they were quite likely to say, 'Toss you to see if I give you thirty pounds or twenty.'

It was a crazy way to carry on, and it nearly broke the heart of Mr Tempest, who had known them from boyhood and in his private capacity was very fond of them. In the

pub he drank with them as a friend; in his office he talked
to them as a stern father. But their mood was a difficult
one to deal with; they were puzzled, angry, bitter, and
rebellious against a changing world which they could not
understand. Their reaction to it was to ride still more
recklessly out hunting. 'Twould save themselves, they said,
and everybody else a lot of trouble if they broke their
necks.

Anarchy in Scarlet

Jerry was one of their company; but Dorrie's gentle hands
held him on a pair of reins, and I thought that with luck
he'd weather the bad times, while Demon's sure-footed
jumping would save him from breaking his neck. He would
often lend me a horse, and it was generally a good one, but
if hounds ran fast I would never see much of Jerry. He rode
always a little way from the huntsman; and if the huntsman
took a toss you would hear Jerry's clear voice calling the
hounds on to the line.

I enjoyed my hunting, and it is something I am glad to
remember and glad I had the chance of doing, though I
don't think I shall ever want to do it again. It seems to me
now somewhat too elaborate a way of doing to death a
rather pleasing little animal. But it has many merits, not the
least of which is that it teaches a lot of people to know the
countryside far better and far more intimately than they
would otherwise do. Of course there is a lot of nonsense
talked in its defence. We are told that it is necessary for the
purpose of 'keeping down foxes' whereas, of course, what it
does is to preserve foxes while to a certain extent controlling
them; that it 'creates employment', which indeed it does
by using up a lot of manhours quite unproductively and
smashing a lot of fences which the farmer's men have to
mend; and that it is very 'democratic', whatever that may
mean.

This is a very curious claim to make for a sport or cere-

mony – it is a bit of both – which automatically divides its
followers into two classes: those who can afford to ride and
those who can't. Yet I suppose fox-hunting is 'democratic'
in one respect, for it cuts clean across all the customs and
traditions relating to private property. Its defenders never
attempt to make this point; perhaps they dare not; but it is
a fact that there is an aspect of fox-hunting which is not so
much democratic as anarchic. Boundaries, fences, gates, all
the great and little walls which man erects against man,
mean nothing whatever to the fox-hunter. It doesn't matter
whether he rides on a five-hundred-guinea horse, pedals a
bicycle, or goes on foot: if he is following the hounds he will
ignore your 'Trespassers will be prosecuted' board, enter
your orchard, wander at will about your fields, go crashing
through your plantations, and even invade your back-
garden. He is the despair of keepers; for the most notorious
poacher, if the hounds are near, will claim the right to loaf
about at the covertside. The veriest ragamuffin, discovered
in a lord's most sacred preserves, will have a good answer
to the question, 'What right have you got here?' if he can
say, 'Following the hounds, sir.' For it is a poor man's
right as well as a rich man's; and it is indeed a right, and a
very ancient one, for there is no offence in trespass unless
damage is done, and trespassers cannot be prosecuted under
English law. Fox-hunting reminds us of our old rights and
confirms them; it also provides us with a useful remedy
against such as lock their gates and deny access to their
land. For if a landlord in a hunting country fails to welcome
the hounds, with all their rag-tag-and-bobtail followers,
then woe betide him. There are social sanctions more powerful far than economic or legal ones.

So I suggest that the sport is essentially anarchic, though
it is practised by those who most fear anarchy. On the
flimsy excuse that a small red animal has run through your
garden a crowd of scarlet-coated men, fierce women, and
half the loafers of the nearest town will appear upon your
lawn, and if by chance the terrified creature has taken refuge
in your chimney they will establish themselves in a circle

round your domain whence you will not easily dislodge them. Indeed unless you take the firmest stand against them they will attack your house with crowbars and pull it down brick by brick until they have achieved their strange desire, which is to tear the little creature limb from limb. Having done so, and the demoniac frenzy having left them, they will assume once more their normal and respectable characters, Lord X, Lady Y, Sir Lionel Z, Mr A the chartered accountant, his daughter Polly, and Mr B who keeps the sweet shop in the village. They will apologize most politely for any trouble they have caused you, smile charmingly, and take off their hats to you as they ride away down the road.

Sporting Encounter with the Colonel

It was out hunting that I encountered again that roguish, gnomish, remarkable man whom I first saw through the Tudor House window when I was a child: 'the Colonel', whom I had since discovered lived at Brensham, where he had a small farm. 'Encountered' is the right word; for Jerry had put me on a horse which was too fresh for me, and it was running away with me down a steep lane on Brensham Hill when I met the Colonel coming up on foot. I did the best I could to avoid him, but the horse was going too fast; the sharp toe of my hunting-boot caught him right in the midriff and he collapsed with a loud grunt on the ground.

As soon as I had stopped the obstreperous horse I rode back to apologize. The Colonel had picked himself up, and if you can imagine an infuriated gnome you will understand how truly formidable he looked. I approached him timidly and penitently, hat in hand. He was making a loud spluttering noise which was not recognizable as speech. His long walrus moustaches bristled; his little blue eyes were popping out of his head; his face was purple, bright purple as a Victoria plum, and yet it had also a sort of pallor of rage which was rather like the bloom on a plum.

'I'm most awfully sorry—' I began; but that was as far as I got. If I was timid, my horse was thoroughly scared. It took one look at the Colonel, flexed its ears, and shied; then, seizing the bit between its teeth, it spun round in the lane and galloped back madly down the hill.

Social Encounter with the Colonel

A few days afterwards I met the Colonel again in the Swan bar.

It was just before noon. The bar was empty and I settled myself in a chair in the corner with a pint of beer and *The Times* which happened to be lying on one of the tables. A moment later the Colonel entered. He took off his battered deerstalker, hung it up on a peg behind the door, and advanced towards the bar. He caught sight of me, his bright blue eyes stared angrily, he took three purposeful steps in my direction.

'*Sir*,' he said. '*Are you aware that you are sitting in my seat?*'

I hastily apologized – he was really a very terrifying old gentleman – and moved to a neighbouring chair. He grunted, ordered a whisky, and sat down. I thought I would placate him, and show deference to his grizzled hairs. I folded up *The Times*.

'Would you care to read the paper, sir?' I said.

He glared at me. His moustache twitched. He looked as if he were about to spring, as if he would leap over table, chairs, whisky and all to assault me.

'*It is for that purpose, sir*,' he said in a dreadful voice, '*that I order it to be delivered here every morning.*'

I was utterly abashed. I passed him the paper with mumbled apologies and tried to hide myself behind my beer. He was indeed a terrible and a wonderful old man; and I couldn't help admiring his gesture in having the paper delivered to the pub, where after all he spent half his time. (The other half was spent in the pursuit of various animals, birds, and fishes, during which *The Times* would have been an encumbrance.)

I became aware that he was staring at me over the top of his paper. I felt very frightened indeed; but as he slowly lowered the paper I perceived that his extraordinary face was undergoing a metamorphosis. A thousand wrinkles appeared all over it, as if a catspaw of wind blew across the sea. His blue eyes disappeared between folds of red weather-beaten skin. His turkey-cock neck shook and quivered. I suddenly realized that he was laughing. Out of his open mouth came suddenly such clear and merry laughter as I had never heard before, such laughter as the Greeks called Ionian laughter which matched the mirth of the Ionian springs. It was rare and beautiful and unexpected laughter and I was entranced as I had been entranced by his mischievous grin, some fifteen years before through the nursery window.

'God damn it, my boy,' said the Colonel, 'what a bloody old fool I am. Let's have a drink!'

Regulars at the Swan

I shall have much more to say about this remarkable Colonel, but first I must describe his habitat, which was the Swan bar.

Every country town has a bar like the Swan, but you will not find such a place in any city or suburb or village. It belongs absolutely to the small market town. It isn't a 'local', in the sense that villages and city streets have their 'local'; it has a different atmosphere altogether. It isn't 'commercial' and travellers avoid it like the plague. It isn't a stopping-place for motorists. And it certainly isn't a smart cocktail bar.

You could call it a kind of Town Club; but people belong to it who would never be elected to any respectable club, and many good clubmen are made so unwelcome that they stay away. It is not class-conscious in any ordinary sense; and yet one has the feeling that the people who regularly go there do represent a class. I cannot put a label to the class; I can only tell you who were the regulars in the Swan about 1930.

There was the Colonel; and he was certainly the Chairman, for he was the only one who possessed, as it were by prescriptive right, his own chair. There were two of his especial cronies, a genial fat lawyer called Johnnie Johnson and a merry little 'gentleman-farmer' called Badger Brown. There was Mr Chorlton. There was Mr Brunswick the haberdasher, Men's and Women's Sana in Corpore Sano. There was the Mayor. There was his most active political opponent, a cobbler called Anderson. There were two or three more Town Councillors; a tailor; a jobbing carpenter; a pensioned sergeant-major; a retired gardener. There was Mr Tempest, the bank manager; Mr Rendcombe, the editor of the *Elmbury Intelligencer and Weekly Record*; and Mr Benjamin, a bookie, a Jew, and a good fellow who was generally in trouble with the police. And there was an idle little ruffian called Sparrow who ran illicit errands for Mr Benjamin, poached, and was reputed to be a dog-stealer. He lived in a caravan surrounded by ramshackle kennels full of barking and whimpering mongrels, which he had the impertinence to call the Sparrow Dog Farm.

These fifteen or so constituted the usual company at the Swan in the evening. There were others who dwelt as it were on the fringe; and of course there were occasional visitors, though strangers were not as a rule very welcome.

Now I cannot for the life of me tell you what it was that these members of the inner circle had in common. It wasn't class in the usual meaning of the word; for there were gentry, tradesmen and working-men. It wasn't politics, for the Mayor was a Diehard and the cobbler was a Red. It wasn't money or the lack of it; for the lawyer and Mr Benjamin were both rich men, whereas the cobbler, the sergeant-major and the gardener were comparatively poor.

It wasn't respectability, for Mr Benjamin notoriously kept two mistresses and Mr Sparrow occasionally went to prison. And it wasn't disreputableness, for Mr Chorlton was a justice of the peace and the Mayor was a churchwarden.

Yet the company was homogeneous: so much so that if you entered the bar as a stranger you felt as if you had barged by mistake into a private room which had been hired for an annual reunion of old schoolfellows. And the longer you remained there, the more of an alien you would feel. These men of Elmbury didn't *mean* to be unwelcoming; they were kindhearted and friendly people. But because they were knit into so close a fellowship – by what mysterious bond I have never really discovered – they simply could not help appearing to a stranger to be a kind of secret society into which he had intruded.

And yet there was nothing sinister about their strangely-assorted companionship. They didn't, as you might imagine, order the affairs of Elmbury from the Swan bar. No Council confidences were shared there. No tradesmen's secret deals were done there. No scandal was spread. The conversation of the Swan regulars was singularly innocent and inoffensive; being concerned chiefly with the following subjects:

The weather; the backwardness or forwardness of the season; gardening; crops; the price of plums; sprouts, and other local products; the behaviour of familiar beasts and birds; the rise or fall of the river and the likelihood of flood or drought; fishing; guns, dogs, horses and hounds; local topography especially in relation to short cuts (a most fruitful source of argument); old times, and their superiority in all respects over today; and, once more, again and again and yet again, the weather, past, present and future, yesterday's hailstones, this morning's white frost, the probability of tomorrow's thaw.

Miss Benedict

I have said the talk was innocent; it had to be. Miss Benedict saw to that. She was exactly the opposite of everything a barmaid is supposed to be. She was middle-aged, tight-lipped, prim and proper. She always wore a high-necked tight-fitting black dress with innumerable jet buttons upon it. Her hair was scraped back in a bun. She had rimless glasses. She didn't smoke, she didn't drink, and she didn't permit the least familiarity from her customers. Whenever she poured you out a drink, she did it with the air of disapproving of your buying it. She was the very spit of a Victorian nursery governess caricatured on the music-hall stage. And her Christian name was Prudence. We learned this when she went to court to give evidence about a waiter who had stolen a bottle of gin; we would never have known it otherwise. To all her customers she was Miss Benedict; though she had served them drinks for twenty years.

Twenty years! She must have known more about Elmbury than any man knows; far more than I know, who have the presumption to write a book about it. She must have learned, as she stood severe and disapproving behind her bar every day from ten to two and six to ten, the comic and the tragic, the drab and the spectacular truth about a very large proportion of its inhabitants. She must have carried the stuff of a hundred novels behind that forbidding brow. But whatever she knew, Miss Benedict kept to herself. She spoke when she was spoken to; she never gossiped. And if you asked her a question about one of her customers she would reprove you with a stern glance. 'I'm afraid I don't inquire into the gentleman's business,' she would say.

Somehow or other she suited the Swan. I can't tell you why any more than I can tell you why Mr Chorlton and Mr Benjamin, Mr Brunswick and the dog-stealer Sparrow, the Colonel, the cobbler and the Mayor, found fellowship and cheer in each other's company there. They were a kind of club; and she was a kind of club-servant; and she matched their mood so that after twenty years they all felt that the place wouldn't be the same, they would be curiously unhappy, without her. The warm-hearted Effie and Millie, who were just right at the Shakespeare, would have been all wrong at the Swan. One could not imagine a pert and peroxided blonde presiding there; and before long I too grew curiously fond of our little schoolma'am, who would greet us when we came back from duck-shooting in the evening with solicitous admonitions:

'You're wet through, both of you! I can't understand why you do it, reely I can't! Standing up to your waists in water! You'll catch your death! Come close to the fire now. Beer? A nice cup of hot Bovril would do you more good than cold beer. And Colonel, I must ask you to take those horrid waders off and not to drip all over the carpet. Oh, you men!'

The River-god

The Colonel and I had quickly become friends, and whenever the floods were out we went duck-shooting together in the evenings. The old man was bent and badly crippled with arthritis; his joints were as knobbly as the roots of a tree. But this did not prevent him from standing waist-deep in icy water waiting for the evening flight. He was sixty-five and it was a wonder he had survived so long; for he spent much of his time in the water, otter-hunting in the summer, duck-shooting in the winter, and at all seasons pottering about on his wet and marshy farm. The rest of the time he spent in the Swan: 'water outside, me boy, and whisky inside'. I have seen him crawl along a ditch *à plat ventre*, stalking a flock of geese, when the ditch was half full of water so that at times he was nearly submerged. I began to look upon him as a kind of water-creature: a river-god. It was wonderful to see him coming up out of the flooded meadows on a moonlight night after duck-flighting, crunching his way through the cat-ice, amorphous in his huge waders and loose-fitting jacket, deerstalker hat pulled down over his eyes. Thus must the Old Man of the Sea look when he comes ashore.

Geese were the ruling passion of his life. He would suffer any hardship, endure the utmost privation, for the chance of a shot at the grey-lags, white-fronts, and pink-feet which came to our meadows in great flocks during the late winter. When he had located a flock he would sit down and seriously plan a campaign against it. 'You've got to put yourself in their place,' he would say. 'You've got to *think like a goose*.' Then, because I was silent he would look up and see my smile; his face would crumble away into that marvellous grin, and he'd say: 'Well, perhaps I do, perhaps I do.'

If there was snow on the ground he would wear his sister's nightdress for camouflage, covering his hat with a white handkerchief. Out of the whiteness his red face glowed and burned like a sun rising through the mist on the river.

He was – even at sixty-five – the best shot I have ever seen, the best stalker, the best naturalist, and incomparably the best fisherman. Yet his fishing tackle was almost as primitive as a schoolboy's. His greenheart fly-rod, which must have been as old as himself, had a kink in the middle joint and two kinks in the top joint; it was nearly as crooked as an apple bough, or its owner's legs. But in his hands it was a magic wand with which he would conjure up fishes when nobody else could catch anything. In the little brook which ran through his farm, a mere runnel overgrown with reeds, bushes, and willows, he discovered a few trout where lesser men would have found only bull-heads, gudgeons and eels. He caught two or three every season in the mayfly time, using only the top joint of his rod and dabbling a fly between the branches. The biggest was two and a half pounds, and he got it out from between the roots of a great willow. I swear that no other man could have landed it in such circumstances.

The Colonel didn't mind what he fished for so long as it swam, what he hunted so long as it ran, nor what he shot so long as it could fly. There were eels in his brook as well as trout and it was his custom to fish for them on Sunday afternoons, an otherwise barren time when there was no hunting and no shooting and the pub was shut. His method of fishing was original (for the Colonel was nothing if not experimental in his approach to every kind of sport). He used no less than six cheap cane rods, which he distributed at intervals along the bank. His lines were baited with lobworms. To each rod-point he fixed a small bell, such as might hang round the neck of a cat. He sat down in the middle of the line of rods, smoked his pipe, and took an occasional swig out of his flask of whisky. Whenever the *tinkle-tinkle* of a bell called him from this pleasant occupation, he strolled leisurely to the appropriate rod and landed his eel. He said that the bells, besides being useful, made the sport more exciting. The tinkling sound, now coming from one rod, now from another, now from two or three at once, gave to the pastime a sense of urgency which eel-fishing generally lacked.

Having caught his basketful of eels, and eaten them for supper, the Colonel nailed up their skins on his barn door and when they were thoroughly cured he oiled them and cut them into narrow strips and used them for bootlaces. I still possess a pair; and they are stronger and more supple than any other laces I have ever seen.

'A Rat! A Rat! Dead for a Ducat, Dead!'

The Colonel loathed and detested rats. For all other animals, birds, and fish he had the queer sort of paradoxical friendly feeling that men have for the creatures they persecute. But rats he abominated. He used to sit for hours with his ·22 rifle, stern and purposeful, waiting for the chance of a snap shot at a rat in the dusk. He rigged up in the rat-runs the most ingenious little springes of bent willow twigs with nooses lightly pegged to the ground; and again he would sit for hours in the hope of actually seeing a rat run into one.

This, on the rare occasions when it occurred, gave him the most exquisite delight: to see the rat flicked high by the straightening twig, wriggling and kicking and swinging in the wind, like a highwayman upon the gibbet.

In his very last days rats obsessed him; and he wrote to me a short time before he died a postcard in which occurred the phrase, twice underlined: *Rats are getting at my walnuts.* But whether these were real rats or creatures of his phantasy I do not know.

Big Game

He, who with infinite care and wonderful cunning would set his springes for 'rats and mice and such small deer' had once been a famous hunter of big game. Habits engendered by long days on shikari never left him; he always noticed footprints, for example, and he was more than a match for any of our local and amateurish poachers. I have been walking with him on his land when he has picked up and pocketed an unfamiliar cartridge-case. 'That belongs to our friend Mr Sparrow.' That night in the Swan he handed it back to the wretched Sparrow. 'I think, sir, that you left this in my ten-acre meadow last Saturday.' Sparrow never poached the Colonel's land again.

One day I was driving with him in his rackety old car – which he drove with fierce and murderous recklessness – when we came across three enormous turds on the road. They were simply mountainous: they were super cowpats. I was astonished and filled with wonder; but the Colonel, swerving to avoid them, was scarcely moved. 'Hm . . . elephant,' he said; and sure enough just round the bend of the road we came upon a travelling circus.

I'd Give a Hundred Pounds . . .

He was eccentric, pugnacious, and often rude; but everybody liked him, and I loved him as if he were my father. I have never met anybody like him, and I don't suppose I ever shall. Mr Benjamin, who was a great fancier of spaniels, expressed what we all felt when he said to me, long after the Colonel's death: 'It's like this, John; it's the same with men and dogs. You can look back upon your life and even if you've known hundreds there's one stands out. There's one which makes all the others seem not to matter. I've had one dog like that, it was a black cocker called Sweep, and I'd give twenty pounds just for one Sunday afternoon walk with Sweep at my heels. And I've known one man like that, out of all the thousands I've met, and I'd give a hundred pounds just to buy him a drink again and see him sitting there in his old chair!'

It would be worth it: to see him come hobbling through the door into the Swan bar promptly at six on a winter's night, dripping wet, kelpie-like, amorphous, a couple of mallard bulging out his 'poacher's pockets', deerstalker over his eyes . . . He peels off his waders with grunts and curses, damning his stiff joints. He says, 'It's going to freeze sharpish,' and you know that it *will* freeze sharpish, because he is never wrong about the weather, he feels it in his bones, he sniffs it with his nostrils, he is one with the wind and the rain and the frost and the sun, he is Protean. 'It's sleeting tapioca already,' he says; for he has his own vivid phrase for everything, he doesn't talk in clichés as the rest of us do, he is something of a poet, he sees things more sharply than we do and matches his words to what he sees. He sits down in his familiar chair and takes a long drink and stretches his legs; and you can hear his knee-joints crackling. You can see him wince; but however sharp the pain he will not confess it, he is indomitable, and he finds something funny even in his own infirmity. He makes an almost Elizabethan joke about being stiff in the wrong places. His wonderful old face disintegrates into the merriest grin that man ever saw; and everybody in the room looks up, smiles, feels his heart grow warmer and the sour world turn merry, at the sound of his Ionian laughter.

PART FIVE

THE CHIMES AT MIDNIGHT

(1935–189 ?)

Rosemary for Remembrance – Those Were the Days – Mr Benjamin – The Jew of Elmbury – Mr Sparrow – 'More to be Feared than a Thousand Bayonets' – The Journalist – Laudator Temporis Acti – Market Ordinary –Mop Fair – Bribery without Corruption – Clem and Fred – The Moral Story of Clem – The Mysterious Story of Fred – The Fatal Train – The Chimes at Midnight – Once More Farewell

Rosemary for Remembrance

ON WINTER NIGHTS when the frost bit keen, Miss Benedict fetched out an iron 'shoe' – a utensil made by the blacksmith for this especial purpose – and heated it in the fire. She placed in it some brown ginger and some spice and a sprig of rosemary, and kept it filled with beer. It was a drink to warm the cockles of your heart. It loosened the old men's tongues, and perhaps the rosemary loosened their memories. At any rate on these occasions there was always good talk in the Swan . . .

Those Were the Days

'Rosemary,' said Wilfrid Jakes the old gardener, 'I minds the time when there was a bush of rosemary in every cottage garden, and d'you know why? Almost every cottage had its own pig in them days, yes, and killed its own pig and cured it, and lived half the year on good bacon. Better nor this Danish stuff they sell us now in the shops. Well, the rosemary was used to flavour the lard, see? Wonderful stuff – I can taste it now – was lard flavoured with rosemary.'

'You never stop talking about the Good Old Times,' said Anderson the cobbler, who was always ready for a sociological argument. 'But my father started work as a ploughboy at three bob a week, working from six in the morning till six at night. When he was a grown youth he often stayed in all day on Sunday while his mother washed and mended his only shirt. If those were your Good Old Times you can keep 'em!'

'But every cottage had its pig,' said Wilfred obstinately, 'and I'd rather have three bob a week and a full belly than thirty bob a week and be half starved, which a lot of lads is today. When I was a boy I used to work for Mister Jeffs' father at the threshing. Five bob a week we got, and thought we was lucky to get it. It was hard work in threshing time, too; we'd work till seven or eight in the evening, and no overtime. But I'll tell you this, Mister Anderson: I never went hungry; and I never knew any honest workman as did. We all sat down in the big kitchen at the farm. And first we'd have an apple pie: 'twas as big across as a cartwheel and there was more where that one come from. You had your helping of apple pie and you could have a second helping if you liked; but there was thirty pounds of beef on the table. And you could cut and come again at *that* too: only you had to have the apple pie first, see, to fill you up a bit. And each man had a quart of cider, to help him along with the work a bit. And I've known old Mr Jeffs, on a cold day at the sprout-picking, pour a bottle of rum into the cider barrel before the cider was handed out. I can't see many farmers doing that today!'

The cobbler shook his head.

'You was dependent on charity, that's the truth of it. Of course there was good employers, just as there was bad ones. But it doesn't alter the fact that they was getting your labour for five bob a week.'

Badger Brown the farmer butted in. He was known as Badger Brown by reason of his extraordinary addiction to badger-digging. I could never see any fun myself in this cruel and tedious sport. You went to a badger-earth at about nine o'clock in the morning and if you had reason to think that the badger was at home you put in your terriers and listened. You lay uncomfortably in the mud with your ear to the ground until you heard various thumps, grunts and yelps which suggested that your terrier had got hold of the badger or, more likely, that the badger had got hold of your terrier and was chewing its face off. You then began to dig. You dug all day like a navvy but without being paid for it, and towards evening, having shifted several tons of earth, you recovered from the bottom of the chasm your bleeding and moribund terriers and a live and angry badger, which you pointlessly slaughtered. Quite possibly it bit you before it died.

Badger Brown, however, was devoted to this pastime, and was equally proud of his scarred and blinded terriers and his own scarred and mangled hands, which had already lost one finger. He spent more time digging for badgers on other people's farms than in cultivating his own; but apart from his mania for persecuting this harmless and attractive animal, he was a decent enough fellow, the last of a long line of yeomen and little squires. He said now:

'In many cases the farmers got their labour for nothing. My grandfather farmed two hundred and fifty acres and kept forty milking cows; but he never employed a man.'

'How did he manage that?' we asked.

'No, he never employed a man nor a woman either. He had twenty-one children. Two died, so he had nineteen left to do the labour: eleven girls and eight boys. The girls did the housework, the dairy, and the milking, looked after the poultry and fed the pigs; the boys did the work in the fields; while my grandfather lived like a lord.'

'What about your grandmother?' we asked. 'She seems to have done a bit of work too!'

'She died with her twenty-first.'

'There you are,' said the cobbler. 'There are your Good Old Times. Ask any woman today whether she'd like to go back to them.'

'Grandfather,' said Badger Brown, 'had peculiar views about women. He used 'em rough and he brought 'em up hard. You talk about your modern girls knowing everything about everything – the Bishops are always preaching that they know too much; and you talk about the Victorian maidens fainting at the sight of a mouse. But my aunts, bless their hearts, used to regard it as one of their ordinary feminine duties to take the cows to the bull. And I suppose the girls today, who know all the facts of life, would think *that* pretty shocking!'

The Colonel nodded his old grizzled head. 'Reminds me of a story,' he said. 'A prim old lady walking down a lane meets a little girl leading a cow. "Good morning, little girl," she says, "you're very small to be leading such a big moo-cow. Where are you taking her?" "To the bull, Ma'am," says the little girl. "Dear, dear," says the old lady, very shocked indeed. "Dear, dear, how dreadful. Couldn't your father do that?" "No, ma'am," said the little girl politely. "It has to be a bull."'

The Colonel threw back his head and laughed his delightful laugh. But Miss Benedict's disapproving eye was upon us; and we knew that it was high time to change the subject.

Mr Benjamin

Mr Benjamin, I suppose, was the person you'd least have expected to find among the Swan fellowship. At times he looked utterly incongruous. These were the occasions when he was going to Birmingham or had just come back. 'Got a little business in Brum,' he would say; and we accepted the formula, knowing perfectly well that his little business was a red-headed widow (for Sparrow, his hench-man, had told us so). In his Birmingham clothes, his cheap city suit, light-grey homburg, diamond tiepin and all, Mr Benjamin looked flashy and cheap: completely alien to the Swan and to Elmbury. And yet somehow or other he belonged, he was part of the pattern of Elmbury's life. I sometimes thought he had a chameleon quality. When he went to Birmingham he became a Brummagem Jew; back in Elmbury, in workaday clothes, with his spaniel at heel and a gun under his arm, he seemed to change – not his race, he could never change that – but at any rate his whole attitude to life. He became one of us.

He was fond of all kinds of sport, especially shooting, and he didn't mind getting wet, which was rather remark-able in a Jew; for they are a people who like to keep their feet on dry land. Everybody liked him, for we knew of certain great kindnesses he had done to foolish gamesters who had betted themselves nearly into bankruptcy. There was a story that Jerry, in his madcap youth, had owed Mr Benjamin both his horse and his motor-bike, these being the only possessions he could offer in settlement of a debt of nearly two hundred pounds. Mr Benjamin kept them long enough to teach him his lesson, then sent them back with a note:

'I am too fat to ride your horse and I should break my neck on your motor-bike. It will save me a lot of doctor's bills if you will allow me to call it all square.'

Yet as soon as he got on to a racecourse Mr Benjamin was metamorphosed back into the quick-witted cheapjack Jew who made his living by his wits and his slick patter.

The Jew of Elmbury

You don't as a rule find people of Mr Benjamin's race in small country towns. They are happier in urban com-munities. But our local historian, Mr Rendcombe, discovered in an old chronicle a curious anecdote about a Jew who lived in Elmbury in 1259.

'A Jew at Elmburie fell into a privie upon the Saturdaie, and would not for reverence of his Sabboth bee plucked out, wherefore Richard de Clare Earl of Gloucester kept him there till Monday, at which time he was dead.'

This story delighted Mr Benjamin, who maintained that it was evidence of our ancient and deep-rooted anti-Semitism which, said he with a wink, made it practically impossible for him to earn a living among us. But we thought it showed that our sense of humour hadn't changed much in seven centuries and we were secretly rather proud of it; feeling that we should do the same thing today if we got the chance, not because the man was a Jew, but because he was such an awful prig; and prigs we abominate.

I think Mr Benjamin rather liked being teased about his unfortunate predecessor. He had learned this much about us: that we only teased people we liked.

'Take care,' we would warn him on Saturday, 'take particular care not to fall down the privy today!'

'Down the plug-'ole,' Mr Benjamin would say. 'That's me. Poor old me. Ho! ho! ho! Down the plug-'ole. Poor old me!'

Mr Sparrow

Of Sparrow, who served Mr Benjamin with dog-like devotion and seemed almost to follow him at heel like another spaniel, it is more difficult to find good things to say. He was an unmitigated rascal, entirely without shame; indeed perhaps it was because of his very shamelessness that we tolerated him. He was said to have stolen a puppy one Saturday afternoon from a rich old lady called Mrs Fothergill and to have sold it back to her for five guineas on

Sunday morning, calling at her house and saying how sorry
he was to hear of her loss, 'but as it so happens, ma'am, by
a lucky chance I've got a pup that's the very spit-image of
the one you lost.' The story goes that he got away with it
and even boasted afterwards that he took the risk out of
sheer kindness of heart. 'I thought the poor old leddy would
be lonesome-like without her pup.' It may be true; he was
impudent enough for anything.

He was a fisherman (like almost everybody else in
Elmbury) and a great liar. The fish he caught always
weighed about three times as much as anybody else's;
we thought they must be filled with lead. 'Caught a chub
this evening,' he'd say, 'and he's four pound and three
ounces by the kitchen scales; I'll go t'ell if 'e 'ent.' That
was his favourite oath with which he concluded every
sentence: ''Tis true; I'll go t'ell if it 'ent.' We thought
Mr Sparrow would go to Hell anyhow. He caught roach
weighing two pounds and pike weighing fifteen, and if we
doubted he assured us it was true, he'd go to Hell if it
wasn't, he'd weighed the fish. We couldn't argue with the
kitchen scales.

One day his wife had a baby, and the district nurse,
having left her spring-balance behind, used the kitchen
scales to weigh it. It was certainly a fine fat baby. It was
just a shade less than twenty-two pounds.

'More to be Feared than a Thousand Bayonets'

Mr Rendcombe, the editor of the *Intelligencer*, besides
being the local historian of the Swan company was also the
one who had the longest memory; it was to him that people
would refer to settle arguments about such questions as
whether the great frost was in 1894 or 1895, or who was
Mayor in the year of the Queen's Jubilee. He was a dapper
little man of more than seventy whose paper maintained
on a parochial scale the traditions of freedom, integrity,
and independence upheld by the great *Manchester Guardian*

itself. Woe betide the person, Party, or sect that attempted to challenge that independence. The *Intelligencer* was a dangerous animal which when attacked defended itself; and Mr Rendcombe, in his day, had put Mayors in their places and even dared to write a critical leading article about the Justices of the Peace. Indeed, the Council so greatly feared his lively comment – and, even more, his too-accurate reporting – that they had lately taken to transacting most of their business in Committee, to which the Press was not admitted. The *Intelligencer* was swiftly roused by this threat to its freedom; and its leading article thundered with the authentic thunder of which from time to time we still hear a faint rumbling in the leaders of Old Auntie *Times*.

One Councillor, a remarkably illiterate man, complained to Mr Rendcombe (who politely paraphrased his speeches) that he was being unfairly reported. Mr Rendcombe promised to put the matter right; and next week he did.

'Mr Goodacre rose and said, "What I means to say Mr Mayor and what I means is I have riz to take up your valuable time to say as how I feels, and there's many in this Chamber and out as feels with me, as how I feels that the Council if you sees what I means is wasting of a lot of valuable time by argifying about this matter about which I feels, and there be others as feels it too, 'tis not worth the argifying about, being something about which you feels just how you feels and nothing what anybody else can say will alter what you feels nor make you feel any different about the matter which I thinks should never be allowed to take up the valuable time of this 'ere Chamber and of you Mister Mayor and my fellow members who feels, I'll venture to say, very much the same about it as I feel . . ."'

Mr Goodacre didn't complain again.

The Journalist

Within the limits of his splendid integrity, Mr Rendcombe managed to make his paper much livelier, it always seemed to me, than many a consciously-bright London news-sheet. Even his reporting of the most trivial cases in the Magistrates' Court was vivid and readable. If a vagrant was fined for being drunk and incapable, Mr Rendcombe was not content with the bare statement:

'Alexander MacDougall, of no fixed abode, was fined ten shillings,' etc . . .

He began his report in a way which compelled you to read it:

'A sinister, uncouth-looking man, calling himself Alexander MacDougall . . .'

Laudator Temporis Acti

But Mr Rendcombe could talk as well as he could write; and he was at his best in the Swan bar on a winter's night when Miss Benedict had warmed the beer and spiced it with rosemary to set his tongue wagging. He would talk, as a rule, about old times; and in particular about the weather and about local politics, both of which it seemed had been far more spectacular in the old days than they were today. He would say, in reply to the Colonel, who was prognosticating a hard frost:

'No doubt, Colonel, we shall have a frost, but I doubt if it will be a hard one. We don't get the weather we used to. Now take the frost of 1895. It started freezing about Christmas and continued until well into March. That was a frost if you like! I remember Mr Jeffs – not the present Mr Jeffs, but the old gentleman, who died in 1914 – I remember him driving his pony and trap all the way from Elmbury to Dykeham along the middle of the river.'

'There was a fairish frost in 1917,' said Anderson the cobbler. 'I minds them roasting an ox on the river in that year.'

Mr Rendcombe, to whom anything which had happened in the twentieth century was recent history and scarcely worth talking about, dismissed the frost of 1917 with a gesture. 'Your memory plays you false, Mr Anderson! There was a frost in that year; but it was nothing to that of 1895. And you may be sure they didn't roast an ox in 1917, for it was during the war, rationing was in force, and such a thing would never have been permitted. No: the ox-roasting was in 1895. The beast was given by Mr Trewin's father and slices were sold at twopence each in aid of the Elmbury poor. And very good they were, too. I well remember it. The roasting was arranged by Mr Nixon, who was at that time the proprietor of the Shakespeare. And the heat from the fire melted the ice, but 'twas freezing as fast as it melted. We also erected a printing-press on the river.'

'What on earth did you do that for?' interrupted the cobbler.

'We printed, in the form of a single sheet, a special souvenir number of the *Intelligencer*. I have a copy in my office now; and you are welcome to see it, Mr Anderson, if you like. It is a very unique and curious thing: a copy of the *Intelligencer* printed on the river, right in the middle of the river, right in mid-stream!'

Market Ordinary

According to Mr Rendcombe, almost everything had deteriorated both in quality and quantity since the beginning of the twentieth century. Everybody agreed about beer and whisky; but even food wasn't what it was.

'You ought to have known the Market Ordinaries in the

old days,' he would say. 'In this very hotel, or in the
Shakespeare when Mr Nixon had it. Calves' heads; roast
beef; mutton and caper sauce; and that wasn't what they
call a choice, mind you, a man could have the lot – and
did, if he called himself a man. And in their season there'd
be elvers, or salmon, or eels. People despise eels nowadays;
but we Elmbury folks used to think of them very highly,
very highly indeed. It was always the head of the house
who cooked the first dish of eels in the autumn; and a very
elaborate business it was, I can tell you, nine different
sorts of herbs and spices, and first the frying, and then the
stewing: it took two days to prepare 'em! And by then you
were so hungry having smelt the delectable smell of 'em
hanging about for so long, that you filled your belly so
that you never wanted to see another eel, not till next
autumn came round. Yes, we did ourselves well, we knew
how to eat, in those days.'

Mop Fair

It was rather depressing, talking to Mr Rendcombe, for it
made one realize how much, apparently, one had missed.
Our annual Mop* Fair, for instance, which always seemed
to me sufficiently rough and riotous, was nowadays in
Mr Rendcombe's view more like a Mother's Meeting than
a real Mop. 'Have I been to the Fair?' he'd say. 'Yes, I
have taken a walk down the street; but I don't call it a
Fair. What did I see? I saw a few stalls selling brandysnaps – but they don't taste like the brandysnaps used to –
and a few young men who looked like nancy-boys lobbing
balls at coconuts. If you hit a coconut when I was a boy
you were expected to smash it; for it'd never fall off its
stand unless it were smashed. What else? A few giggling

* Years ago, the 'Mop' was a hiring-fair, at which farmers hired
their labourers and masters their servants. A carter would carry a whip
to identify himself, a wagoner would wear straw in his cap as a mark
of his trade. But that ended long ago; and now the Fair is given over
entirely to fun.

wenches on the swings. (*We'd* have given 'em something to giggle about!) A few mangy animals in cages; and a couple of booths which promise you all kinds of sights to tickle up your appetite, only when you get inside it's nothing but a couple of girls in tights. Our appetites didn't need that sort of stimulus.' And Mr Rendcombe would sadly shake his head.

Goodness knows what the Mop must have been like in his youth; for it was pretty orgiastic even in 1930. It shocked the parsons even then, and caused astonishment to visitors from the cities who didn't understand Elmbury. We were a pretty highly civilized community really; and we were homogeneous. We could be trusted with a degree of liberty, even of licence, which would have turned the heads of a younger and more mixed people. At least, I think that was the explanation of the fact that our Mop, which happened every year on October 10th, never did us much harm, although it was the occasion for more drinking, fighting, and love-making than you'd see elsewhere in a month of Saturday nights. Such an affair as Elmbury Mop could not, I think, have taken place anywhere but in an English country town; it would have been ugly in Wales and it would have been murderous in Scotland. (In the former they daren't even hold village dances for fear of the Devil which broods over their savage hills; in the latter they have to shut the pubs on every possible occasion lest the whole population drink itself into homicidal frenzy.) But Elmbury was grown-up. We'd been doing this sort of thing since the fifteenth century. We were old enough to be trusted with fire; and the Mop was a veritable bonfire of morals at which once a year we warmed, but did not burn, our hands.

Bribery without Corruption

Local politics, it seemed, had lost, like the Mop and the weather, the rough turbulence and hardihood they once had. Politics today, according to Mr Rendcombe, were wishy-washy. There were too many doubters on both sides; men lacked the fierce and flaming convictions they used to possess, which would lead them to bash one another on the nose for what they believed to be right. Council elections in the 1890s were rough-and-tumble affairs; and there were always a few black eyes next day and sometimes a few broken scalps. Political colours meant something in those times; a Liberal's red rosette was, to a Tory, literally a red flag to a bull. Men played practical jokes on their opponents, jokes carried out on a huge and majestic scale, as when the houses of all the prominent Liberals were painted bright blue in a night by dozens of painters employed by the Conservatives.

'Your uncle played a part in that prank,' said Mr Rendcombe, looking at me. I couldn't imagine my gentle and courteous old uncle doing anything of the kind; but if Mr Rendcombe said so it must be true. He went on:

'Yes, that was the first year he got into the Council, in 1892. I well remember old Fred Pullin – he was young Fred Pullin then – going into the Anchor with a bagful of half-crowns and jingling them while he called out as bold as brass: "Who's going to vote for Mr Moore?"'

'Tory graft!' grunted the cobbler.

I was scandalized.

'But do you mean,' I said, 'that *my uncle* had given him the half-crowns?'

'Lord bless you, yes. They all did it, in those days: the Radicals and the Conservatives. It was the accepted thing. Your uncle is an upright and honest man and always was; but he gave the half-crowns because it was the proper and traditional thing to do. 'Twas all fair and above board. The candidates would go into the bank quite openly the day before the election and draw out ten pounds, all in half-crowns. I've seen some of the older ones nearly bent double carrying it away.'

The cobbler groaned. 'And they call it Democracy.' Mr Rendcombe fixed him with a stern eye.

'And so it was democracy,' he said. 'Do you think that a man who was capable of voting against his own convictions for half a crown would be content with *one* half-crown? He'd take half-crowns from everybody, see; and then he'd vote according to his conscience, though most likely he'd be so drunk that he'd forget to vote at all. But the stalwart fellows who were already determined to vote for Mr Moore, well, they took his half-crown just to drink his health and wish him luck. And a very good practice it was, to my mind. It made many a poor man merry on Election Day.'

He laughed, and added for my benefit:

'You can look shocked, all of you; but if Mr Moore is bold enough to ask his uncle one day, he'll be able to tell you I'm speaking the truth. I'll tell you another thing. Have you ever heard of the Booth Vote?'

We said we hadn't.

'I don't mean a voting booth,' said Mr Rendcombe, 'if you'll pardon the pun. I mean the voting power of the Booth family, which used to be, and probably still is, about 200 strong. There are Booths, as you know, in every alley in Elmbury; they breed like rabbits. They're a very clannish family and they all vote the same way; it's said that they leave the decision to the head of the family, whoever he is, the patriarch Booth, and vote for whoever he tells 'em to. Now the Booth Vote is pretty important; I think I'm right in saying, Mr Mayor, that it can swing an election?'

The Mayor nodded.

'Well, you can imagine that old grandfather Booth, who could bring 200 votes along with him, was worth more than half a crown. He certainly thought so. He stuck out for ten bob; and regularly every year on the first of November he got his ten bob from each of the candidates. In a good year it totted up to at least a fiver; and you ought to have seen old Booth that evening. Drunk? I should say so! Most years they took him to the police-station; but once or twice he had to go to the hospital.'

'And did the Booths vote as he told them?' I asked.

'To a man. A very well-disciplined family; they've got gipsy blood in them, and they live according to the patriarchal idea. They fear neither God nor Devil but they fear the head of the family very much. They vote in a solid block, all for the same candidate. I think they vote for you, Mr Mayor, each time you come up for election?'

'I'm told so,' said the Mayor cautiously.

'Of course,' added Mr Rendcombe mischievously, 'I'm not suggesting that the – er – practice I have described still goes on.'

The Mayor looked uncomfortable and Mr Rendcombe hastened to add: 'Times have changed, of course; and we are inclined to think that bribery and corruption are very wicked now. All the same I'd rather see the traditional half-crowns handed out in the pubs on Election Day on behalf of honest men who want to get on the Council with the idea of serving their town than hear the plausible lying vote-catching speeches which some of our candidates make today. If I were a poor man I'd rather take half a crown for my vote than a promise which the candidate knows he'll break as soon as he gets elected. And I'd rather see the kind of graft going on which means a few pints of beer to whet a poor man's throat, than the kind which consists of sly understandings over ten-thousand-pound contracts and generally results in the poor man losing his shirt. And that's flat,' said Mr Rendcombe, glaring fiercely round the company; for there had been a scandal in the Council about housing contracts and the *Weekly Intelligencer* was on the warpath. Mr Rendcombe's leader last week had been deliberately libellous. He could print things which *The Times* would not have dared to print; for he knew that nobody would have the courage to bring an action against him. His defence would have been to repeat the libel in court and produce the evidence. He was the Man Who Knew Too Much.

Clem and Fred

A lot of secrets would be buried for ever when Mr Rendcombe went to his grave; for he knew a great deal more than he could print, courageous though he was. It was from him, one night in the Swan, that I heard the full story of my two cousins, Clem and Fred – although cousins they were born twenty years before me – who had vanished out of my ken when I was an inquisitive little boy spending my days in the window-seat of the Tudor House nursery. 'Railway trains', you will remember, were somehow connected with their disappearance – or rather their disappearances, for the two events had happened at different times; and my family was obviously ashamed of the whole business, for I could discover nothing more by asking questions than this vague sinister hint of 'railway trains'. As I grew up, of course, I picked up fragments of the two stories; but it wasn't until I sat late one night with Mr Rendcombe and with Johnnie Johnson the fat lawyer that I learned all. At least I learned as much as anybody knows; because nobody knows the end of Fred's story, and it is unlikely that anybody ever will.

The Moral Story of Clem

Clem's story comes first, chronologically; and it belongs especially to the Swan bar because most of it happened in the Swan bar.

Clem, you may recollect, was the clever member of our family. He was indeed the only clever one; and he was brilliant. While he was still very young he made a name for himself as a barrister, practising in a provincial city, but travelling to and fro every day by train. He had great charm, wit, and an acute and restless mind: he was to the rest of the family as champagne is to madeira. A wonderful future was prophesied for him: a KC then politics or the

Bench. Our part of the world, people said, would soon be too small to hold him. He'd have to go to London . . .

One morning Clem missed his train.

Now thanks to that purblind generation of Elmburians who thought that the railway would interfere with their amenities, the journey to our county town was extremely complicated. As the crow flies, the distance was fifteen miles; as the train crawled, it was about thirty. You had to change twice; and the connexions were bad. So if you missed the morning train, it was hardly worth while going at all. It would be time to start back as soon as you got there.

Accepting this with mild annoyance, Clem shrugged his shoulders and resigned himself to a day's enforced holiday. He walked back from the station, and having nothing better to do he decided to drop in at the Swan for a glass of beer. It was still quite early – about nine o'clock; but the pubs opened at seven in those days.

Clem enjoyed his holiday morning. One by one his friends came in for their 'elevenses'. Soon there was much the same company as I have described as typical of the Swan's regulars. The Colonel was surely there; and Mr Benjamin; and Johnnie Johnson, who remembers talking business with Clem and offering him a brief; and Mr Rendcombe. There was good talk of fishing and shooting and cricket and boats. For his part, Clem enlivened the bar with his incomparable wit. It wasn't often that the Swan heard such talk. Lucky for us, said the cronies, that young Clem missed his train. They hoped he'd miss it again.

Next day he didn't feel very well. He told himself that since he'd taken one day's holiday he might as well take another while he was about it. He'd been overworking lately . . . He'd got no very pressing business on hand . . . Those two briefs could wait . . .

He decided he wouldn't catch the 8.30 train that morning.

He never caught it again.

The Decline and Fall of Clem was slow and majestic.

Morning after morning, night after night, his brilliance gradually burned itself out in the Swan Hotel. Leaning against the bar, a Triton among minnows, he held forth upon every subject under the sun, Science, Art, Law, Poetry, Philosophy and Religion, so bemusing his listeners that often they forgot to go home to their dinners. The world was Clem's oyster. While he was talking, the small cramped bar seemed to grow, to expand, to become gaily cosmopolitan. Hushed and attentive, the company ceased to be conscious of time and space. Clem's wise and witty talk ranged here and there over the whole earth, Africa, America, Asia, Australia; though, in fact, he had never set foot in any continent but Europe. His rhetoric, thriving on whisky, became more flowery and more fantastical; and his notions grew wilder and stranger to match it. Indeed, one morning he announced with certainty that beneath Brockeridge Common, two miles from Elmbury, lay a rich seam of coal. He had incontrovertible proof of it, he said; and with a finger moistened in whisky he drew geological maps of the strata on the bar counter. Not one of his listeners doubted that he was right, for Clem could make juries believe whatever he told them, and men in a pub are made of the same stuff as a jury. So even to this day there are people in Elmbury who want to dig up Brockeridge Common to look for coal, although any geologist could tell them that in its Inferior Oolite they'd find nothing more valuable than the bones of an ichthyosaurus.

Clem died, said the stolid respectable Moores, through being too clever. It endears them to me that they would never use his sad story as an example of the Evils of Drink; but simply as an example of the Evils of Cleverness. His terribly restless mind, they declared, had needed whisky to quieten it. Restless minds were dangerous; cleverness was dangerous; the thing to do was to jog along quietly and then you wouldn't come to a bad end.

The Mysterious Story of Fred

It was left to Cousin Fred to demonstrate that this maxim didn't always work. Fred was not in the least clever; Fred was not in the least eccentric; but he succeeded in doing the most eccentric thing that any man in his situation could do. Fred jogged along very nicely and quietly for years; and yet he came to a bad end. At least he came to a very mysterious end; and I suppose you might call him the skeleton in the family cupboard, if anybody had the faintest idea where his skeleton lay.

Fred, as you know, used to pass our window on his way to the office, he was so regular in his hours that you could set your watch by him. And he always wore a buttonhole; and in summer he wore a straw boater (which was the fashion in those days) and in winter he wore a bowler hat. He was a perfect example of the creature of habit: so much so that he was a bit of a joke.

He had a sufficient, comfortable practice. He was unmarried. He had no apparent troubles, financial or domestic, no known love-affair, and no known vices; except the habit of having a small bet, well within his means, with Mr Benjamin each day. He walked one day to Elmbury station and bought a ticket to the county town. He appeared to be cheerful and well. He was seen to get into the train; and since then he has never been heard of. A few years ago permission was given to presume his death.

Consider what a remarkable feat this disappearance was. Fred left his affairs in perfect order; he took no large sum of money with him (in fact the amount he was supposed to have in his pocket was one pound seven and sixpence); and he was qualified, as far as one knows, for no trade or profession other than his own. Professional qualifications are bound to a man's identity; if he loses the latter, the former are lost too. If he started again as a lawyer he began at the beginning: a man with no name and no con- nexions and no money. The point is, if Fred lived, *how* did he live? – for he wouldn't even have been much good as a navvy.

Again, why should he choose to run away and what was he running away from? He hadn't embezzled his clients' money; he wasn't in debt; he hadn't got a nagging wife; his life up to the moment he disappeared had been smooth, untroubled, and supremely unadventurous.

On the other hand, he was not the sort of man whom anybody would be likely to kidnap or murder; and if he took it into his head to commit suicide (although he seemed perfectly sane and had no reason to do so) where did he manage to conceal his body, and why was it never found? Indeed, if Fred committed suicide, he committed the most ingenious suicide I've ever heard of; and Fred had shown no signs of being an original or ingenious man. A great deal of trouble was taken over the search for him. The rivers were dragged for weeks, the whole district was quartered, bushes, quarries, ditches, ponds, the police all over England published his description; and a very ordinary description it was.

His money at the bank accumulated compound interest; his investments, carefully managed by Mr Tempest, grew bigger every year; but Fred never came back to claim them. There was a vague unsubstantiated report that he had been seen somewhere in South America; but that was never confirmed, and nobody took it seriously. Why should Fred want to go to America anyway?

But perhaps after all it was true. Perhaps one day there occurred to Fred one of those revelations, sudden, cataclysmic and complete, which happen sometimes even to ordinary men. I do not mean that Fred went mad; I mean that he became suddenly sane. I suggest that he said to himself: 'This is perfectly absurd. Here I am, a man of thirty, and I've never done anything exciting in my life – scarcely ever travelled more than a few miles from Elmbury, in fact! And yet there are millions of places to go to and millions of new and strange things to see; there's even a place called Popocatapetl' – Clem had probably told him that – 'and it would be sheer folly to die without seeing places with names like Popocatapetl. It would be ridiculous, in fact it would be mad!'

So off he went to South America. At least I like to think that is the truth of it; but Mr Rendcombe favours the grimmer alternative and believes that somewhere, in some bramble bush, in some thicket, the white skull of Fred lies waiting to be discovered and grins at the sky, as if it were grinning at the excellent joke its owner has played on the stolid respectable Moores, the ponderous substantial Moores, who would never believe that a man could walk clean out of the world by way of a railway carriage.

The Fatal Train

As for me, I never go to Elmbury station, the funny little branch-line station among the allotments, without being reminded of the stories of Clem and Fred, and without recapturing for an absurd moment my childhood impression that it was the starting-place for all disappearances, the setting-off place for all adventure. The ancient station-master looks at his turnip watch and blows his whistle, the little fussy train puffs away, and I remember Fred catching his train, which bore him out of the world, and Clem missing his, with roughly the same results. Chuffle, chuffle, puff, the train rounds the bend on its way to the junction; and thus, I remember, it disappeared with Fred on board it, and thus Clem watched it disappear as he cursed its unusually prompt departure, and turned back resignedly towards the Swan.

The Chimes at Midnight

It wasn't very long before that fussy little train bore me away on the first stage of a long journey. What we now perceive to have been the first skirmish of the greatest war the world has ever known was taking place in Spain. I left Elmbury about Christmas-time and went to Madrid. My reasons for going need not concern this book. Curiously enough I wasn't the only man of Elmbury who made that journey. Bardolph, when he had served his two months for his enterprising theft of the policeman's bicycle, decided that England was too orderly a place for his opportunist temperament, falsified his age by ten years, and enlisted in the International Brigade.

The night before I left I went duck-shooting with the Colonel, and afterwards we spent the evening at the Swan. I remember that evening best of all the evenings, because in a sense it was the last; for somehow the place didn't seem the same when I got back to it.

Also, we shot a goose. It must have been the Colonel's last goose: a solitary grey-lag winging its majestic way across a lemon-coloured sunset, and turning suddenly for no obvious reason to pass right over our heads. We both fired at once and it came down like an inside-out umbrella to fall almost at our feet. It was a gift from the gods; and to the Colonel, who died before the geese came back next season, it was a farewell gift.

Perhaps he knew this; at any rate he determined to celebrate it. He laid it on the bar in the Swan and said:

'Drinks all round! Who'll drink to our goose?'

'Reely, Colonel,' said Miss Benedict, 'I must ask you to take the nasty thing away. It is making my clean bar all bloody.'

'Dear me, what language,' said the Colonel; and Miss Benedict blushed.

The grey goose was handed round and everybody guessed its weight. Badger Brown was there, and Mr Chorlton, and the lawyer, and the cobbler and the Mayor, and Mr Rendcombe, Wilfrid Jakes the gardener, and Mr Benjamin dressed in his flashiest, for he'd just come back from his bit of business in Birmingham.

We all sat down and drank to the goose. The Colonel stretched his legs and we heard his joints crackling.

'It's the wet weather gets into 'em,' he laughed. 'There's a lot of rain coming. The clouds are right down on Brensham; and you know the old rhyme: "When Brensham Hill puts on his hat, Men of the Vale, look out for that!"'

Old rhymes, old proverbs, old wise sayings, are much loved of Elmbury men. They decorate and flavour their conversation with them as good wives decorate and flavour their dishes with thyme and marjoram, with mint and borage, with rosemary and angelica; and indeed the old sayings are somehow aromatic, evocative and nostalgic like the herbs.

The talk of the men in the Swan was always so spiced and peppered with proverb and rhyme, as if they were aware that they talked plain common-sense and deliberately decked it with a sprig of poetry; and when I try to recollect what we talked about, on that last night of the Swan's ancient glory, I am aware of the flavour of it, pungent and aromatic in memory, although I cannot remember much of what was actually said.

I remember the Colonel talking about the habits of robins, which he loved, and telling us how they each had their own bit of territory jealously guarded against intruders, their own beat as it were: 'Just like prostitutes,' said the Colonel, laughing his merry laugh. He described the robin at his back door in phrases rather like this: 'You look at him from behind and he's a round-shouldered disillusioned business man wearing a brown mackintosh that's too big for him. He's so dowdy that however many times you've seen him it's always a surprise when he turns round and you see his red waistcoat.' The Colonel's little blue eyes were as sharp as Gilbert White's; if he could have written as well as he talked we should have had another book as good as *Selborne*.

It was his custom to mix with his talk a number of old phrases and country expressions which in a long life he had picked up from his labourers and from the cottage people and had made his own. On a drizzly morning, when the outlook was uncertain, he'd say: ''Tis a mizzling

day, neither Jim Cook nor Mary-Anne.' If the wind was
backing, he'd say, 'The wind's going downhill.' He spoke of
green woodpeckers as stock-eagles. ('The stock-eagles be
rating, we shall have rain,') and moles he always called
Oonts. Molehills were Oonty-tumps, a phrase which he
loved and which always made him chuckle. Yet he used
these country terms not academically nor in affectation.
They had become part of his normal speech, they belonged
to him just as he himself belonged to the countryside from
which they sprang like the wheat and the grass.

There was talk of the weather, of course, on that last
night, and there were tales, I am sure, for there were
always tales told in the Swan; and there was a long argument on some matter of local politics between the cobbler
and the Mayor; and there was reminiscence about cricket
and about Gilbert Jessop's big hits on to our pavilion roof.
Mr Rendcombe, backward-looking as usual, regretted that
cricket was no longer what it used to be. It had lost its
vigour, like the weather, the Mop, and local politics.
'They don't hit the ball as hard as they used to,' he said.
He shook his head sadly. 'The sting's gone out of everything,'
he said. Winters were milder, elections were duller, the
Mop was less riotous, and batsmen played pat-ball: a wishy-
washy world.

'Your uncle,' he said to me, 'he could hit sixes. He could
bang the ball about the field. Wilfrid Jakes'll remember
fishing the ball out of the brook with a net on the end of a
long pole – the brook which had little sallies planted along
the edge of it – You recollect it, Wilfrid?'

'They be grown willows now,' said Wilfrid Jakes.

'Aye. That's fifty years ago,' said Mr Rendcombe. 'And
Mr Moore's uncle was a lad.' My old uncle had just died,
and Mr Rendcombe heaved an appropriate sigh. 'He was
a great loss,' he said. 'Another of the old ones gone.'

One always had a sharp sense of mortality when talking
with Mr Rendcombe. After all, he wrote fifty obituary
notices a year; it came natural to him to speak of graves
and worms and epitaphs. And he was not by nature a

gloomy man; it was a gentle and not unpleasing melancholy which he wore on those occasions when he talked of his old friends who had died. 'Thinning 'em out,' he would say, with a shrug of his shoulders. 'Thinning 'em out.'

'Another of the old ones,' he repeated now. 'Aye: thinning 'em out.' He looked at Wilfrid Jakes, who was the only one of the company as old as he was. 'He was a young spark, was Mr Moore's uncle. We could tell a thing or two about him.' He turned to me. 'Ah, Mr Moore, if you'd seen the times that Wilfrid and I have seen!'

Mr Chorlton, in the corner, suddenly looked up. He glanced sharply at Mr Rendcombe and then back at me. He raised his eyebrows. I had caught an echo somewhere, but I was slow-witted. Whatever was the purpose of Mr Chorlton's glance I seemed to have missed the point. Mr Rendcombe went on:

'You wouldn't have thought it, but he was a great one for the girls in his youth, was your uncle.' He chuckled. 'Do you remember, Wilfrid, Jennie Greening that was old Greening's daughter from the Mill? The black-haired one? A little hussy! – Is she still alive, I wonder?'

Wilfrid Jakes nodded.

'She's getting on,' he said.

I was conscious of a memory just round the corner, just behind Wilfrid Jakes' or Mr Rendcombe's shoulder there was a huge and significant shadow. Mr Chorlton was smiling happily; but I was still groping in the dark.

'She must be,' said Mr Rendcombe. And then I had it. It fell into place in my mind almost with a click. Mr Chorlton glanced at me again and I nodded. He pulled out a pencil and began to scribble on the back of an envelope.

'Yes, yes, she must be,' repeated Mr Rendcombe. I had a beautiful and terrible sense of the continuity of English life and English talk and English men; and Stratford, I remembered, wasn't very far away.

Mr Chorlton passed me the envelope. In the familiar

scrawl with which he had corrected so many of my Latin exercises he had written:

> '*Old, old, Master Shallow — Nay, she must be old; she cannot choose but be old; certain she's old ... Ha, that thou hadst seen that this knight and I have seen: — We have heard the chimes at midnight, Master Shallow.*'

Once More Farewell

It was closing-time. I put on my coat and stood for a moment warming myself before the dying fire. I didn't want to leave; and I was conscious of my long journey on the morrow and of strangeness and uncertainty at the end of it. The embers were bright in the great fireplace, and the room was warm also with a glow of good fellowship. There were Christmas decorations over the mantelpiece, a sprig of holly above the bar, a big bough of mistletoe hanging as it happened over the Colonel's seat in the corner. I thought: 'It'll all be different when I come back, and perhaps I shall be different too.' I said goodbye to Miss Benedict, and we shook hands. She said:

'Take care of yourself among all those foreigners.'

The Colonel was dozing, or had fallen into a reverie. His chin was slumped on his chest. I called out:

'Goodbye, Colonel. I'll be back in time for the may-fly.'

He woke with a start and shivered. Then he grinned.

'A goose walking over my grave,' he said.

Miss Benedict had picked up the grey-lag and now she handed it to him.

'Don't leave it behind, Colonel; I don't want the horrid thing littering up my nice clean Christmassy bar.' She added: 'Why, you're cold! You're all shrammed with the cold! Let me help you on with your coat, you'll catch your death else!'

The Colonel stood up stiffly, and as he did so Miss

Benedict did the most extraordinary thing. Never in all her life, I'll swear, had she done such a thing nor ever would again. She blushed bright pink to the roots of her hair and kissed him on the forehead, underneath the mistletoe.

PART SIX

INDIAN SUMMER

(1937–9)

*Festival – Blood and Thunder – Slums and Slum Land-
lords – Mr Councillor Chorlton – Freedom's Battles – A
Debt Repaid – Time's Revenges – I'd Best Go Willing –
Death of the Colonel – Goodbye to the Swan – The Shakespeare – Silence at Adam's Norton – The Millionaires Come
to Elmbury – Moths and Men – Munich-time – Twilight in
the Shakespeare – Soldiers and Guns*

Festival

I WAS BACK in time for the mayfly, and found Elmbury, at
high summer, livelier and more crowded than I had ever
known it. Cars and charabancs poured ceaselessly through
the town. It seemed that those secret springs whence Money
comes, which had dried up in 1931, had suddenly started to
flow again; the motors, the buses, the sedate tourists and the
cheap trips from Birmingham which flooded through our
streets were the visible manifestations of that invisible stream.

Elmbury, revived, was bubbling with all sorts of activity.
It looked as if both the Council's brochures were bearing
fruit at last; for the town now suffered a regular weekend
invasion of paper-hatted holiday-makers visiting 'unspoilt
Elmbury', and two aircraft factories were being built on the
outskirts. There was a Fishing Match (five hundred anglers
from all over Britain drank us out of beer, threw huge
quantities of bread into the river and caught an average of

three ounces of fish per rod: Mr Chorlton called it a modern version of the parable of the Loaves and Small Fishes). There was a cricket week. And there was Elmbury's annual festival of plays.

I had had some part in promoting this festival. Some years previously our old vicar, hounded and pursued by his creditors, had been compelled to give up the living, and shortly afterwards, having reached his wits' end, had died tragically by his own hand. The new vicar was an enthusiast for the stage, and since the Abbey badly needed repair we decided to try to raise the money by means of plays performed beneath the walls of the Abbey itself. There was good precedent for this; for in 1600 the churchwardens, faced with a similar urgency, had 'adventured upon themselves' to raise the necessary funds by 'setting forth three stage plays within the Abbey on the first days of Witsunweek'. Their accounts for that year contained various items relating to the hire of 'players' apparell' such as:

'Item iiij. Capps of green sylke.
  Item viij. Heades of haire for the apostles and x beardes.
  Item.   A face or vysor for the devyll.'

It was this which gave us the idea. We started in a fairly small and amateurish way, but the floodlights in the dark churchyard playing upon the tremendous west front of the church discovered a strange and unearthly beauty that was not of our making and we knew that we had embarked almost by accident upon a great adventure from which there was no turning back. Amateur actors, however competent, were dwarfed by that huge and fantastic backcloth; the thing must be done professionally or not at all. So the next year we engaged a professional company, and timidly spent what seemed to be a great deal of money on lighting, amplifiers, costumes and props. But our fears were ill-founded. The weather miraculously kept fine, visitors came to our plays from all over England, and the annual Elmbury Festival became an established event.

Elmbury, of late years, had seemed to grow old and slumberous and apathetic – Mr Rendcombe had reason to shake his head over it and complain that its atmosphere was wishy-washy and, like modern beer, lacked the tang and bite which once it had. Our Festival seemed to give new life to the place; and this new life manifested itself not only in enthusiasm but in vigorous opposition. Before long we were involved in a storm in a teacup which was none the less tempestuous because the teacup was small. We were accused of blasphemy, irreverence, sacrilege, immorality and even drunkenness (because we had asked the magistrates to grant an extension to all the pubs during Festival Week); and nothing loath for a good row we accused our critics of narrow-mindedness, hypocrisy, puritanism, and the Nonconformist conscience. It seemed that some old puritan yeast, which had lain dormant through the years, had suddenly thrown Elmbury into a ferment. The town split into two factions: those that were for the plays and those that were against them. The matter was fiercely debated in pub and pulpit. Even families became divided against each other. Mr Rendcombe, when he walked down the street, looked younger and more dapper, and less melancholy. This was more like old times. 'He smelleth the battle afar off and cries Ha Ha!' said Mr Chorlton. The correspondence columns of the *Elmbury Intelligencer* were full of angry letters. Everybody was happy, everybody enjoyed the civil war.

And now I came back from another civil war, a fierce and fatal quarrel which was soon to engulf the world, and found Elmbury in the midst of its annual summer controversy. The actresses wore indecent dresses, said some; they danced upon the graves, said others; blasphemy, blasphemy, cried the Nonconformist conscience; drunkenness and debauchery, whispered the teetotallers. And the Vicar got up in the Abbey and preached a gallant and glorious sermon in praise of beer.

Blood and Thunder

If we had awakened an old puritanism, we had also stirred into life something equally old and deep-rooted: a delight in pageantry, dressing-up, and acting, so that I felt almost as if Merrie England was reborn. Everybody in Elmbury (except the puritans) seemed to have caught the theatrical fever. The Operatic and Dramatic Societies flourished; and a deputation from the latter waited upon Mr Chorlton, who was known to have produced plays at the prep school, to ask if he could suggest a suitable piece for their next season's production.

'You want a costume play?' said Mr Chorlton; and they agreed, yes, it was fun to dress up, they would like a play in costume.

'And, of course, a thriller?' Mr Chorlton went on.

'Of course,' they said.

'With two or three good murders?'

Yes, they said, murders always went down well in Elmbury.

'And lots of blood?' asked Mr Chorlton.

They approved of lots of blood.

'Excellent,' said Mr Chorlton. 'We will produce *Macbeth*.'

And now they were all learning their parts. You heard the mighty majestical lines of Shakespeare in every shop, every pub, even at the Alley's mouth. 'How now, you secret, black and midnight hags?' said Mr Brunswick when he came upon his wife gossiping with two old women in the street. 'What bloody man is this?' was the housewife's greeting to the butcher delivering the meat. It was a good game and almost everybody played it; and the unfamiliar words didn't come awkwardly from Elmbury lips, our rough country talk and our rather broad accent didn't mangle the lines but gave them freshness and clarity and a new vigour. They suddenly seemed to belong to our own times; and one was reminded that Shakespeare's speech was probably not unlike our own, and that Burbage, far better than many a drawling actor of today, could have made himself understood in Double Alley.

Slums and Slum Landlords

All this liveliness, the Festival controversy, *Macbeth*, the new factories a-building, the charabancs full of trippers and fishermen, caused Elmbury's queer hotch-potch to boil and bubble merrily all through the summer and autumn. The periodic row about slums and housing blew up again in the Council. Elmbury was making an honest attempt to clean up its appalling alleys and had built a small satellite town, consisting mainly of workmen's cottages, on some parkland two miles away. There were plenty of sites where more houses could be built if necessary, but this didn't entirely solve the problem. In the first place it was often difficult to persuade the slum-dwellers to move; for many of the older people, strange as it may seem, had a sentimental attachment to their own hovel and to their own squalid surroundings. The new housing estate, with its gardens, its trees, its little patches of green, seemed to them a howling wilderness. They said in effect: Our alley may not be very beautiful or very comfortable, but it is all we know, all we have ever known; surely you will not uproot us at our time of life? As far as the old people were concerned, the plea seemed justified. Unfortunately they generally lived with their children, upon whom they were dependent and who in turn had young children; and it was these whom we wanted to save from the slum.

The second difficulty was the cost of the new houses. The rents were higher than many of the alley-dwellers could afford; and the twopenny bus fare into Elmbury, if they worked there, or if they wanted a drink in the evening, was an additional charge upon their slender means. The tee-totallers had seen to it, of course, that there was no pub in the satellite town; and this was another hardship on the old people who while they lived in Elmbury had always been able to hobble across to the Wheatsheaf or the George but who were too infirm to manage the longer walk to the bus-stop and the journey in the crowded bus. The warmth, the cheer, the fellowship of their local pub had meant a great deal to them. Fresh air, clean wallpaper, a bath they didn't use and a garden they couldn't cultivate were no adequate substitutes.

The third problem was, of course, the attitude of the slum landlords, some of whom sat on the Council. The only way of shifting the population of the alleys was to condemn the least habitable dwellings; and the Council showed itself extremely reluctant to condemn houses owned by such people as the Deputy Mayor, the oldest Councillor, and the most influential Alderman.

I don't mean that there was any deliberate 'graft'. Apart from two or three careerists who were out for what they could get, the Councillors were ordinary decent citizens who were mostly tradesmen and had the outlook of tradesmen. It is a first principle of trade that you don't offend your best customer if you can help it; indeed you will be prepared to stretch your conscience a bit to avoid offending him. This was precisely what occurred in the Council. Mr Y, let us say, is a prosperous baker who happens also to own a few slum cottages. You, who sit in the Council with him, are a builder by trade and you have good reason to suppose that Mr Y is going to invest in a new bakery and will give you the contract to build it. He has also bought a bit of land and is thinking of building a house for himself to live in when he retires; you are likely to get the contract for that too. Now when the question of condemning Mr Y's slum cottages comes before the Council, are you going to speak and vote in favour of it? Mr Y is your friend as well as your potential customer; but he's a man who is easily offended, touchy, a bit awkward-tempered. You know he'll never forgive you if you vote against his interests. He won't even understand that you were actuated by conscience; he will persist in believing that you were satisfying some private grudge

against himself. 'What does *he* want to butt in for?' Mr Y
will say, 'it isn't any of his concern. I've always been his
good friend; I've never hurt *him*.' And indeed, if things had
been the other way round, Mr Y wouldn't have dreamed of
'putting his spoke in'. He will be genuinely hurt by your
action; and you certainly won't get the contract for the new
bakery.

Knowing all this, what do you do about it? If you're a
man of very high principles you'll vote according to your
conscience; if you're a bit of a hero you'll even speak in
favour of condemning Mr Y's cottages. But suppose that
times are bad and you've got an overdraft at the bank and
your son is a clever lad whom you want to send to college –
and that contract might make all the difference to his
career?

Then perhaps you will persuade yourself that Mr Y's
tenants are really quite happy where they are (which is
probably true) and that Mr Y, who is quite a good landlord,
will probably do the cottages up, and make them habitable
(and incidentally give you that little job as well). So you
decide to lie low and say nuffin'.

That's why Elmbury had such a job to clear its slums. The
Council didn't consist, as some people tried to make out, of
a lot of wicked men; but merely of a lot of fallible men.
The evil lay not in their hearts but in the system they
served.

Mr Councillor Chorlton

Mr Chorlton, who had a small pension from the school and
a very small private income, was probably the only Councillor who was capable of giving an independent and un-
biased judgement on every issue. The others feared him for
this reason and also for his wit, which was sharp and mordant
and of a kind unfamiliar to them who hadn't experienced it
in their schooldays. He puzzled them; and they complained
that 'they never knew where they were with him', they

never knew which side of the fence he was going to come down. The Conservatives always voted as good Conservatives; and the Liberals always voted as good Conservatives too unless the issue were connected with beer*; and the two Labour members, of course, always voted against all the rest. This was a reasonable state of affairs because you knew exactly where you were; but Mr Chorlton was an uncertain quality, he changed sides as frequently as Warwick the Kingmaker and at times he even voted with the Labour members. This annoyed everybody; for the Labour members, both of whom were excessively stupid, felt certain there must be a trick in it if the solitary representative of the 'gentry' voted on their side, while the Elmbury Diehards complained that Mr Chorlton was being 'disloyal to his class'. (Surely the most fantastic loyalty that any man could be expected to observe!) The whole Council was disturbed by his refusal to play the game according to the rules.

As Independents must, he offended everybody in turn. He made a blistering speech about the Deputy Mayor in the debate on slum clearance. He fought hard for a pub on the new housing estate and tore the Liberals to bits when they opposed it, telling them they had forgotten the very meaning of the word Liberal. He described the workhouse, criticizing its severity and its barrack-room atmosphere, as 'that concentration-camp for the old and helpless' and the new Town Library, which had been designed by the borough surveyor, as 'that perfect example of the public lavatory style'. A notice pointing the way to the real public lavatories excited his scorn by referring to them as 'public conveniences' – in Gothic lettering. A proposal to cut down some fine old trees in the public gardens (which, to the distress of our puritans, were much frequented by lovers at night), provoked him to plead for their reprieve on the grounds that they were 'more sinned against than sinning'.

What most dismayed his fellow Councillors was their own uncomfortable suspicion that he was very often right. The

* In which case they voted as Liberals, ie, against liberty.

Mayor put their feelings in a nutshell when he got up,
bewildered and half-apologetic, to defend the sign which
pointed the way to the public lavatories. 'We all know Mr
Chorlton has had the benefit of a very good education and
he ought to know what's good taste and what isn't. I saw
that notice before it was stuck up and I thought the lettering
was very nice and dignified; but Mr Chorlton says it's
vulgar. And I thought it was nicer to say conveniences and
more decent; but Mr Chorlton says that's vulgar too. Now
I always thought it was vulgar to say lavatories; so I don't
know if I'm on my head or my heels.'

Freedom's Battles

The only people in Elmbury who really approved of Mr
Chorlton were the alley-dwellers and Mr Rendcombe. The
latter, of course, saw him as a survival of the 'good old days'
when gentlemen sat on the Council and spoke their minds
freely and firmly, having no customers to please and no
vested interests to serve or fear. (Incidentally, Mr Chorlton's
speeches and interpolations provided the *Intelligencer* with
plenty of good copy.) The alley-dwellers loved him for his
independence and for his stout-hearted defence of all kinds
of freedom. Everybody, of course, praised Freedom with a
capital F – the abstract idea of Freedom; the Liberals and
the Nonconformists praised it more than anybody else. But
whenever there arose a particular issue in which freedom
was involved it seemed to the poor men of Elmbury that it
was Mr Chorlton who fought for it and the Liberals and the
Nonconformists who opposed it. They voted, whenever they
could, to restrict a man's freedom to drink a glass of beer.
They voted against the cinema opening on Sunday. They
voted against dances being held in the Town Hall. They
voted, every time they got the chance, against Fun, while
paying lip-service to something they called Freedom which
seemed to mean their own freedom to stop people having
fun.

But Mr Chorlton fought stoutly for all these little, personal freedoms; and Double Alley gave him their votes and their gratitude to a man.

A Debt Repaid

Double Alley, however, was unlikely to survive much longer. The elder of those two tomboyish girls, Dick Perkins' daughters, who as long ago as 1917 shocked their neighbours by putting on breeches and going to work on the land, had inherited her father's little estate when he died. He had been a successful cattle-dealer, and had invested his profits in Double Alley itself, buying up his neighbour's dilapidated hovels one by one as they came into the market. When he died it was discovered that he owned almost every cottage in the Alley: twenty-nine cottages which brought in a total rent (in the unlikely event of every tenant being able to pay) of less than three pounds a week. His daughter, meanwhile, had married; and her husband, an enterprising young greengrocer, had just got himself elected to the Council . . .

There had recently been a number of cases of TB and the Medical Officer of Health wanted to condemn every house in the Alley. At last the way was clear; for there was no opposition from the new slum landlord who but twenty years ago had been a slum-dweller herself. She had no memories of the place which were not horrible; now she would wipe out Double Alley and those memories with it, and reckon her life from that fortunate day in 1917 when she strode boldly past the scandalized neighbours, into the green fields, into a new world.

Time's Revenges

The Victorians who saved Elmbury from the railway junction which they thought would blacken the countryside and destroy their quietude must now have turned in their graves; for Elmbury, where three roads met, had become a junction indeed and the traffic which came together at its Cross was far noisier, far more destructive of amenities, and incidentally far more dangerous to life and limb than the railway would have been.

On Saturdays and Sundays, and especially on Bank Holidays, it was practically impossible for any but the most agile to cross the High Street. The noise was so great that gossipers had to shout to make themselves heard; and even at night during holiday-time the flow of cars and charabancs did not pause and the noise would have kept us all awake had we not developed some sort of defensive mechanism so that we ceased to hear it; as men who live beside a waterfall become oblivious of its roaring and would only hear the silence, a terrible roaring silence, if the waterfall should suddenly dry up.

However much we might regret our lost quietude, there was no remedy; and even if there had been I daresay the majority of Elmbury people would have put up with the traffic for the sake of the trade which came with it. By no means all the charabancs passed through; you could see a score of the green or red monsters drawn up in the town's new car park almost any afternoon – and probably fifty or a hundred cars. The streets, the shops, and the pubs were always full, the tradesmen prospered, and the long queue of unemployed shrank to a few dozen unemployables.

Mr Parfitt, during these halcyon days, should have made a small fortune; for it was he who had first taught Elmbury how to pick the well-lined pockets of tourists and holiday-makers. But somehow or other he seemed to have lost his touch. He did well enough with postcards and models of the Abbey in Festival time; but for the most part the new generation of holiday-makers merely glanced at his dusty shop window and passed by. Perhaps he had gone out of fashion; for even the Long Man had ceased to be popular and a dozen of the figures littered the dark corners of his shop, unwanted, neglected, and covered with dust. It was a sign of the times, he told me, as he picked up and mourn-

fully dusted one of these masterpieces which looked particularly woebegone by reason of its having been broken at its
most vital joint. 'People today,' said Mr Parfitt sadly, 'would
be downright *frightened* to have one of these things in their
bedroom. What they want is something with the opposite
significance. They don't want to have children; and more's
the pity, say I.'

But Mr Parfitt's genius had deserted him. Puzzle his old
head as hard as he might, he could not think of a charm
against child-bearing.

I'd Best Go Willing

The autumn, of course, brought the international crisis
which we had already learned to associate with August and
September. It blew over and life in Elmbury went merrily
on. There were less trippers, for these were summer migrants,
but in consequence of the crisis work was speeded up on the
aircraft factories. There was employment and good money
for everyone; indeed, there was a local shortage of labour
and about a hundred Irishmen came to the town to make it
good. The pleasant, unfamiliar brogue of County Cork
introduced a new gaiety into our streets; its owners brought
to Elmbury also the filth, the fights, and the squalor which
accompany Irishmen wherever they go upon the face of the
earth.

The crisis had one other consequence. The Elmbury
company of Territorials, which at that time I commanded,
received a sudden unexpected influx of recruits. During the
early Thirties it had dwindled to a mere handful; one August
I had marched shamefacedly to camp at the head of seventeen men. Now, with the new recruits, I had nearly seventy.
This was not due to a sudden access of patriotism; the lads of
Elmbury were not at all anxious to go to war. But they had
suddenly realized that if there was war there would certainly
be conscription. They hated the idea of 'being fetched'. I
asked one sullen-looking and unmartial youth why he had

joined up. 'If there be a war,' said he, 'they'll come and fetch I. I'd best go willing.'

Elmbury men were known in the battalion for their tireless marching and their good night-fighting (which was not surprising for almost all were poachers) but also, I regret to say, for their obstinacy. They were easy to lead, but hard to drive. Even in khaki they kept their sturdy independence. Sometimes they sang a song they had learned from their fathers: 'We won't be buggered about, we won't,' and they meant it. They made first-class soldiers; but if they were badly handled they quickly came near to mutiny.

I now handed over the command of these stout-hearted and turbulent citizens in uniform to a lad of nineteen who was, like them, an incorrigible poacher, who could stalk, shoot, fish and ride, and who being anarchic himself could understand their particular brand of anarchy. For my part, I had determined that when war came – we no longer thought of it as 'if' – I should fight it in the air; for I had just learned to fly a Moth, had discovered a brave new world of cirrus and cumulus, and was bemused by the strange beauty of the sky's snowy regions, its unearthly continents of cloud.

Death of the Colonel

But when the crisis was over, we bundled away the thought of war for another year, accepting the respite but knowing it was only a respite, and, heedless once more, polished our hunting-boots and wiped the oil off our gun barrels. Winter came early, in a swirl and scurry of November snow, and we listened for the honk of the first geese on the north wind. I did a reconnaissance of the flooded, frozen, river-meadows with Michael, the boy who had taken over my Territorials; we promised the Colonel to let him know as soon as the grey flocks arrived.

But they were tardy, and when they came at last it was too late. Just before Christmas I met the Colonel out partridge-shooting. It was rough, hard walking, and by mid-morning I realized he was in a bad way. Our host didn't know it, and set a good pace for the guns as they walked in line over the wet, feggy fields. The Colonel couldn't keep up, so I dropped back and walked at his side. He put his hand up to his heart. 'It gets me here,' he said. But he wouldn't give up. Slowly and painfully he dragged himself along.

We came to a tall fence. I got over first and took his gun. He climbed up somehow or other on to the top of the fence and put his hand on my shoulder. He must have been in agony, for his face was quite grey. He had angina, though I didn't know it at the time. There was an awkward ditch on my side of the fence. 'Sod it,' he grunted, 'I shall have to jump.' I stood ready to catch him. I loved him very much, and it was awful to see the sweat running down his grey haggard face which twitched with pain. But he was in-domitable. I saw his face suddenly crumple into a grin. The thousand creases, the little crows' feet around his eyes, appeared as if by magic and for a moment he was his old self again, gnomish and naughty, mischievous as a boy.

'By God,' he said. '*I wish I had a good fat woman to fall on.*'

He jumped down and I caught him; he was as light as a child. We walked on for a little way, but the ground was squelchy and soft. He had to give up at last, and I took him home in my car. On the way he said: 'John, I shan't shoot again.' I tried to cheer him up. 'Nonsense,' I lied, 'you'll be better in a day or two,' but he had felt that invisible dagger in his chest and he knew, I think, that its wound was mortal. He slowly shook his grand old badger-grizzled head.

I saw him once again, about a week later, when I called to ask how he was. He had just finished planting an oak tree, but even that little task was too much for him, and I had to help him into the house. He had always been a great one for planting trees; his farm was dotted all over with saplings in various stages of growth. I think his choice of an oak to plant on that last morning, a tree so slow-growing and so long-living, was a sort of gesture of defiance to the blind Fury with the abhorréd shears. It would stand there with luck, beside the little pool in his Home Field, for hundreds of years after he had gone. His great-grandchildren might know the summer shade of it. There was a sort of continuity, a sort of comfort, in that.

Late that night he died.

Goodbye to the Swan

His death marked the end of a phase in the life of Elmbury; for almost at once that queer little company who had sat night after night in the Swan began to break up, the oddly-assorted fellowship ended, as if it had been only he who had held it together. For a long time his chair in the corner remained empty; nobody liked to sit in it; and gradually the 'regulars' ceased to be regular. Badger Brown stayed in his own village, Johnnie Johnson joined a club where he could play billiards, Mr Benjamin paid more frequent visits to his little business in Birmingham, Wilfrid Jakes the old gardener fell ill with lumbago and kept to his house. Soon Miss Benedict herself left; for the bar was altering its character, her new customers demanded new drinks with strange names which she had never heard of, motorists were more frequent and they scandalized her by bringing their women-folk into the bar, 'commercials' refused to be frightened away, one Saturday evening there was an invasion of paper-hatted women, part of an outing, who demanded fourteen Guinnesses and look snappy, miss, or the charry will leave us behind. Miss Benedict looked snappy all right; the thought that the charry might indeed leave them behind made her serve the Guinnesses with frantic haste, although they were frothy and difficult to pour out. But that night she gave in her notice; and Mr Rendcombe, the only one of her old customers who remained faithful to her, saw her burst into tears. When the last 'commercial' had taken his leave, our little Miss Prunes-and-Prisms caught the old man's arm and suddenly broke down. Perhaps he was the only man who had ever seen her cry; the only man who had ever looked

behind her stern and schoolmistressy façade. We may be
sure he patted her on the shoulder and said: 'There, there,
my dear ... Times change. We get old, and things aren't
what they were. Thinning us out, we old ones ... thinning
us out.'

The Shakespeare

Mr Chorlton and I, when we met for a drink, now went to
the Shakespeare, which was a warm and cheerful pub
peopled by no ghosts and with no empty chairs in the corner.
Effie and Millie still reigned there as co-equals, dividing
their long bar by means of the beer-engine in the middle, so
that Effie held sway over the territory north of it while
Millie was queen of the south. The darts board still hung in
the same place, and it was the same dart board, with the
worn patches near the treble twenty and the treble nineteen.
The picture of the landlord as a Royal and Ancient Buffalo
still hung over the fireplace, flanked by notices about forth-
coming meetings of the Cricket Club, the Football Club, the
Conservative Association, the Labour Party, and the Flying
Club (which flew not aeroplanes but racing pigeons).

If the Swan, in its heyday, was representative of one aspect
of Elmbury, the Shakespeare was typical of another. It was a
kind of club too, but less esoteric than the Swan. I could
never quite define, or even decide in my own mind, what
held the Swan fellowship together; unless it were a con-
glomerate consisting of weather-lore, interest in civil affairs,
guns and fishing-rods, recollections of hearing the chimes at
midnight, plus something else which was quite undefinable.
But it is easy enough to say what common interests were
shared by the customers of the Shakespeare: horses, cricket,
football, motor-bikes, and girls. It was the meeting-place of
the young limbs from the country round Elmbury; in some
respects it was more a country pub than a town pub. The
farmers' sons filled it on market days, on Friday mornings
when they came to draw the wages from the bank, and in the

evenings before a dance or after a cricket-match. Mr
Sparrow, as perky, as cheeky and as prospective as the bird
his namesake, used to call there every day on behalf of Mr
Benjamin for betting-slips. Before he entered, and when he
came out, his little head would waggle from side to side on
his long thin neck as he looked about him anxiously for the
patrolling policeman.

The Cricket Club held its annual meetings at the Shakespeare; and every year the notice over the fireplace was in
similar terms: *There will be a meeting next Friday at eight o'clock
to discuss plans for cricket next season and ways of raising money to
wipe out the club's debt of £29 4s 11d.* We were always confronted with this dreadful deficit in the accounts and Mr
Jeffs, who owned our cricket-field, always forgave us the
rent, grumbling nevertheless, 'Them as wants cricket ought
to pay for it.' Usually we decided to make somebody else
pay for it; and so we arranged a Rummage Sale or a dance.
But the mysterious deficit always appeared again next year,
and Mr Jeffs, still grumbling, had to guarantee our overdraft at the bank.

The Shakespeare was also the headquarters of the Darts
League. Darts playing would have been unthinkable at the
Swan; it was customary, it was traditional, in the Shakespeare, where Millie could get you a double top with one
dart out of three almost any time, and Effie had been known
more than once to put three darts running in the treble
nineteen.

And there was another thing you could do at the Shakespeare which you would never dream of doing at the Swan.
You could sing. There was a piano in the corner, and both
girls were capable of strumming out, perhaps a bit clumsily,
almost any tune you asked for from *Mademoiselle from Armen-
tieres* to *Billy Boy*. Indeed, such was the Shakespeare's renown
for singing that men from Adam's Norton (where, as you
will remember, the people sang like crickets all day long)
would often visit it when they were in Elmbury. In particular
there was a merry and chirruping fellow called Tommy
Dove, whose curious trade was that of a gelder: he travelled

about the countryside castrating horses, cattle, sheep and pigs. He brought from Adam's Norton a good tenor voice and a wonderful assortment of old songs, some of them so old and traditional that they were almost unintelligible. His favourite was the strangest song of all, which belonged to Adam's Norton and was sung to the best of my belief nowhere else in the kingdom. I never knew what it was about; but its chorus went like this:

> 'The prickolye bush,
> The prickolye bush,
> The prickolye bush so sore.
> If I ever get out of the prickolye bush
> I'll never get in it no more.'

Certainly the Shakespeare was very different from the Swan! But it was a pleasant little pub and it was not unimportant in the life of Elmbury.

Silence at Adam's Norton

It was about this time that a little tragedy occurred at Adam's Norton; and the story is worth telling as an example of the enormous difference in outlook between the city and the countryside.

The landlord of the Adam's Norton pub – the Salutation Inn, the pub with the crooked chimney – was a kindly old man and a great songster, and he'd been there for twenty-five years. He was in the habit of obliging a few of the Birmingham fishermen with a drink about half past six on Sunday, which was half an hour before legal opening-time. The village policeman knew of this, and shut his eyes to it, being aware that the train to Birmingham left at five past seven and the fishermen wouldn't get a drink otherwise.

But one day a policeman from Birmingham, being off duty, came down with the fishermen for a day by the river; and at half past six they brought him up to the pub. He waited till the first round of drinks had been bought and paid for, slipped out quietly, and called the village police-man, who was having a quiet sit-down by the fire.

The village policeman protested. 'You've no call to inter-fere. You don't know the village. It's a decent, quiet, well-conducted pub.' 'If I show you my warrant,' said the Birmingham man, 'you've got to come and you've got to make a case of it, or I'll have you out of your job.' He didn't even give Constable Roberts time to put on his boots. The poor man came along reluctantly in his carpet slippers, and took everybody's name, and even carried away a sample of beer in a bottle; because the Birmingham bobby made him do that too.

So there was a charge against the landlord of 'selling drinks outside permitted hours', and he lost his licence, and had to leave the pub; although the magistrates were privately sympathetic with him and would have dismissed the case if they had dared. He died six months later, of a broken heart, it's said; and the new landlord of the crooked little pub didn't sing and didn't approve of singing, for fear it would get him into trouble with the police. Adam's Norton, that had been so merry, became as silent as the grave. The people there no longer holler the old merry tunes with the absurd, irrelevant, traditional words.

'They shut their doors in the evening; and they know no songs.'

But the extraordinary thing about the incident is this: the Birmingham policeman really thought he was being 'smart' in making what he'd probably have called 'a good cop' when he was off duty; and quite a lot of his Birmingham friends thought he was smart too. They told us that although he wasn't a very nice fellow they expected he'd go far. But we were shocked; not so much angry as shocked; and we regarded him, not as wicked exactly, but as worse than wicked: as a sort of diseased creature whom we must shun lest he infect us. Because of his wanton, stupid, childish action we can't ever feel friendly towards the Birmingham fishermen any more; and more than ever we feel that we have nothing in common with the cities, where men think it's clever to do things like that.

The Millionaires Come to Elmbury

The local Point-to-Point was held in March, and Jerry rode his last race on Demon; the old horse broke a blood-vessel and had to be shot. You can see his picture if ever you go to the Shakespeare; it is on the wall between 'The Midnight Steeplechase' and the 'Royal and Ancient Buffalo': a faded photograph of a great raw-boned horse with huge shoulders and tremendous haunches, and Jerry, lean and graceful, upon his back sitting as easily as if he were in his armchair before the great fire at Hill Farm.

With the spring came more trippers, more prosperity and, following the prosperity, more Chain Stores. Elmbury already had two of these; and now two more bought shops in the town. Each one brought ruin to two or three of our little tradesmen who couldn't compete with the huge organization, the ingenious advertising, and the ruthless price-cutting of these million-pound concerns, these nation-wide butchers, grocers, fishmongers, haberdashers and whatnot. Mr Patterson, the fishmonger, who had been trading in Elmbury for thirty years, was compelled to shut up shop in April; for Elmbury being far from a port, he lived precariously at the end of long lines of communication, and he couldn't compete with the well-organized combine. In May Mr Brunswick went out of business too; and his opposition, Ye Olde Vyllage Shoppe, celebrated the occasion by a big advertising campaign to get more customers, filling the windows with summer frocks at 'half-prices' and cheap slogans such as 'Spend the rent and let the landlord wait'. Elmbury, goodness knows, held landlords in no great affection; but this piece of silly slick vulgarity, with its implied invitation to poor people to get themselves into trouble for the sake of a new dress, roused even our slow tempers and provoked Mr Chorlton, in the Council chamber, to speak of 'millionaires without morals who corrupt and cheapen whatever they touch.' The little tradesmen in the Council, who had never loved and often feared him, discovered in him a Daniel come to judgement, recognized him as their champion, and rose in their seats and cheered.

Moths and Men

But Mr Chorlton, these days, was not often roused to anger. He was getting old, and he confessed that as each year passed there seemed fewer things worth getting angry about. Instead, like the Greek philosophers whom he loved, he mocked with gentle and mocking laughter at a world which appeared to him increasingly absurd. I visited him in the spring, on a day in mid-May when a sudden chilly wind was scattering the apple petals over his lawn. He looked out of the window and quoted A. E. Housman:

'There's one more spring to scant our mortal lot,
  One season ruined of its little store.
May will be fine next year, as like as not,
  Oh aye. But then we shall be *sixty*-four.'

'Sixty-four,' he repeated. 'You begin to count the springs then; though the delights they bring with them are ever less sharp. There was a time when each May presented me with at least half a dozen days which were so exquisitely beautiful that they were scarcely bearable; now they don't hurt so much. If the years dull your pleasure they also deaden your pain. I'm no longer visited with that divine frenzy of the spring night when one feels an inescapable compulsion to make love or get drunk or write a poem. On the other hand I no longer feel it is in the least tragic or even very regrettable that I can no longer do these things. I merely experience a mild disappointment that May hasn't brought me a milk-white magpie moth this year!'

'How's the breed going?' I asked; and he led me to the

cabinet in the corner, pulled out a drawer, and showed me his long rows of delicate moths, arranged in order from the darkest to the lightest, so that those in the last row were practically snow-white, as white and satin-smooth as plum blossom, save for the faintest speckling which blemished each, a few black freckles, the scantiest dusting of grey.

'You see, I'm getting near it,' he said. 'But even in moths which produce two generations a year the path to perfection is long and hard. How about man, who reproduces himself perhaps once in twenty-five years?'

I laughed:

'And you know what you're breeding for in moths! You happen to want an immaculate one. In mankind you don't know if you want a Tarzan or a motor-mechanic or a Newton or a Keats; or a Ginger Rogers.'

'Indeed.' Mr Chorlton nodded. 'But there is a greater difficulty. My moths have a God. Oh yes, they have. He has smudges of cigar-ash on his waistcoat and he drinks too much port, but he is God nevertheless; he is omnipotent as far as they are concerned. Each generation he picks out with his rather shaky fingers the whitest, the most worthy, and in His temple – that jam jar in the corner – he places them together, where in obedience to the God's wishes they mate. So there is a reasonable expectation – since offspring tend to vary within narrow limits on each side of the parental mean – that their progeny will contain a certain number of yet whiter examples, fit candidates for the priesthood. Understand?'

'Yes.'

'Well, mankind may or may not have a God; but He's either incapable of practising selection, or too disinterested to do so. Therefore man does the selection himself; and a nice mess he makes of it. Double Alley, bless its heart, breeds at a rate approaching that of rabbits. You and I, for various social reasons, don't breed at all. Likewise an able fellow out of Double Alley, who gets on, learns a trade, marries a decent wife and saves a bit of money, has perhaps one or two children; he wants to give them a good schooling and a better

chance than he had, so he doesn't have any more. His nitwit
brother, who's too lazy to work, remains in his pigstye,
marries a slut, who may indeed be diseased or moronic, and
proceeds to have no less than twelve equally anti-social
children to multiply by twelve the mess he's made. A mad
world, my master. And since it seems to me to be utterly
beyond my power, or anybody else's, to remedy' – Mr
Chorlton chuckled – 'can you blame me if I devote my
declining years to Mr Cockburn's excellent vintages, the
Greek crossword in *The Sunday Times*, and the amusing
exercise of trying to breed *Abraxas grossulariata* ab *lacticolor*?'

Munich-time

Soon it was Festival time and once more – but surely, we
thought, this must be for the last time? – we lit the floodlights
in the churchyard and let them gild against the July night
our huge incomparable backcloth of stone. Little Tobias
triumphed over the demon Asmoday and watched the
serving-man who had helped him throughout his long
journey change to a shining angel before our eyes. Out of the
shadows of the dark funereal yews a youth, naked save for a
blood-red loincloth, ran breathless into a pool of cold white
light to tell in Milton's imperishable words the story of the
death of Samson. And, in the play *Everyman*, from the very
rooftop of the great church towering above the heads of the
audience God spoke to a terrible shadow that shone with
the faint green dreadful light of corruption and rose, it
seemed, out of the very tomb: *Where art thou, Death, thou
dreadful messenger?*

So, in a dozen evenings of brief and breath-taking beauty,
another Festival ended; and we suddenly became familiar,
some of us for the first time, with the name of a place called
Sudetenland. Would God indeed call his dreadful messenger
this autumn? No: it seemed we were to be granted another
reprieve. There occurred what sentimentalists were only too
willing to call the miracle of Munich; though why there

should be anything miraculous in a doddering old statesman sacrificing his country's honour for the sake of a few months of uncertain peace was not very clear.

We were told that in London the Munich Agreement was the signal for dinner-parties and celebrations; that the hotels and restaurants sold more champagne on that night than they had sold for years; and even that bands of young men roamed the streets until the small hours singing patriotic songs such as *Rule Britannia*.

I don't know if this was true. I was in Elmbury at the time and I can only speak for Elmbury. I can affirm that we didn't have any inclination to celebrate in the Shakespeare or the Swan. I remember Millie, pouring out a pint while she listened to the wireless and saying: 'Well, I calls it a bloody shame, I does, reely.' I remember Mr Chorlton telling me: 'I believe that history will write down that remark about "Peace in our Time" as the most inane statement ever made by a British Prime Minister.' And I remember Jerry, on that evening of Munich, deciding that when war came he would sell Hill Farm and join up with his friends. It would be tough on Dorrie, he said, but she would understand; he couldn't just stay behind and make money . . .

No; London folks that night may have been merry and mad: but in Elmbury we knew better. The pub was soon empty; and we went soberly back to our houses, for very shame.

Twilight in the Shakespeare

The last fantastic months went by. We made plans for the future with a sense of horrible unreality: as if we were citizens of a sick world which nevertheless was possessed by a kind of *spes phthisica*, a frantic feverish hope against hope that the inevitable wouldn't happen after all. We held our annual cricket-meeting – it was about the time when the Germans marched into Prague – and sought ways and means as usual to wipe out our usual deficit. We needed a new mower, and I remember old Mr Jeffs, in the chair, muttering: 'Them as wants mowers ought to pay for 'em,' but a few minutes later offering to buy us the mower all the same. After the meeting we went into the bar and listened to the news. There was nothing new, save the usual vague talk of negotiations and mobilizations going on simultaneously; but the sense of crisis persisted, we were aware, as countrymen can smell the approaching rain, of the vast storm brewing. I heard Mr Jeffs, who'd fought against the Boers and who'd lost his two sons in the Great War, say briefly and finally: 'We'll have to stop un next time. We'll have to cry Halt.' There was a murmur of approval; and Jerry said sombrely: 'Aye. We'll have to go, I reckon.' 'Yes,' said Mr Jeffs. 'You wouldn't hang back, Jerry; nor the rest of you neither. You'd have to go.' I knew then, more sure than if a Cabinet Minister had whispered it to me, that we should be at war within six months. For that was the temper of England; and old Mr Jeffs spoke for England, though he knew well what was the cost of war in sons.

Soldiers and Guns

'Soldiers and guns! Soldiers and guns!
These for your daughters, and those for your sons!
What if your children be comely or tall?
When soldiers and guns come, down they will fall!'
ERIC LINKLATER.

We had one season's cricket nevertheless, and we had one more Festival, lit the great lamps for the last time before the black-out, and then it was September.

I stood, in strangely-assorted company, on the pavement outside the Anchor Inn and watched the Territorials march away with young Michael at their head. Mr Chorlton was there, Mr Jeffs, and Mr Rendcombe; Mr Benjamin and Mr Sparrow; Millie and Effie; Pistol, Nym and Bardolph, who had come back from the Spanish war minus an arm.

I counted the columns of three as they went by. There were nearly ninety men. Not bad for Elmbury! I half wished I were going with them; but I should be leaving by a later train to join my Fleet Air Arm squadron.

Mr Rendcombe said:

'I stood here and watched them go off to the Boer War; and in August, 1914; and now again. Three times in a man's life is too much.'

I waved Mike goodbye. He shouted: 'This'll be livelier than goose-shooting!'

'Good luck!' I shouted.

'Good luck!' he waved back.

I remembered sitting in the Tudor House window-seat and watching the soldiers march off on that day in 1917. I remembered Black Sal pirouetting after them and Double Alley cheering them as they went by. I remembered Mr Jeffs – a larger, more substantial Mr Jeffs – on the same morning quarrelling with the old vicar about Tithes – was it the same morning or did memory telescope the two events into one? I couldn't be sure; but I heard him mutter now, as he stood at my side: 'Them as wants wars ought to fight in 'em,' and I remembered that he had paid this grimmer, inescapable tithe which we pay each generation to our own folly and the world's.

Farmers' sons, tradesmen's sons, poachers' sons, the khaki files went by. Pistol, Bardolph and Nym came stiffly to attention beside me. Millie and Effie were crying, and sharing the same inadequate white handkerchief. Mr Chorlton quoted grimly: ' "War for his meals loves dainty food" – Aeschylus.'

Then suddenly the soldiers started to sing. It was the same song, the same foolish simple parody, as their predecessors had sung in 1917. Perhaps the same bittersweet Elmbury humour stirred them; perhaps some of them remembered their fathers singing it as they stood, ill-clad guttersnipes, at the mouth of the Alley.

'Farewell—Double Alley,'

they sang,

> 'Goodbye—Ulmbree Cross!'

and round the corner into Station Street swung the last of the files, so beautifully in step, so perfectly dressed by the right, so purposeful and yet so gay, that it broke your heart to see them go.

POSTSCRIPT IN NORMANDY

(1944)

I AM writing this in Normandy, in a once-pleasant little village which before our bombers visited it must have looked very much like any one of those dozen little villages which lie in a ring round Elmbury. Away to my left about the great cathedral of Caen burns a town which may for all I know have looked like Elmbury itself. The church tower reminds me sharply of Elmbury Abbey.

In the field where I sit a peasant who might by his appearance belong to Brensham or Tirley is doing exactly what any of our peasants would do in similar circumstances: he is trying to remove a bomb-splinter from the hindquarters of his cow and cursing, in a slow, sombre, hopeless monotone, the kicking beast, the Boches, the British, and the war.

We have just received our first mail since we left England; and I have got a long letter from Mr Chorlton. It contains the latest news of Elmbury; it brings the portrait up to date. So here it is:

'It is D-Day at last,' writes Mr Chorlton, 'and even I, who loathe the wireless, have switched it on a dozen times and even I, who am not accustomed to praying, have breathed a prayer to whatever gods there be that you may fare well.

'It has been a little D-day for me also, for there emerged this morning, and slowly spread out before my unbelieving eyes its immaculate wings, my milk-white unspotted *lacticolor*. She is very beautiful. There is not a speck nor a blemish upon her. She is white as driven snow.

'Mars, and you his servants, have robbed me of most of my triumph. Even a doddering old fool of over seventy who is now cynical about almost everything cannot be expected to feel that a little moth is very important on a day like this.

'Still, I have done it. And it took ten years! I am satisfied, and since my own time for pupation, or at any rate going to earth, cannot be far off, I can say "Nunc dimittis".

'Meanwhile you may like to hear the latest news of Elmbury.

'The town looks much the same and so far it hasn't had a bomb on it, although Double Alley gives the impression that it has been the target for a block-buster. We have torn down all the filthy hovels and after the war we propose to make a little park there, or at any rate a green space with a few trees. Black Sal would laugh. Perhaps she will haunt it. She would be an alarming ghost, I think, to the pure-minded and hygienic citizens of 1950.

'Outside the town there are bigger changes, and I'm sorry to say that the aircraft factory which now sprawls for miles has recently engulfed the Colonel's farm. All the trees he so lovingly planted are down, and he has no longer any memorial; unless he was, as you once suggested to me, Protean, and lives on in the rain, the wind, and the grass.

'His chair is still in the same corner of the Swan bar but the new generation is not shy of sitting in it. The Swan no longer stands for what it used to (whatever that was: I was never quite sure). Frippits and flibbertigibbets behind the bar serve beer to American GIs – when there isn't any whisky.

'Millie and Effie have gone into the ATS where they no doubt encourage the troops as they did our young farmers. They'll be back after the war, I bet, to re-establish their matriarchy in the Shakespeare.

'Farther down the street Mr Parfitt's shop looks very dusty and unprosperous. Mr Parfitt himself is old and infirm. He haunts his premises hungrily like an old unsuccessful spider whose inept web fails to catch a warier generation of flies. He ought to be able to make something out of the Americans, but he hasn't the spirit to try. The only thing in his window, bait for the archaeologists and folk-lorists who come here no more, is obviously a toasting fork labelled "Ancient Eel-spear circa 1700".

'Our soldiers, as you know, have done great deeds since you and I and the rest of us watched them march away on that lovely morning in September: a morning which seems so long ago that it is already almost lost in its own September mists. Outside Dunkirk they fought a savage rearguard action and young Michael got the MC for using his Bren gun carrier as if it were a tank. Then they went out to Egypt and marched from Alamein to Naples. Doubtless they are now on the path to Rome. Michael writes to me from time to time telling me of the various snipe, geese, hares, etc, which he has killed; but it appears he has slain a great many Germans too. Sometimes in his letters I get the impression of the Colonel's shadow on the page, and seem to hear a faint whispering echo of his laughter.

'Jerry, of course, went into the Yeomanry, who were converted to what I think are called cavalry tanks. He was killed in Tunisia; and with him three of the others who rode that crazy Midnight Steeplechase from Brensham to Elmbury Cross long ago. Thus "history repeats itself" (what a silly phrase!): they died as their fathers died; and the people who make the next war will have to look elsewhere for the sacrificial stuff, for we have no more. Whole families have ceased to exist, the breed is wiped out.

'Mr Jeffs went back to Hill Farm to manage it for Jerry; but the strain and the shock of Jerry's death was too much for him and last autumn he died in harness, worn out (as he told me a little time before he died) by filling up endless forms which he didn't understand for the benefit of the clerks and the "jacks in offices" whom he so heartily hated.

'Pistol, Bardolph and Nym (old soldiers never die) are in the Home Guard, which gives them better opportunities for poaching than they have ever had before. But I must not traduce them. There was a time, when we were expecting the Germans to arrive any day, when the sight of Pistol's sinister spidery figure, sloping down the hedgerow, and Bardolph's red nose behind a tommy-gun, gave me a kind

of comfort. I should have feared them had I been a German
soldier! Yesterday I saw them all three engaged in some
furtive business at the corner of Dogleg Spinney and last
night by chance I found an old rhyme that exactly describes
them:

> Mychers, hedge creepers, fylloks and luskes,
>   That all the somer keep dytches and buskes,
> Lawtryng, and wandryng, fro place to place,
>   And wyll not worke but the bypaths trace
> And lyve with haws, and hunt the blakbery,
>   And wyth hedge brekyng make themself mery . . .

I don't know what a "fyllok" is, nor yet a "lusk" but I bet
Pistol is both. Yet the absurd disreputable creature is not
without a sense of what is proper; he has a profound though
inarticulate belief in the dignity of man. Early in the war,
when an ARP warden brought him a gas-mask to try on, he
protested hotly. "No, thank 'ee, sir! No thank 'ee! No gas-
maskses for me! I woan't put un on, I tell 'ee! If so be as
Hitler drops gas on us, and it's come my time to die, I'll
die natural!"

'That's about all our news, except that the Council is very
disturbed because some earnest statistician has discovered
that Elmbury contains 1,509 houses of which only 248
possess baths. Maybe I am growing old and apathetic; but
the disclosure scarcely moves me. Mr Rendcombe, however,
made a headline of it; he thrives and flourishes, though he
compares the present war unfavourably with its predecessors. Mr Benjamin also is still with us, but he has recently
lost his little business in Birmingham and this has broken his
heart. He creeps about mournfully, a sad Semitic shadow.
Sparrow, on the other hand, is chirpy as usual: in mysterious
ways he is making a fortune out of the Americans.

'Yes; we have thousands of Americans in the district; and
thousands more are streaming through every day down the
main road with a rumble and a roar louder than that of the
charabancs on Bank Holidays. Their impact upon Elmbury

has produced interesting results, but good ones, on the whole, both for them and us. Recently a battalion of Negro soldiers arrived, to the great delight of some of our silly little wenches who were soon to be seen "walking-out" with them. The people who were most shocked by this were, of course, the Americans themselves; and the local American commander called a meeting of all the "public and religious bodies" in Elmbury – the Town Council, the Chamber of Commerce, the Parochial Church Council, the Nonconformists, the district visitors, the Salvation Army, the Mothers' Union, you know the sort of thing – and apologized very politely for the presence of the coloured troops who had come to fight in our war. "You're an ancient, peaceful town," he said, "and you've got a tradition hundreds of years old; we shall very deeply regret it if things happen which seem to do violence to that tradition." We honestly didn't know what he meant, and we all felt vaguely uncomfortable. He went on: "You may wish to make certain local regulations and if so we shall give you every help to enforce them. You may wish, for example, to put the public houses out of bounds to the coloured men; and of course you wouldn't like to see them dancing with white girls, so the dance halls can be put out of bounds as well."

'Well, there was a rather long silence, and then suddenly the meeting (which was representative, mind you, of all that is most prim and pious in Elmbury) did a very astonishing thing. Speaker after speaker got up and said that if any dances were held in Elmbury the coloured men would be as welcome as the white. Mr Patterson the fishmonger who's a Rechabite or something frightful of that kind said that drink was an Evil, but if public houses existed no man must be barred from them except by his own conscience, etc, etc. Little Mr Brunswick, who is Methody and strait-laced, said that he didn't much hold with dances but he supposed that black soldiers had as much right as anybody else to attend them. Even the Chairwoman of the Moral Welfare Committee, while she deplored all manner of goings-on, declared stoutly that she would have no part in differentiating between black and white. "No, Colonel," she said. "I'm sorry. But you spoke of our ancient tradition. Well, there it is. We don't do things like that in England."

'I was never so proud of Elmbury as I was then.

'And of course – in the good American phrase – we can take it. We are old enough and wise enough and adaptable enough. So one sees the unusual sight of a great chocolate-coloured coon grinning behind his pint with our locals in the Shakespeare, or playing darts for Elmbury against Brensham, while the white chaps from Virginia and Alabama and South Carolina, somewhat disapproving, take themselves off to the seclusion of the Swan. On the whole, it works pretty well; for there's plenty of natural courtesy on both sides. I suppose we shall pay for our broadmindedness with a few coffee-coloured bastards, but if so, what of it? A spot of miscegenation never did any harm. It gives what's called heterosis vigour to the race – which incidentally my magpie moths sadly lack. Mr Sparrow, by the way, supports this view. Discussing the problem the other day, "Nothing like a good mongrel," he said. "I've got cross-bred pullets and they're the best layers I ever had, I'll go t'ell if they 'ent."

'But seriously: these little invasions, by black or white, won't hurt us. We can absorb and we can assimilate, and we can keep our queer unique "Elmbury" character. (After all, we've absorbed and assimilated Mr Benjamin, and his race is the most indigestible in the world!)

'But we *must* keep our character. I, who am hardly ever serious, am dead serious about this. I want to say something to you – something that I feel is important – about this Elmbury from which in the nature of things I must shortly depart and to which, if the news is as good as it seems, I hope you and Michael and the rest of you will before very long return.

'I see about me a changing world. I had almost said a dissolving and disintegrating world. I'm no prophet, and I can't predict the future of Europe and of England; but I think it's going to be for a time a strange and uncomfortable future. In the end your generation may save its bacon by some sort of internationalism, probably on communist lines. I've got no quarrel with that.

'But meanwhile I visualize a period of something very like anarchy. I may be wrong; I hope I'm wrong. But if I'm right it may be that the remedy – the temporary remedy – will lie not so much in internationalism as in lots of tiny nationalisms. Parochialism, in fact; the little low plant may survive when the great tree is swept away by the wind.

'Parochialism, unlike nationalism, never caused people to go to war. The men of Dykeham think they catch bigger fish than anybody else, and the men of Brensham think the Dykeham folks are a lot of liars. But they don't try to settle the question by bashing each other on the head, and are never likely to. Therefore, I think that the smaller the "nationalism" is, the nearer it comes to internationalism. England, as a whole, finds it difficult to understand Russia, as a whole; but Brensham village can much more easily understand a village in Russia. For example, we can perfectly understand the men of two adjacent riverside villages on the Don or the Dnieper arguing over their vodka about their respective catches of sturgeon.

'Very well; if Parochialism in some sort survives, Elmbury may survive and the entity that is Elmbury life, the idea of the small, intimate, closely inter-related community – when the great winds of the world have swept kings from their thrones, dictators from their seats and scattered like chaff the fortunes of the great financiers and the great banks.

'Now I believe that if this is so Elmbury and all the other country towns like it will have a big part to play in the evolution of England. It seems to me that we – as an American soldier kindly put it to me the other day – "have something". It's not all good: Double Alley is an example of how bad it can be. But the best of Elmbury, I think, is something pretty important and something which the world would be much poorer for losing. We are, in our way, a rather highly civilized community. We have achieved quite a sensible sort of relationship among ourselves. We have evolved in a great many hundreds of years a way of life which seems to me a good way.

'It may be, therefore, that the country towns and villages will be for a period the repositories (like the monasteries in the Dark Ages) of a certain way of life, a certain sort of culture, while the great cities go mad. It sounds fantastic, but I believe it is possible. It may be that they will be the model, the rough prototype, from which a new sort of community will evolve. For, mind you, I don't want to restore the *status quo ante bellum*. Change there will certainly be, and evolution, and perhaps revolution. I merely suggest that the pattern of our English country life has been, perhaps, as good as fallible men could make it and that you and those who come after you might take that pattern as a rough guide and try to devise something better.

'But of course I may be completely wrong. We know enough about evolution now to realize that old dame Nature (or God if you feel that way about it) is experimental and somewhat capricious. Evolution doesn't march along a nice straight course. A promising line is developed (eg, the social insects, the bees and ants) and suddenly it comes to a dead end. Nature gets sick of it and tries another way. Often she contrives something which is in its way quite perfect, something as gorgeous as a bird of paradise, as fantastic as a platypus, as monstrous as a whale, as ingenious as a humming-bird, but for some reason it fails to fit in with her mysterious purposes and she drops it like a hot cake.

'Communities seem to evolve and develop in much the same fashion and with just as many false starts and dead ends. Byzantium left us little but the reflection of its architecture, Egypt little but its tombs, the Incas nothing but broken temples nearly overwhelmed by the green devouring jungle. Athens was perfect of its kind; but it led nowhere. Islam was vigorous and all-conquering and set the Mediterranean afire with its white and searing flame; but it suddenly faded away.

'It may be that in a comparable but much smaller way the kind of English life and tradition which I have conveniently labelled "Elmbury" is a dead end, sterile already, an offshoot which looked promising but which hasn't come to anything after all.

'I don't believe that; but if so, so be it. It was good while it lasted. It was merry and sane and comic and fantastic; and from certain aspects – most of all perhaps from the aspect of an old man who is soon to leave it – it looked very, very fair. As my American friend said, "It had something." I am glad to have belonged to it, to have been part of it.

'FUIMUS TROES; FUIT ILIUM.'

THE BRENSHAM TRILOGY

Holds a mirror to the English way of life. These human and humorous chronicles spring from the soil of Elmbury, a Gloucestershire market town and Brensham, its neighbouring village.

PORTRAIT OF ELMBURY 30p

'Vivid characterization, country lore, humour and fine common sense. It is true to the real heart of England' – THE DAILY TELEGRAPH

BRENSHAM VILLAGE 30p

'Brensham – with its crooked village street and crooked church spire – crack-brained Brensham, is your village and mine' – BBC.

THE BLUE FIELD 30p

'Full of the wisdom of the English countryside, of humanity and kindliness, of insight and humour' – THE SUNDAY TIMES

JOHN MOORE

'One of the most absorbing, warmest-hearted, romantic-optimistic of English novelists' – SUN

THE BRENSHAM TRILOGY

'Breathes the very spirit of our native land' – DAILY EXPRESS

Also available in an attractive full-colour slipcase price 90p

A SELECTION OF POPULAR READING IN PAN

CRIME

Agatha Christie
THE LABOURS OF HERCULES   25p
Victor Canning
QUEENS PAWN   30p
THE SCORPIO LETTERS   30p
Dick Francis
FLYING FINISH   25p
BLOOD SPORT   25p
Gavin Lyall
VENUS WITH PISTOL   30p
James Leasor
A WEEK OF LOVE   25p

GENERAL FICTION

Mario Puzo
THE GODFATHER   45p
Rumer Godden
IN THIS HOUSE OF BREDE   35p
Kathryn Hulme
THE NUN'S STORY   30p
George MacDonald Fraser
ROYAL FLASH   30p
Rona Jaffe
THE FAME GAME   40p
Leslie Thomas
COME TO THE WAR   30p
C. S. Forester
THE MAN IN THE YELLOW RAFT   30p
Arthur Hailey
HOTEL   35p
AIRPORT   40p
IN HIGH PLACES   35p
Nevil Shute
REQUIEM FOR A WREN   30p

NON-FICTION

Harrison E. Salisbury
THE 900 DAYS: The Siege of Leningrad 95p

Explained by David Reuben, M.D.
EVERYTHING YOU ALWAYS WANTED TO
   KNOW ABOUT SEX but were afraid to ask 45p

Peter F. Drucker
THE AGE OF DISCONTINUITY 60p

Norman Mailer
A FIRE ON THE MOON 40p

Leonard Mosley
ON BORROWED TIME (illus) 65p

Adrian Hill
HOW TO DRAW (illus) 30p

edited by Bruce Campbell
THE COUNTRYMAN WILD LIFE BOOK (illus) 30p

Andrew Duncan
THE REALITY OF MONARCHY 40p

Graham Hill
LIFE AT THE LIMIT (illus) 35p

Miss Read
MISS READ'S COUNTRY COOKING 30p

Gavin Maxwell
RAVEN SEEK THY BROTHER (illus) 30p

Obtainable from all booksellers and newsagents. If you have any difficulty, please send purchase price plus 5p postage to P.O. Box 11, Falmouth, Cornwall.

While every effort is made to keep prices low, it is sometimes necessary to increase prices at short notice PAN Books reserve the right to show new retail prices on covers which may differ from the text or elsewhere.

I enclose a cheque/postal order for selected titles ticked above plus 5p a book to cover postage and packing.

NAME ....

ADDRESS ....

....